G. Hutchinson (George Hutchinson) Smyth, G. S. (George Sherwood) Dickerman

The life of Henry Bradley Plant

Founder and president of the Plant system of railroads and steamships and also of the

Southern Express Company

G. Hutchinson (George Hutchinson) Smyth, G. S. (George Sherwood) Dickerman

The life of Henry Bradley Plant
Founder and president of the Plant system of railroads and steamships and also of the Southern Express Company

ISBN/EAN: 9783743467200

Manufactured in Europe, USA, Canada, Australia, Japa

Cover: Foto ©ninafisch / pixelio.de

Manufactured and distributed by brebook publishing software (www.brebook.com)

G. Hutchinson (George Hutchinson) Smyth, G. S. (George Sherwood) Dickerman

The life of Henry Bradley Plant

Henry Bradley Plant.

PREFACE.

IF it be asked why another biography is added to the almost endless number now in our bookstores and libraries, an answer is found in the countless distinctions of individual character, and in the varied experiences which come to men in different walks of life. The botanist says that of all leaves in the forests of the world, no two can be found alike in every particular. The phrenologist says the same of the various forms of the human head, and the psychologist affirms it of the intellects and dispositions of men and women. Hence each life has its own peculiar experience to record for the pleasure or profit of others.

Biography is the most universally interesting and instructive branch of literature; hence the power of the novel and drama, which are merely biographies pictured and acted before us. A study of history shows that the nations' great movements are the work of individual men and women. In illustration of this fact it is needful to mention such names only as Abraham, Joseph, Esther, Joan of Arc, Napoleon, and Washington.

The commercial and industrial occupations from which a nation now derives its strength should be honored as truly as the military exploit, or the scientific achievement. The record of a noble life which, in its sphere of quiet duty, has accomplished much for the good of others, is a lesson in patriotism and a legacy to posterity. The best period of the history of the Cotton States could only be written by taking into account the share which the subject of this biography has had in their development.

It is rare to find a man who has had dealings with so many of his fellows, and who, at the same time, has won the esteem and affection of his associates and employés, as has Henry Bradley Plant in every department of his great railroad system.

The writing of this biography is undertaken in the belief that there are many general readers to whom the record of such a life will be as welcome as it must be to those to whom, in his manifold activities, he has proved a benefactor and a friend.

G. H. S.

CHAPTER I.

The Plant Family—Birth of Henry Bradley Plant—Mr. Plant's Parents—Ancestors Came from England in 1639—David Plant Occupied Many Positions of Honor and Trust—A. P. Plant's Successful Business Career—H. B. Plant on his Mother's Side is Descended from Joseph Frisbee, a Major in Washington's Army—Reverend Levi Frisbee, Father of Professor Levi Frisbee of Harvard College—Connection with Sir William Pepperell, Bart.—The Historian of the Frisbee Family—Richard of the Second Generation Went from Virginia to Connecticut, and Settled at Branford, 1644 —Sketch of Oliver Libby Frisbee, Historian of his Family— Senator Hoar's Relations to the Frisbee Family—Frisbee Patriotism and Services to their Country—They Were Good, Church-going People, mostly of the Puritan Belief—Probability that the Frisbees Came from Wales . . . 1-14

CHAPTER II.

Branford, Connecticut, Purchased by the New Haven Colonists from the Totokett Indians in 1638—First Settlements Were Made in 1644—First Church of Logs Surrounded by Stockade to Protect from Indians—Guards at the Gate during Service —Church and Town Records Preserved at Branford—John Plum, the First Town Clerk—Style of the Second Church Building and Character of its Services—Rev. Timothy Gillett its Pastor—He Taught an Academy in Addition to his Pastoral Work—Prominent Families of Branford—Intelligent Character of the People—De Tocqueville's High Estimate of this "Leetle State"—Branford in 1779 . . 15-22

CHAPTER III.

The Blackstone Family—The Ancestor Came from England before 1630—His Name Was William Blaxton—Settled first in Massachusetts, afterwards Went to Rhode Island—His Beautiful Character and Numerous Descendants—Origin of Yale College of Branford—The Blackstone Memorial Library 23–34

CHAPTER IV.

The Plants Came from England to Branford, between Two Hundred and Three Hundred Years ago—Still Own the Lands first Acquired—Henry's Father Died of Typhus Fever when Henry Was about Six Years Old—His Tender Recollection of his Mother—Henry's First Day at School—His Natural Diffidence—Mr. Plant's After-dinner Speeches—His Mother's Second Marriage—Stepfather Kind to Henry—Thrown by a Plough Horse and nearly Killed—Attended School at Branford—Engaged on Steamboat Line Running between New Haven and New York—On Leaving, Promised a Captaincy—Marriage—Express Business—Leaves New Haven and Goes to New York—Romantic Experience in Florida 35–50

CHAPTER V.

Mr. Plant Goes from New Haven to New York—Captain Stone's Friendship—Mrs. Plant's Health Fails again—Returns to the South—Is Appointed Superintendent of Adams Express Company—His Great Executive Ability—The Civil War—Mrs. Plant's Death—Mr. Plant Buys out the Adams Express Company 51–55

CHAPTER VI.

Relations to the Confederate Government—Jefferson Davis. Gives him Charge of Confederate Funds—Mr. Plant Buys a Slave, who afterward Nursed him through a Severe Sickness—Impaired Health—Goes to Bermuda, New York, Canada, and Europe—Second Marriage 56–67

Contents

CHAPTER VII.

Education from Books and from Experience—Keen Intuitions—Abreast of the Progress—Mr. Plant's After-dinner Speech at Tampa Banquet Given him by Tampa Board of Trade, March 18, 1886—Location of Tampa—In Territorial Days Had a Military Reservation—In 1884 Population about Seven Hundred—Its Cosmopolitan Population now—Many Cubans and Spaniards in Tampa—Tobacco Industry—Phosphate Abounds in this Part of the State—Much of it Shipped to the North and to Europe—Plant System Gives Impetus to the Prosperity of the Place—Its Progress the Last Five or Six Years 68–86

CHAPTER VIII.

Florida Mr. Plant's Hobby—Banquet at Ocala—Mr. Plant's Speech—Sail on Lakes Harrison and Griffin—Banquet at Leesburg—Visit to Eustis—Cheering Words to a Young Editor—Make the Best of the Frost—It may be a Blessing in Disguise—Must Cultivate Other Fruits (and Cereals) besides Oranges—Importance of Honesty—Sense of Justice—Consideration for the Workmen—Unconscious Moulding-Power over Associates and Employees—Letter of Honorable Rufus B. Bullock 87–101

CHAPTER IX.

Mr. Plant's Industry and Power to Endure Continuous Strain—Labor of Examining and Answering his Enormous Mail—Letter from Japan—Mail Delivered Regularly to him at Home and Abroad—His Private Car, its Style, Structure, Hospitality, and Cheering Presence—Numerous Calls—The Secret of his Endurance—The Esteem and Love of the Southern Express Company for its President—Mr. Plant Enjoys Social Life—He is a Great Lover of almost all Kinds of Music—Mr. Plant a Medical Benefactor—Some of the Progress Made in the Healing Art—Bishop of Winchester's High Estimate of the Value of Health—Dr. Long's Opinion of the Gulf Coast as a Health Restorer—Unrecognized Medicines in Restoring Lost Health—Nervousness among the American People—The Soothing and Strengthening Effect of Florida Climate—Mr. Plant's Part in Facilitating Travel and Providing Comfortable Accommodations for the Invalid 102–116

CHAPTER X.

Reason for Submitting Press Sketches of Mr. Plant—*Descriptive America*, December, 1886—*City Items*, December, 1886—*Railroad Topics*—*Home Journal*, New York, March, 1896—F. G. De Fontain in same Journal—Ocala *Evening Times*, June, 1896—*Express Gazette* 117–140

CHAPTER XI.

Mr. Plant's Close and Constant Contact with the Great System as Seen in the Following Letters—Letter Written on Board the Steamer *Comal*—Letters on Trip to Jamaica, West Indies, March 15, 1893, and Published in the *Home Journal* 141–149

CHAPTER XII.

MANAGEMENT OF THE GREAT PLANT SYSTEM WORTHY OF ADMIRATION AND IMITATION . 150–156

CHAPTER XIII.

Plant Day at the Cotton States and International Exposition of 1895 at Atlanta, Georgia—Preparations for its Celebration—Impressive Observances of Mr. Plant's Birthday at the Aragon Hotel—Mr. Plant's Remarks in Acknowledging Presentation of Gifts 157–182

Contents

CHAPTER XIV.

Tampa Bay Hotel, One of the Modern Wonders of the World—Its Architecture, Furniture, Works of Art, Decorations, Tapestries, Paintings, Inlaid Table and Three Ebony and Gold Cabinets from the Tuileries, a Sofa and Two Chairs once Owned by Marie Antoinette—The Dream of De Soto Realized—A Palace of Art for the Delight and Joy of Those who are in Health, and an Elysium for the Sad and Sorrowful 183–203

CHAPTER XV.

Programme of Plant Day Ceremonies—Ringing of the Liberty Bell—Presentation of Addresses to Mr. Plant in the Great Auditorium—His Reply—Resolutions from the Different Departments of the System, from the Savannah Board of Trade, etc.—Mr. Morton F. Plant's Acknowledgments . 204–226

CHAPTER XVI.

Banquet at the Aragon Hotel Ends the Festivities of the Day—Sketch of the Southern Express Company—Distinguished Callers on President Plant during the Day—Many Telegrams and Letters of Congratulation Received—Many Press Notices of the Day, and many Tributes of Respect and Esteem for him who Called it forth 227–263

CHAPTER XVII.

Some Changes that have Taken Place in the Configuration of the Globe—Islands Born and Buried—French Revolution—Napoleon's Influence on Europe—England's Long Wars—Barbarous Treatment of Prisoners—Slavery Abolished—English Profanity and Intemperance—Temperance Movements—Duelling—Penny Postage—Expansion of the Press—Canals, Erie and Suez—Railroads in England and the United States—First Steamer to Cross the Atlantic—First Steamship Line 264–278

Contents

CHAPTER XVIII.

PAGE

Railroads Established—Engineering Progress—Steel, Iron Steamships—Horse Railroad—Kerosene Oil in Use 1830—Sewing Machines — Agricultural Implements 1831–51 — Sanitary Progress—Philanthropic and Christian Progress—Higher Education—Medical Progress—Humane Care of the Insane—Sailors' and Seamen's Home—World's Fairs—Religious Reciprocity—Arbitration—Numerous Inventions and Discoveries—Henry B. Plant in War and in Peace—Testimonial Presented to Mr. and Mrs. Plant on the Twenty-fifth Anniversary of their Wedding 279–306

PLANT GENEALOGY . . 307–337

INDEX 339–344

ACKNOWLEDGMENTS.

The author takes pleasure in acknowledging his indebtedness to many of the Southern Express and "Plant System" officials for their prompt and valuable assistance in the preparation of a biography of their able and esteemed President. Chief among those to whom thanks are due may be mentioned Messrs. A. P. C. Ryan, M. J. O' Brien, D. F. Jack, B. W. Wrenn, and G. H. Tilley. The last named furnished not only much material in manuscript and print, but many valuable suggestions as to their use. The letter of Ex-Governor Bullock of Georgia, published in the volume reveals the noble nature which penned it, far more eloquently than any words which can be written here, and is alike honorable to its distinguished subject and its eminent author.

Acknowledgment is due also to the papers from which extracts have been taken.

THE LIFE OF HENRY BRADLEY PLANT.

CHAPTER I.

The Plant Family—Birth of Henry Bradley Plant—Mr. Plant's Parents—Ancestors Came from England in 1639—David Plant Occupied Many Positions of Honor and Trust—A. P. Plant's Successful Business Career—H. B. Plant on his Mother's Side is Descended from Joseph Frisbee, a Major in Washington's Army—Reverend Levi Frisbee, Father of Professor Levi Frisbee of Harvard College—Connection with Sir William Pepperell, Bart.—The Historian of the Frisbee Family—Richard of the Second Generation Went from Virginia to Connecticut, and Settled at Branford, 1644—Sketch of Oliver Libby Frisbee, Historian of his Family—Senator Hoar's Relations to the Frisbee Family—Frisbee Patriotism and Services to their Country—They Were Good Church-Going People, Mostly of the Puritan Belief—Probability that the Frisbees Came from Wales.

HENRY BRADLEY PLANT was born October 27, 1819, at Branford, Connecticut. His paternal great-grandfather was attached to Washington's army as a private, when Washington was at Newburg, and he was one of the guard of the unfortunate Major André at the time of his execution.

His great-grandfather on his grandmother Plant's side was a major in General Washington's army at the same time.

Mr. Plant's father was Anderson Plant and his mother was Betsey Bradley. They were married December 23, 1818, and were of good old Puritan ancestry who came from England about two hundred and sixty years ago. According to a genealogical table at the end of this volume, it will be seen that John Plant was in Hartford, Connecticut, in the year 1639,—some give the date three years earlier,—and his son, John Plant, is granted a tract of land at Branford in 1667. These people possessed the characteristics that distinguished their race. They loved freedom, were thrifty, energetic, self-reliant, patriotic, and devoutly religious. Many of them were officers, and most of them members in the Congregational Church, which was the only church in the town for the first hundred years of its history.

Some of them occupied positions of honor and responsibility in the State and country.

David Plant was born at Stratford, prepared for college at the Cheshire Academy, graduated at Yale College in 1804, studied law at the Litchfield Law School, and was a classmate of John C. Calhoun. In 1819 and 1820, he was Speaker of the House of Representatives, and in 1821 was elected to the State Senate and twice re-elected. He was Lieutenant-

Governor of the State from 1823 to 1827, and from 1827 to 1829 he was a member of the United States Congress. In politics he was a staunch Whig. He was an influential man in the political circles of his day in the State of Connecticut, and Calhoun, when Secretary of State, offered him any position within his gift; but he refused to hold office under the dominant party.

Another successful man of the Plant family was A. P. Plant, son of Ebenezer and Lydia (Neal) Plant, born at Southington in the year 1816.

Early in life he began to earn his own living, and by industry, economy, and business tact he became in time the head of a large manufacturing establishment. He settled in that part of the town known as the "Corner," a part which rapidly increased in population and soon grew into a prosperous village. It bears the name of Plantsville in honor of A. P. Plant and his brother E. H. Plant. His biographer says: "He made a profession of religion in 1833; and from that time was an influential member of the Baptist Church. In 1850, he was elected a deacon of the church in Southington, and held the office until 1872, when he transferred his relations to the new enterprise started in his own village. To this church he gave liberally, and left it a legacy in his will." He is described as a most faithful and consistent Christian, an esteemed officer in the church, and a firm believer in the presence of the Holy Spirit in the heart of the Christian.

Henry Bradley Plant, on his grandmother's side, is a direct descendant of Joseph Frisbee, a major in Washington's army. The Frisbees were a numerous family, and many of them occupied positions of honor and influence in the history of the country. One of them writing to Mr. Plant says:

"I suppose you have often wondered what has become of my history of the Frisbee family. I have been diligently at work on it since you heard from me. It has grown from a very small beginning to be quite an affair, namely, from looking up my ancestors so that I could join the hereditary societies of the United States, to writing a history of over one thousand of the lineal descendants of Edward Frisbee, the first settler. I find them a noble race, worthy of history. I have also looked up my maternal ancestors and can trace them back to 1497, thirteen generations, among them Sir William Pepperell."

The fitness of the writer, Oliver L. Frisbee, for his task of searching the records of his long line of progenitors may be gathered from another paragraph in the same letter where he says: "My Alma Mater, Bates College, gave me the degree of Master of Arts, last Commencement, for eminent success in business and proficiency in the studies of genealogy, heraldry, and colonial history."

The following sketch, with some slight corrections, is taken from a carefully prepared account, by the same writer, of the descendants of Richard Frisbee, the first-named ancestor of this family.

"Richard Frisbee came from England to Virginia, in 1619, when he was twenty-four years old. In 1642, the Governor of Virginia ordered all those who would not join the Church of England to leave the Colony, and hundreds went to Eastern Virginia, now the State of Maryland. Among these refugees were Richard Frisbee and his two sons, James and William. They purchased plantations in Cecil County and resided on Kent Island, the northern part of Chesapeake Bay.

"At first the Governor of Virginia claimed this island; later, Lord Baltimore and afterwards, William Penn. The latter wrote to James Frisbee, from London, in 1681, instructing him to pay no tax to Lord Baltimore. James Frisbee was a member of the House of Representatives of Maryland, and held other important positions in the State. In addressing a petition to His Majesty, in 1688, he, with others, began their petition thus: 'We the undersigned Englishmen though born in America,' etc. James went back to England, the land of his birth, in his old age.

"Richard, son of Richard the emigrant, came from Virginia to Connecticut, and settled at Branford in

1644, when his brothers went to Maryland. His son John had several children, among them Edward and Joseph. The former was the ancestor of Major Philip Frisbee, of Albany County, New York. He was in the War of the Revolution, and his grandsons belonged to the Sons of the American Revolution, of the State of New York. President Edward S. Frisbee of Wells College, in New York State, is his descendant. The latter, Joseph, your ancestor [referring to Mr. Plant], married September 14, 1712, had a son Joseph who married Sarah Bishop, August 25, 1742. Their son Joseph married Sarah Rogers, March 11, 1773. Their eldest child, Sarah, born May 15, 1774, was your grandmother.

"The name Joseph has been in our branch of the family a long time. My father's name was Joseph. I had a brother Joseph, and my son born this summer is also named Joseph.

"The youngest child of the first Edward was Ebenezer, my ancestor, brother to John, your ancestor. He had two sons, Ebenezer and Elisha. The latter was the father of the Rev. Levi Frisbee who settled at Ipswich, Massachusetts, and was the father of Professor Levi Frisbee of Harvard College, who died in 1820, one of the most talented men that ever passed through that institution. Senator Hoar was named for him, George Frisbie Hoar. Ebenezer's son James, born in 1722, was lieutenant with Captain Paul Jones, and was killed one hundred and fifteen years ago to-day, September 23d, in the engagement between the *Bonne Homme Richard* and *Serapis* in the English Channel. This was my great-grandfather and by right of descent from him I joined the Sons of the American Revolution. His son Darius (born in 1769), my grandfather, settled in Kittery, Maine, and married Dorothy Gerrish, a great-granddaughter of Colonel William Pepperell, a well-known merchant and the father of Sir William Pepperell, Bart., the hero of Louisburg. Dorothy Gerrish was also related to some of the most distinguished colonial families in New England."

The subjoined letters from John B. Frisbee and Senator Hoar will be of interest in this connection.

"LAKEWOOD, N. J., December 16, 1894.

"MY DEAR MR. PLANT:

"This tardy reply to your favor of the 6th inst. is occasioned by illness since its receipt, and which prompted my coming to this place to recruit. I am now rapidly recovering from quite a severe attack of grippe, and hope to be able to leave for Mexico this week.

"Referring to the subject of your letter, I can only give you meagre information. My great-grandfather, Philip Frisbie, was a major in the New York Militia and served under Washington, and I have no doubt was closely related to the Joseph Frisbie you mention.

"I have a first cousin, Mrs. Farman, the wife of Judge Farman, formerly United States Consul-General in Egypt, who has devoted much time and research in obtaining an accurate history of our family. Recently, she went to Europe for the purpose of educating her children in the French and German languages.

"I have written to her, requesting her to advise you directly in regard to the information you desire, hence I feel assured that you will in due time receive a letter from her upon the subject.

"Since we last met I have visited New York several times, and upon each occasion you have been absent from the city, thus depriving me of the coveted pleasure of paying my respects to Mrs. Plant and your good self; with best regards to both, I remain,

"Yours very sincerely,
"JOHN B. FRISBIE."

"UNITED STATES SENATE,
"WASHINGTON, D. C., January 26, 1895.

"MY DEAR SIR:

"I know very little about the Frisbie family in this country. I have no relatives of that name. I was myself named for a very intimate friend of my father, Prof. Levi Frisbie, who was an eminent scholar in his time, a graduate at Harvard in 1802, and afterwards filled two professorships there. His writings, as I dare say you know, were collected with a brief memoir and are occasionally to be found in bookstores. He was son of the Rev. Levi Frisbie, of Ipswich, who delivered several addresses that have been published. Prof. Frisbie wrote some articles for the *North American Review* which you will find referred to in Cushing's lists of the articles. Dr. Holmes wrote me some years ago an account of Prof. Frisbie's personal appearance, which I suppose I can find when I am at home in Worcester, if you desire. Prof. Frisbie was nearly blind and instructed his classes and pursued his studies without being able to read.

"I am faithfully yours,
"GEO. F. HOAR.*

"To O. L. FRISBIE,
"Portsmouth, N. H."

The Frisbee family was patriotic and promptly responded to the call of freedom and independence. There were thirty-five of them from Connecticut in the War of the Revolution. Eleven of them spelled their names Frisbee; seventeen, Frisbie; and seven, Frisby. They continued in the service of their country from the Lexington alarm, April 19, 1776,

* George Frisbie Hoar.

until the disbanding of the army, by Washington, on the Hudson in 1783. A regiment marched from Connecticut towns, in 1775, to the relief of Boston. John Frisbee, son of Titus Ebenezer, represented Branford in the Legislature from 1690 to 1692. O. L. Frisbee writes to Mr. Plant: "Your ancestor was a good churchman. From him, there is a long list of Frisbees in the records of the church of Branford. In 1700, the annals of Branford say that among the families prominently identified with the church, town, and business from 1700 to 1800, the Frisbees, Bands, and Plants head a long list in the order in which I have written their names. This religious element seems to have been with the Frisbees. Rev. Levi Frisbee, father of Professor Levi of Harvard College, was a very pious man.

"He was invited to deliver an oration on Washington at his death. My grandfather was a very pious man; he founded a church at Kittery, Maine. My father, Joseph Frisbee, was a deacon in the church. He and Caleb Frisbee were in the regiment from Branford. I found Noah and Edward Frisbee were members of the company that marched to the relief of Fort William Henry, August, 1757, from Connecticut. I found your ancestor Joseph Foote Frisbee was in the Revolutionary War. He lived to be ninety-eight years of age. About 1700, Samuel Baker and Samuel Frisbee, Jr., bought land for a wharf at Dutch House Point, from Joseph Foote at Branford. Joseph Foote Frisbee might have been named for this man.

"In the church records of Branford there is a great deal about Joseph Frisbee, in connection with the church from 1743 to 1746. I find all the Frisbees good church (Congregational) people, from the first Edward who settled at Branford, July 7, 1644. He and his wife Abigail joined the Congregational church soon after settling in Branford. I should say the Frisbees were good fighters in war, and good church and law-abiding people, with Puritanic principles that helped to build the nation."

In a history of the Wolcotts of Connecticut, it is stated that John Frisbee and Abigail Culpepper, his wife, came from Wales. This may be correct, although in the genealogical sketch already given it is stated that the first of the family, Richard Frisbee, came from England to Virginia in 1619, but the same sketch says that in 1642 the Governor of Virginia ordered all who would not join the Church of England to leave the Colony, and that hundreds went to Eastern Virginia, now called Maryland, and that among them was Richard Frisbee, who with his sons settled in Cecil County, living on Kent Island, the northern part of Chesapeake Bay. Now it is quite common, in the early accounts of immigration to America, to describe the people as English, or as coming from England, when in fact they were Scotch or Irish. But coming from any of the British Islands they were often called English. This would be more likely to be the case with those coming from Wales, which is, geographically speaking, a part of the island of Great Britain. Be this as it may, it is not of great importance. The spirit of dissent from the Established Church was just as strong in England as in Wales. The name Frisbee or Frisby, as its terminal denotes, is of English origin, but it is quite possible that the family came from one of the border countries.

Whether this family came from Wales or England may be only a matter of historic accuracy and personal interest; certain it is the Frisbees are a people who have done honor to their country both in war and in peace. They bore a prominent part in the victorious struggle for the freedom and independence of the American Colonies. They have been the promoters of education, peace, piety, and "the righteousness that exalteth a nation." We have given this account of this people, for four reasons. First, because the historian of the family, with a commendable pride, has collected and preserved the family record of his people, from which the material for this brief notice was placed at our disposal. Secondly, because the family histories of the people who have combined to form the American nation are only beginning to receive a slight part of the attention which they justly merit. Thirdly, because a knowledge of the numerous and varied races that have formed the nation is essential to a correct understanding of the American people. Fourthly, because in the present case, owing to the early death of Mr. Plant's father, the widowed mother was especially dear to him, and is still cherished in his memory with the most tender and affectionate regard.

Mr. Plant's connection with Washington's army during the Revolutionary War was one of the family traditions, but he was not the man to accept honors unless he knew they rightly belonged to him. So after an extensive correspondence, and a thorough investigation of the military register in several States, and at the national capital, he received the following communication, which I have carefully copied from the original.

"Records and Pension Office, War Department, Washington, November 15, 1895. Respectfully returned to Mr. Oliver L. Frisbee, A.M., Portsmouth, New Hampshire. It appears from the records of this office, that Joseph Frisbee was enlisted September 3, 1780, and served as a private in Lieutenant-Colonel Sherman's Company (also designated as Captain Sylvanus Brown's and Lieutenant Joseph Hait's Company), Eighth Connecticut Regiment, Revolutionary War, and was also discharged October 29, 1780." On transmitting the above to Mr. Plant, Mr. O. Frisbee writes from Portsmouth, New Hampshire, December 24, 1895: "Enclosed please find the record from Washington of the service of your grandmother's father, Joseph Frisbee, in the Revolutionary War. He was born August 17, 1745; married, March 11, 1773, Sarah Rogers; had a daughter Sarah, born May 15, 1774, married Samuel Plant, February 11, 1795. These records will enable you and your sons to join in 'The Sons of the American Revolution.'

"O. L. FRISBEE."

CHAPTER II.

Branford, Connecticut, Purchased by the New Haven Colonists from the Totokett Indians in 1638—First Settlements were Made 1644—First Church of Logs Surrounded by Stockade to Protect from Indians—Guards at the Gate during Service—Church and Town Records Preserved at Branford—John Plum the First Town Clerk—Style of the Second Church Building and Character of its Services—Rev. Timothy Gillett its Pastor—He Taught an Academy in Addition to his Pastoral Work—Prominent Families of Branford—Intelligent Character of the People—De Tocqueville's High Estimate of this " Leetle State"—Branford in 1779.

SOON after New Haven was settled, the people negotiated with the Indians for an additional tract of land, some ten miles in length from north to south. It extended eight or ten miles east of the Quinnipiac River. The purchase of this land occurred in December, 1638. It was bought from an Indian sachem named Sorsheog of Mattabeseck. The territory included the land on which the town of Branford was built, and its Indian name was Totokett. It was several years before the purchasers went to live at Totokett. It was early in the year 1644 when the first settlers located upon their lands at Branford. By the first of October of that year, the society was so far organized that their minister could gather them for regular service. The people soon built him a house and a meeting-house, or church. This latter stood in the front of the old burying-ground; it was built of logs and had a thatched roof, and was surrounded by a cedar-wood stockade twelve feet high. A cedar-wood vase made from the wood of this stockade is still in the possession of Mrs. Samuel O. Plant.

During the hours of worship, one or more of the men stood guard near the entrance of the stockade. All carried firearms to church, or when going any distance from home. They were not afraid of the Totokett Indians, but of raiding bands of other Indian tribes who attacked both the whites and Indians. The fierce Mohawks from the neighborhood of the Hudson were often the assailants. The first thing that appears on the ancient records of Branford is the division of lands among the first settlers in the month of June, 1645. It has been said, and often repeated, that in 1666, when so many people went from Branford to settle at Newark, New Jersey, they took the records of Branford with them. These in some way were burned, and thus much valuable history was lost. But such was not the fact.

The town and church records have always re-

Old Homestead of the Plant Family.
Branford, Connecticut.
Birthplace of Henry Bradley Plant.

mained at Branford. They are quite full and in a reasonably good state of preservation. In a manuscript history of Branford from which the above account is taken, the name of the first town clerk, John Plum, in 1645, and a list of his successors, are given with the date of their service. It is interesting to note how much alike are the ways and customs of this old Puritan town to those of the town of Harlem, built by the Dutch a little later and now part of New York City. In both places the history of the town and the history of the church are one. They are so interwoven that they can hardly be separated. The division of the meadow-lands is the same; mutual protection from the Indians, and the manner of defence are also alike. The official appointment, by the town, of a man to gather in all the cows of the settlers, take them out to graze in the morning, and bring them back at the proper time to be milked, and many other such customs, are very much alike in both settlements.

The second church, or meeting-house, was built on the common, of wood, and was succeeded by the present house of worship, which is built of brick. Mr. Plant remembers the high galleries in the old church where the seats were arranged in slips, the boys on one side, and the girls on the other; neither could see the minister, and it is very doubtful whether any of them heard him. There were no children's sermons in those days. The babes, of whom Paul writes, were not fed on milk, but on strong meat, which even the rigorous doctrinal appetites of the fathers sometimes found hard to digest. Some of the modern church movements, such as women preaching, and Salvation Army barracks, would have sufficiently alarmed those good orthodox people to make them call for a day of fasting and prayer. Nevertheless they were a noble race, among whom misappropriation and embezzlement of funds, trust swindling and corporation stealing and political corruption were unknown.

The pulpit was the old-fashioned barrel-shaped structure, and, like some of the sermons, was high above the heads of the people. There was a great sounding-board over the head of the preacher, and it used to be a subject of calculation with the boys, whether this board would not some day fall on the devoted head of the speaker and stop the sound altogether. This church had the old family square pew, and in front of the pulpit was a bench for the deacons. The people were classified in their pews according to age, and the oldest, perhaps on account of their difficulty in hearing, occupied the seats nearest the pulpit. The church building was not warmed, save by the fervid sermons of those grand old Puritan divines. That, however, reached only the head and heart, hence, for the feet, they made stoves of sheet iron, over which was a perforated tin casing, and over this a hardwood casing. Coals from corn-cobs, or seasoned hickory, as being the most durable, were placed in this stove, which was carried in the bottom of carriage or sleigh to church, where its heat would last all forenoon. At the close of the forenoon service, the people went to the neighboring church house, which was warmed by a log fire. Here they ate their luncheon, and then returned to the church for another two hours' devotion.

The Rev. Timothy P. Gillett was pastor of this church in Mr. Plant's boyhood. He taught an academy—Mr. Plant being a scholar for several terms—in addition to his ministerial duties of preaching, visiting, and catechising the church people. He was a sober, solemn, orthodox clergyman of the old school, scholarly and dignified both in and out of the pulpit. It is only a hint of the changes that time brings, and no reflection on this good man's charity to say that, had he seen one of the modern ministers visiting his flock on a bicycle, he would have had him deposed from the sacred office. Some unfortunate misunderstanding came between him and his congregation in the latter part of his ministry, so that his wife refused to have his remains interred in the church burying-ground. She afterwards relented, was herself buried in the church cemetery, and left in her will two thousand dollars to defray the cost of removing her husband's remains thither, and for erecting a suitable monument to his memory. The sacred dust of both pastor and wife rests, as it should, among the people to whom they ministered for some fifty years or more. The town of Branford was composed of an intelligent, industrious, and religious people, mostly farmers and well-to-do citizens. The academy presided over by the Rev. Timothy P. Gillett constituted a centre of intellectual, moral, and spiritual development that inspired the life and elevated the character of the people.

The following account from the *Branford Annals* is only one of the many testimonies that might be recorded of the patriotism and courage of this people :

"No town in New Haven County was more important during the war of independence than old Branford. Her citizens proved very patriotic. She had a few royalists who were somewhat troublesome. But most of her people were self-sacrificing in a special degree in sustaining the federal cause. No town surpassed her in furnishing men and means. Most all of her able-bodied men were in the army, responding promptly at every call. Col. William Douglass' regiment, which did most effective service, was largely recruited from Branford. The coasts and harbors of Branford exposed her to visits from the vessels of the enemy. Coast-guards were needed, and were kept night and day at Stony Creek, Indian Neck, Town Neck, and at Branford Point. At the approach of the enemy, two reports of a cannon were to call out all the people to repel invasion. Expresses were kept in readiness to hasten to the remote parts of the town with the alarming news. When New Haven was invaded, patriots from Branford were quickly on hand to help. A company of her men were in the battle at Milford Hill. Two Branford men, Goodrich and Baldwin, were killed, and several others wounded at that battle. The attack of the British on the east side of New Haven harbor was repelled by the Branford home guard mostly. Those from Branford were supported by men from Guilford, who hastened to the rescue.

"At that time a new vessel, a brig named the *New Defence*, was at Branford wharf almost ready to sail against the enemy. She had been built and manned at Branford. Her future history was tragical. At the first alarm of the landing at New Haven the guns of this vessel were taken out and hurried over the hills to East Haven. There mounted and vigorously used and well supported by the brave minute-men with their muskets, the invaders were compelled to hasten a retreat. One of the reports made by the British officers speaks of the strong force and 'great guns' encountered in that direction. There is an old record at Branford showing that Mason Hobart, of that place, was paid £5 for carting two cannon to East Haven from the brig *New Defence*, July 5, 1779."

Connecticut, though one of the smaller States of the Union, has ever maintained a high standard of patriotism, education, and moral power in the progress of the country. De Tocqueville was in the habit of saying, "All de great men in Amerique comed from dat leetle State dey call Connecti-coot." Branford is an old seaport town. Its ship-building, fisheries, West India trade, two hundred years ago, were quite extensive for that day. It is also a seaside resort in summer, being half-way between Boston and New York.

Branford was for many years the Governor's seat of the colonial government of Connecticut. The house of Governor Saltonstall is still standing. Many of the useful and prominent men of the country were born and reared in this quiet yet enterprising little town, founded more than two and a half centuries ago by the Puritans of old England. Among its noted and worthy families were those of the Plants and Blackstones, of whom we shall speak in the following chapter, as the two families became connected by marriage, and are still warmly attached to their native town.

CHAPTER III.

The Blackstone Family—The Ancestor Came from England before 1630—His Name was William Blaxton—Settled First in Massachusetts, afterwards Went to Rhode Island—His Beautiful Character and Numerous Descendants—Origin of Yale College of Branford—The Blackstone Memorial Library.

FROM a pamphlet history of the Blackstone family, in which the name is spelled Blaxton, we gather the following interesting account:

"For several years before Winthrop came, in 1630, William Blaxton constituted the entire population of this peninsula [Massachusetts, of which the present Boston Common was then a part], at that time an unbroken wilderness of woods traversed by savages, by wolves, and other wild beasts almost as dangerous. Here he dwelt alone, exposed to dangers, many and great. He was a man of culture, refinement, and gentlemanly bearing, amiable and hospitable, liked by Indians, and indeed by everybody. These noble traits, this love of nature, his sacred calling, his trusting faith, invested whatever belonged to him with a romantic interest. He was a clergyman of the Church of England, born in 1595, graduated from Cambridge, England, in 1617, and died 1675, aged eighty years. Blaxton took orders in the Episcopal Church, but it seems that he never had a cure, though he still wore his canonical coat, which would indicate his attachment to the English Church, yet some have represented him as a non-conformist, 'detesting Prelacy.' He had in his library ten large volumes of manuscript books, presumably sermons, all of which were burned in his house during King Philip's War. Blaxton came to America in 1623 with Robert Gorges."

The father of Mr. Plant's first wife was Captain James Blackstone. He lived to the ripe old age of ninety-seven. His son, Timothy B. Blackstone, is building a public library in Branford to the memory of his revered father. The following extract of a letter to the donor from one of the trustees of this library, Mr. Addison Van Name, will be of interest in this connection, showing, as it does, the origin of Yale College. The letter is dated from Yale University Library, and runs as follows:

"My fellow-trustees asked me to procure a design for a book-plate, and one is herewith submitted for your approval. It seemed to us that a memorable incident in the earlier library history of Branford might appropriately be commemorated here, and this has been attempted in the vignette, in the upper right-hand corner of the plate. You are no doubt familiar with the story, but President Clap's *Annals of Yale College* is not a very common book, and I may be excused for quoting his exact language.

"In the year 1700, 'The Ministers so nominated met at New Haven, and formed themselves into a body, or society, to consist of eleven ministers, including a rector, and agreed to found a college in the colony of Connecticut, which they did at their next meeting at Branford, in the following manner, viz.: Each member brought a number of books and presented them to the body, and laying them on the table said these words, or to this effect, " I give these books for the founding a college in this Colony." Then the trustees, as a body, took possession of them, and appointed the Rev. Mr. Russel, of Branford, to be the Keeper of the Library, which then consisted of about forty volumes in folio.'"

The story is so good that, if there were not the best of reasons for believing it true, one might easily suspect it to have been invented. But in his preface President Clap says: "Several circumstances [and among them we may well suppose the incident in question] I received from sundry gentlemen who were contemporary with the facts related, among whom were some of the founders of the college with whom I was personally acquainted in the year 1726."

The following account of Mr. Timothy B. Blackstone is taken from the New York *Herald* of April 12, 1896:

"Mr. Blackstone was born in a part of Branford known as Blackstoneville, on March 28, 1829. His father, Captain James Blackstone, in whose memory he erected this building, was a well-to-do farmer and stock-raiser. He derived his title of captain from being elected to that position in a company of local militia. He was elected to the Legislature in the sessions of 1825, 1826, and 1830, and was elected State Senator in 1840.

"Timothy attended the public schools here until he was eighteen years old, when he left, and obtained employment as assistant to a civil engineer, who was at that time surveying on the construction of the New York and New Haven, now the Consolidated, Railroad. After finishing this piece of work he became an engineer, and was appointed assistant engineer of the Stockbridge and Pittsfield Railroad, a short line constructed in 1849, and now a part of the Housatonic road. After this road was completed, Mr. Blackstone went west in 1851, and took charge of the construction of a portion of the Illinois Central Railroad. He settled at this time in La Salle, Ill., and was Mayor of the city for one year. In 1856, he became civil engineer of the Joliet and Chicago Railroad, which ran from Joliet via Lockport to Chicago. After this he was employed in surveying the land over which the Chicago and Alton Railroad now runs.

"Mr. Blackstone first began accumulating wealth while this road was being built. He purchased land ahead, and then sold it at a profit. He then invested in stock, and held several responsible offices until he attained his present position—president of the great system."

On June 17, 1896, the magnificent library was dedicated with appropriate ceremonies, and called forth much enthusiasm from the townspeople.

In the course of his speech on this occasion, as reported in the *Daily Palladium* of New Haven, Judge Harrison said:

"While the primary purpose of the generous donor of this building, and its endowment fund, is to benefit the people of the town of Branford, it will never be forgotten that it serves also as a memorial to Hon. James Blackstone, who spent his long life of ninety-three years in this town, where he was born, and to the welfare of which he devoted so much time during the years of his young and mature manhood. For nearly two centuries the Blackstone family has occupied a conspicuous place in this community, and for the same length of time representatives of the family have been tillers of the soil, the title to which has always been in a Blackstone.

"We cannot properly dedicate this building to the purpose for which it is intended without calling your attention briefly to James Blackstone, his life, his family, and his ancestors. He was born in Branford in 1793, in a house located nearly opposite that home which was during nearly his whole life his residence, and where he died on the 4th of February, 1886. His first ancestor in this country was the Rev. William Blackstone, a graduate, in 1617, of Emanuel College, Cambridge. He received Episcopal ordination in England after graduation, but, like John Davenport of New Haven, he soon became of the Puritan persuasion, left his native country on account of his non-conformity, and became the first white settler upon that famous neck of land opposite Charlestown, which is now the city of Boston. When the Massachusetts colony came to New England they found William Blackstone settled on that peninsula. He had been there long enough to have planted an orchard of apple trees. Upon his invitation, the principal part of the Massachusetts colony removed from Charlestown and founded the town of Boston, on land which Mr. Blackstone desired them to occupy. He was the first inhabitant of the town, and the colony records of May 18, 1631, show that he was the first person admitted a freeman of Boston. His house and orchard were located upon a spot about half-way between Boston Common and the Charles River. A few years passed by, and the peculiar notions of the Puritans of Boston on the subject of church organization and government, had satisfied William Blackstone that while he could not conform to the church of Archbishop Laud, neither could he conform to the Puritan Church of Boston, and when they invited him to join them he constantly declined, using this language: 'I came from England because I did not like the lord-bishops; but I cannot join with you because I would not be under the lord-brethren.'

"In 1633, an agreement was entered into between himself and the other old settlers, in the division of the lands, that he should have fifty acres allotted to him near his house forever. In 1635, he sold forty-four of those acres to the company for £30, retaining the six acres upon which was his orchard, and soon afterwards he removed to Rhode Island, living near Providence until the time of his death, which occurred on the 26th of May, 1675. A few years after leaving Boston he sold the orchard of six acres to a man named Pepys. He was not in any manner driven away from Boston by the Puritan Fathers, but holding certain ideas which did not agree with those of his neighbors, he concluded to move to a new location, from similar motives to those which led John Davenport to leave New Haven and go to Boston after the union of the New Haven colony with the Connecticut colony at Hartford. All of the accounts and records of Rev. William Blackstone show him to have been a religious man, with literary tastes, of correct, industrious, thrifty habits, kind and philanthropic feelings, living for several years on Boston Neck, and demonstrating the ability of the white man to live in peace with only Indians for his neighbors. While living in Rhode Island he frequently went to Providence to preach the gospel, and was highly esteemed by all the settlers of that colony. In July, 1659, he married a widow named Sarah Stevenson, and by her he had one son, John Blackstone. The inventory of his estate after his death describes him as having a house and orchard, 260 acres of land, interests in the Providence meadows, and a library of 186 volumes of different languages. A river of Rhode Island and a town in Massachusetts were named Blackstone in his honor.

"His only son, John, married in 1692, and about 1713 moved to the town of Branford, where he took up his residence on lands southeast of the centre of the town, and bounded southerly by the sea.

"The son of this John Blackstone was born in 1669, and died in Branford, January 3, 1785, aged nearly eighty-six. His son, John Blackstone, was born in Branford in 1731, and died August 10, 1816, aged eighty-five. The son of this last John Blackstone, Timothy Blackstone, was born in Branford in 1776, and died in 1849, at the age of eighty-three. This Timothy Blackstone was the father of Hon. James Blackstone, who was born in Branford, in the old homestead of his father and grandfather, in 1793.

"Here were five generations of the Blackstones living and dying upon the old family farm in Branford. All of them seem to have possessed many of the traits of their first ancestor in this country. They were noted for their force of character, industry, modesty, and marked executive ability. James Blackstone, like his ancestors, was a farmer. At the age of twenty he was elected a captain in the Connecticut militia, and as such commanded his company for several months while serving as coast-guard on Long Island Sound during the war of 1812–15. He held at one time or another during his life the important local offices of the town, such as assessor and first selectman. Before the separation of North Branford in 1831, the township of Branford, as one of the original towns, was entitled to two representatives in the General Assembly, and on several occasions Captain James Blackstone of Branford and Captain Jonathan Rose of North Branford were the representatives of the town at Hartford and New Haven. In 1842, James Blackstone represented the Sixth District in the State Senate. In politics he was a Federalist, a Whig, and a Republican. His advice and counsel were sought by people, not only of his own town, but of neighboring towns, when occasions arose concerning the settlement of estates or other matters, where the opinion and advice of a man of marked good judgment were needed. The first time I ever saw Captain James Blackstone, he was pointed out to me by a resident of the town, as he was driving past the old public square, with the remark: 'That is Captain James Blackstone. When he rises in a town meeting and says, "Mr. Moderator, in my humble opinion it is better for this town that a certain course be taken," the expression of his opinion always prevails with the majority of the voters in the meeting, so great is the confidence the people of the town have in his judgment.' His character and remarkable ability can be easily read by any student of physiognomy who will look at the admirable life-size portrait of him now placed in this building. If his tastes had led him to a larger place for the exercise of his ability, no field would have been so large that he would not have been a leader among men.

"Yet here he chose to dwell, performing his part well through the whole of his long life. . . .

"The donor of this library was the youngest son of James Blackstone. To many of you his history and life are well known. He left the east more than forty years ago to pursue his chosen profession. He married, in 1868, Miss Isabella Norton of Norwich, and since that time his home has been upon Michigan Avenue, in that great metropolis of the west, Chicago. There, for over thirty years he has managed with consummate skill the affairs of the most successful of all the great railroads of the west. Of him, his character, his generosity, and his remarkable modesty, but great ability, I am not at liberty to speak . . . but this is not complete as a memorial of James Blackstone unless I mention briefly the other descendants. The eldest son of James Blackstone, George, died in 1861, never having been married. The eldest daughter, Mary, married Samuel O. Plant. One of her daughters, Ellen Plant, is with us to-day. Three grandchildren of Mrs. Mary Blackstone Plant, being the children of her daughter Sarah, are William L., Paul W., and Gertrude P. Harrison.

"The second son of James Blackstone, Lorenzo Blackstone, who lived for many years in Norwich, and died there in 1888, had five children. The eldest, De Trafford Blackstone, has one son, Lorenzo. The second child of Lorenzo is Mrs. Harriet Blackstone Camp of Norwich, who has three children, Walter Trumbull, Talcott Hale, and Elizabeth Norton Camp. The second daughter of Lorenzo is Mrs. Frances Ella Huntington of Norwich. The fourth child of Lorenzo Blackstone is William Norton Blackstone of Norwich; and his youngest son, Louis Lorenzo Blackstone, died in 1893.

"The second daughter of James Blackstone, Ellen Elizabeth, married Henry B. Plant, now of New York City. She died in 1861, leaving one son, Morton F. Plant, who is married and has one son, Henry B. Plant, Jr. James Blackstone's third son was John Blackstone, who died several years ago, leaving three children, George and Adelaide Blackstone and Mrs. Emma Pond.

"Sir William Blackstone, the great authority upon the common law of England, was a cousin of the fifth degree to our James Blackstone, and the portraits of the two men bear a marked family resemblance.

"Ten years ago James Blackstone passed to his reward. His influence for good still exists in this community, where the old New England ideas are yet strong, though modified by the leaven of modern industry, education, and thought."

CHAPTER IV.

The Plants Came from England to Branford, between Two Hundred and Three Hundred Years ago—Still Own the Lands First Acquired—Henry's Father Died of Typhus Fever when Henry was about Six Years Old—His Tender Recollection of his Mother —Henry's First Day at School—His Natural Diffidence—Mr. Plant's After-Dinner Speeches—His Mother's Second Marriage— Stepfather Kind to Henry—Thrown by a Plough Horse and nearly Killed—Attended School at Branford—Engaged on Steamboat Line Running between New Haven and New York—On Leaving, Promised a Captaincy—Marriage—Express Business—Leaves New Haven and Goes to New York—Romantic Experience in Florida.

THE Plants settled in Branford at an early date, and their descendants still own the lands on which their ancestors first settled over two hundred years ago. It will be seen, by referring to the genealogical table at the end of this volume, that Anderson Plant was of the fifth generation from John Plant, who resided in Hartford, Connecticut, in 1639. Anderson Plant was the father of Henry B. Plant, the subject of this biography. He is described as a farmer in good circumstances, of amiable disposition, fond of outdoor sports, gunning being a favorite amusement. He died when Henry was six years of age, and, consequently, Mr. Plant does not remember much about his father. He can recall, how his father once came in, with a friend, from a morning's duck shooting, and threw down half a dozen ducks on the floor. At another time, his father took him by the hand to see something that was happening in the town which had drawn out the people, but he does not remember what it was. His father died of typhus fever, and he himself also had the fever, and was so ill that he knew nothing of his loss until he was partially recovered from the dreadful disease.

One week after the father's death, the father's youngest sister died, and Henry's sister also died a few days following, when she was about a year old. He was then left alone with his mother.

She was the only daughter of the Honorable Levi Bradley. He was a member of the Legislature and also a musician who taught a singing school. Mr. Plant remembers that his mother sat with the choir in front of the pulpit and led the singing in the Congregational Church. She had been brought up in the Episcopal Church, and though her father did not approve of it, she deemed it her duty to go with her husband to his church.

"One of the first recollections I have of my mother," says Mr. Plant, " was on a Christmas Eve, when she dressed me up neatly, took me on her knees, talked affectionately to me, and sang that beautiful vesper hymn, 'Adeste Fideles'; even now, whenever I hear it, it brings tears to my eyes." This explains tears the author has seen in his eyes while listening to the orchestra in the music-room, but knew not then what were their tender and sacred association. Little did that mother realize the mighty power, the subduing influence, the enduring benediction to her child of that simple act, the outgoing of the maternal heart. The hallowed influence of that sacred hour has never been effaced through long years, in the whirl of business, in the varied conflicts incident to a public life, in close contact with civil war, within sound of the booming cannon, and the groans of the dying, away in far distant lands, and on stormy seas. Yet amid all, the hallowed influence of that sacred hour, when a mere child on a mother's knee, has never been effaced. How well it accords with what the poet wrote:

> "I had a mother once like you,
>   Who o'er my pillow hung,
> Kissed from my cheek the briny dew,
>   And taught my infant tongue.
>
> "She, when the nightly couch was spread,
>   Would bow my infant knee,
> And place her hand upon my head,
>   And kneeling, pray for me.

"Youth came; the props of virtue ruled;
  But oft at day's decline,
A marble touch my brow could feel,
  Dear mother was it thine?

"And still that hand so soft and fair,
  Has kept its magic sway,
As when amid my curling hair
  With gentle force it lay.

"That hallowed touch was ne'er forgot,
  And now though time hath set
Stern manhood's seal upon my brows,
  These temples feel it yet.

"And if I e'er in Heaven appear,
  A mother's holy prayer,
A mother's hand and gentle tear,
That pointed to a Saviour dear,
  Will lead the wanderer there."

Mr. Plant's first day at school is another tender memory connected with his mother. She had dressed him up in new clothes and talked to him about going to school and learning to read, and becoming a good scholar, and doubtless much more that her kindly mother-heart would suggest to awaken interest and stimulate ambition in the boy. Then she took him outside the gate, pointed out the schoolhouse, kissed him, and told him to go thither and give his name to the teacher as a scholar. His mother intuitively knew her child's sensitive disposition, and had her misgivings about his being able to carry out her instructions; so she concealed herself and watched him till he reached the school door. Here poor little Henry's courage failed him, and he came running back to his mother, not to be scolded, but to be encouraged and helped over his childish timidity. His mother this time went with him to the schoolhouse, took him in, and made him acquainted with the lady teacher. Thus began, more than seventy years ago, the first lesson of this most successful man. The scene is as vivid in his mind to-day as it was on the day when it was enacted. How little that teacher knew of the man that was enfolded in this timid child, and of the great privilege, as well as great responsibility, that was hers, thus early preparing him, in part, for his great career.

Henry was a very diffident child, nor did his diffidence quite cease with childhood, for even in manhood at public dinners when he suspected that he might be called on for a speech, it took away his appetite if not the enjoyment of the otherwise pleasant occasion.

This will surprise many of Mr. Plant's friends who have listened to him with pleasure and profit on many occasions. He rarely prepared his speeches, but drew his ideas from that knowledge and experience which he possessed on so many different subjects, and always spoke intelligently in plain, clear, well-chosen words, without any attempt at oratorical display. Of this we shall speak in another place.

"Some time after my father's death, perhaps three or four years," says Mr. Plant, "my mother married again, a man by the name of Philemon Hoadley. He was a very religious man, and was exceedingly kind to me; he said I was the best boy he had ever seen. He lived in New York State, and mother left Branford and we moved to his home at Martensburg, New York. I lived part of the time with her there and part of the time with my grandmother Plant at Branford. She always attended church on the Sabbath, and took me with her, never failing to carry a good luncheon, which we ate in the church house at the close of the morning service."

An incident of Mr. Plant's boyhood was sent to the writer by one who has known him long, and esteems the President of the Southern Express Company, (of which he has been a faithful and efficient agent in North Carolina for many years) very highly, and loves him with a genuine, manly affection. He writes thus:

"The following incident which occurred in Branford during Mr. Plant's boyhood may be of interest to you, in showing how near the country came to being deprived of his great usefulness and noble life. When a boy of about eight or ten years of age, he was one day riding a plow horse at work in the field. The horse became frightened and ran away, carrying plow, boy, and all with him. Barefooted and bareheaded, the brave lad clung to the horse until entirely exhausted, when he fell and was severely injured. He was found in the woods by friends who carried him into their house. After several hours' hard work by the doctor and others, he revived sufficiently to be taken to his home. The fight for life was severe and protracted, but he bore it heroically.

"I wish I could express all I feel towards Mr. Plant. I have been in his employ thirty-eight years —with the Southern Express Company. During all these years he has been a friend to me in all that that word implies. I am sure I voice the sentiments of thousands of his employees when I say that he is one of the noblest and best of men.   A. P. B."

After his mother married and had lived for some time at her husband's home in New York State, they went to live at New Haven and Henry made his home with them, often visiting his grandmother Plant at Branford. The grandmother wanted him to go to Yale College, doubtless in the hope that he might enter the ministry, for few took a college course in those days unless they intended to enter the ministry. But Henry was not particularly fond of study. He had attended the district school at

Branford, and had studied for a time at the Gillett Academy, and at Lowville, New York State. He had also studied under John E. Lovell, a famous teacher in New Haven, whose birthday was celebrated in New Haven, long after his death. He was the founder of the Lancastrian System of instruction in America. Henry did not accept his grandmother's offer of a college course at Yale. He was anxious to try his hand at some active occupation. He attempted several things, none of which seemed to suit him. At last, in 1837, he engaged himself to a steamboat line running boats between New York and New Haven.

The boats of the line were named respectively, *New York*, *New Haven*, *The Splendid*, *The Superior*, and *The Bunker Hill*.

Henry began as captain's boy and worked his way up, filling various positions for some five years, to the entire satisfaction of the company, so that on leaving it he was promised a captaincy of the next new boat if he would remain with the line. The following account, taken from a recent issue of *The Marine Journal*, shows how young Plant would pocket his fastidiousness, and stand up to manly duty like a true American. This recalls the story of a man in a Philadelphia market who tendered his services to an Irish coachman, who was troubled to find a man to carry home some fish which he had bought for his master.

Arriving at the fine mansion on Chestnut Street the Irishman offered to pay his porter, who respectfully declined saying: "Oh, no, I only just carried the fish to oblige you. I do not need pay. I am a United States Senator. Good morning."

"There are few men who can call to mind more interesting reminiscences of 'Auld Lang Syne,' and tell them in a more agreeable manner than Henry B. Plant. Referring to his early manhood, Mr. Plant said recently: 'I got my first experience in the express business when performing the service of a deckhand on a steamboat running between New Haven and New York in the latter part of the "thirties." At the time referred to I was employed on the sidewheel steamer *New York*, which had for companion steamers the *New Haven*, *Splendid*, and *Bunker Hill*, on each one of which I served at one time or another. It was on the *New York*, however, that I spent the most of my apprenticeship. The deck-hands slept below in the forecastle, an uncomfortably small space in the "eyes" of the boat, and took our meals in the kitchen, standing up. Take it all in all it was rather rough on a fellow that had just left a good home, and when some of my towns-people would come aboard and catch me with swab or broom in hand I didn't feel altogether happy, but had too much pluck to quit. One winter the *New York* had been laid up for new boilers, and I was transferred to the *Splen-*

did till the *New York* was ready for service, and when she came out in the spring it was quite an event. She had two new copper boilers, one on each guard, the first to be placed on the guards.

"'Up to this time a considerable lot of package freight, express matter, began to be sent back and forth. This was stowed in different places about the boat and not properly cared for, until one day the captain conceived the idea that a big double stateroom forward of the wheel could be used in which to store it, and I was given the duty of looking after it, and a berth was put up there for me to sleep in. As I look back upon my career in those days, the one on which I was transferred from the dingy forecastle to the express room was by far the happiest, and it was there that I took my first lessons in the express business.'" Those who are familiar with the extensive business of the Southern Express Company, of which Mr. Plant was the founder, and which begins at Washington and extends throughout the railroads south of Washington and the Ohio, excepting the Illinois Central, and to Cuba by the Plant Steamship Lines, can understand why it has taken nearly a lifetime of earnest toil to get it up to its present magnitude. It is a monument to the enterprise of the youngster from Connecticut, who got his first idea of the express business on a steamer between New Haven and New York nearly sixty years ago. The other large undertakings of Mr. Plant in railroads, steamships, hotels, etc., that have helped make the State of Florida the garden spot of the United States in winter, were easy as their necessities developed, in comparison to the Southern Express business which was the foundation of this enterprising citizen's fame and fortune."

Captain Stone was very fond of young Plant, and deeply regretted his loss to the service. It was during Mr. Plant's engagement with this company, in 1842, that he married Miss Ellen Elizabeth Blackstone, daughter of Hon. James Blackstone, one of the Blackstone family already referred to in this biography. One son was born to him, a promising child, who lived only eighteen months. His second and only living child is his son, Morton Freeman, now associated with his father as his assistant, and Vice-President of all the interests of the "Plant System," over which his father presides. Mr. Plant's position on the steamboat line plying between New York and New Haven, entailed a frequent absence from his home in New Haven, and he therefore decided to be more at home. At this time he went into the express business of the line conducted by Beecher and Company. At first he had charge of the business at New Haven, but afterwards went to New York City, still keeping up his connection with the boats. When the Beecher Company was consolidated with the Hartford and New Haven line, owned by Daniel Philipps and C. Spooner of Hartford, Mr. Plant was placed in charge of all the express business of the New Haven line in New York. Subsequently the business was acquired by the Adams Express Company, and was transferred from the steamboat line to the railroad, and Mr. Plant was transferred with it. While thus employed, young Plant was economical and saving. He received his pay monthly, and instead of wasting it in folly and dissipation he gave his earnings to his mother, and she banked it for him. He then bought some stock in a New Haven bank which he still retains. His stepfather, being a religious man, advised Henry to buy a pew in a new church which the Congregational Society was building at New Haven. This he did, and in after years, on the failure of the church, when the property was sold, he got back his money. His stepfather died at New Haven about 1862 or 1863.

It was in 1853 that Mrs. Plant was seized with congestion of the lungs, and Doctors Delafield and Marco advised that she be at once taken to Florida. On March 25, 1853, Mr. Plant started with his sick wife from New York City to Charleston, South Carolina, by the steamer *Marion*. From Charleston he sailed on the steamer *Calhoun* to Savannah, Georgia. And from Savannah he went by the steamer *Welaka* to Jacksonville, Florida. It took over eight days to

Ellen Elizabeth (Blackstone) Plant.

make the journey which is now a delightful trip of one day, for he left New York on the Sabbath morning and the next Sabbath evening he arrived at Jacksonville, which was a small village then with only one poor wharf and not a vehicle of any kind to carry passengers or baggage. He succeeded in getting some negro boys to carry his trunk to a poor hotel where he remained only one day. Through some persuasion he found a man to take him into his private house at Strawberry Mills, seven miles in the country from Jacksonville, across the St. John's River. Here Mrs. Plant's health greatly improved, her cough disappeared and she was so much better that by the first of May, Mr. Plant was able to leave her and return to New York. Early in July, Mrs. Plant came back to the city apparently in good health. The following almost romantic story is told in the New York *Times* of their first experience in Florida.

"In the winter of 1853, a Northern man with an invalid wife brought her down to Jacksonville to benefit her health. The present metropolis of Florida was then a settlement of five or six houses, one of which was called a hotel, but the hotel was so badly kept that the gentleman was cautioned against going to it, and he found accommodations in a private house. He had letters of introduction to a Florida settler, whose home was six or eight miles out of

Jacksonville, and as soon as he could communicate with him through a stray traveller, the settler sent his boat after the Northerner and took him to his house. The boat was an immense 'dug-out,' made from a single mammoth log, manned by a crew of uniformed blacks, who handled their oars in man-of-war style. At this settler's house a hospitable and comfortable stopping-place was found.

"In the course of the winter the lady's health improved to such an extent that her husband decided upon taking her to St. Augustine for a pleasure trip. There was in the household a beautiful Indian girl, the daughter of one of the Seminole chiefs, who afterward became the wife of the settler I have mentioned, and she volunteered to accompany the lady on what was then the long and difficult journey. The only road between Jacksonville and St. Augustine was the old Spanish highway known as 'the king's highroad,' and this was so grown up with trees and bushes that it was barely passable. But even this road lay five or six miles from the settler's house, and to reach it it was necessary to drive through the trackless woods. The gentleman and his wife and the Indian girl set out in a buggy, their host going before them on horseback to select the road and blaze the trees between his place and the king's highway, to enable the strangers to find their way back.

"The journey was made in safety; but the return trip took a little longer than was intended, and the party found themselves at the point where they must leave the old highway and turn into the forest just as the deep shades of a Florida night were about to fall. They found the blazed trees, but were unable to follow them. The gentleman, however, managed for some time to pick his way by finding the indistinct wheel tracks in the sand and the broken twigs; but as the darkness increased this became impracticable, and there was every prospect that the invalid lady and her husband and the Indian girl would be compelled to spend the night under the pine trees. But their host was better acquainted with blazed trees, and, as they did not arrive when expected, he set out on horseback to hunt them up, and his shouts soon gave them welcome assurance of succor. The lady's health was so much improved before the winter ended that she returned home comparatively well, and during the remainder of her life every winter was passed in Florida. Her husband has not since that time missed his annual winter trip to Florida, and he is now spending his thirty-ninth winter in the State.

"The gentleman who found Jacksonville a settlement of a few shanties, and who came so near passing a romantic but uncomfortable night in the woods with his wife and the Seminole girl, told me the story of his adventure a few days ago, while I sat with him in his gorgeous private car, so far down in the State of Florida that, in 1853, few white men had reached it. The Florida climate never did a better winter's work than when it restored the health of this gentleman's wife, and thus interested him in the new country, for the gentleman was Mr. H. B. Plant, who no longer does his Florida travelling in a dugout, but sends his own cars over his own tracks to the farthermost corners of the State."

CHAPTER V.

Mr. Plant Goes from New Haven to New York—Captain Stone's Friendship—Mrs. Plant's Health Fails again—Returns to the South—Is Appointed Superintendent of Adams Express Company—His Great Executive Ability—The Civil War—Mrs. Plant's Death—Mr. Plant Buys out the Adams Express Company.

WHEN Mr. Plant first went to New York City he boarded at the Judson Hotel, then kept by a Mr. Judson of Hartford, Connecticut. A little incident of that period shows the high estimation in which he was held by Captain Stone, Superintendent of the New York and New Haven steamship line. Captain S. Bartlett Stone brought his son George to board at the Hudson Hotel, saying, "Henry, when you were a boy I took charge of you; now do you the same for my son." Mr. Plant remained in New York until October, when the fall weather of the North began to affect the health of his wife unfavorably. He then started South by the steamship *Knoxville*, which ran to Savannah. When he reached Savannah he commenced to exercise his appointment as superintendent of the Harnden Express, which forwarded express matter from New

York by steamer to Savannah, and thence to Augusta, Macon, and Atlanta, by the Central, Macon, and Western Railroads; and also in Charleston, of the Hoey Express, by which goods were forwarded by steamer from New York to Charleston and were then distributed through the interior by the South Carolina Railroad.

About this time, Adams & Company had organized under the corporate title of the Adams Express Company, and had acquired all these express interests above mentioned. This was in March, 1853, and April, 1854. The chief shareholders of the company were Alvan Adams, of Boston; William B. Dinsmore, of New York; Edward S. Sanford, of Philadelphia; Samuel S. Shoemaker, of Baltimore; James M. Thompson, of Springfield, Massachusetts; Johnstone Livingstone, of New York; and R. B. Kinsley, of Newport, Rhode Island. When it was found necessary for Mr. Plant to go south again on account of his wife's health he was appointed superintendent of the Adams Express Company. This was in 1854, and he was placed in charge of all the interests then controlled by that company, and all that might be acquired by the company in the South under his management or through his efforts.

During Mr. Plant's administration of the Adams Express Company, the lines were extended over all the railroads south of the Potomac River, namely, Norfolk, Richmond, and Lynchburg, Virginia; Louisville, Kentucky; Cairo, Illinois, and over all the railroad lines constructed in the South, and over all the navigable rivers on which at that time there was steamboat connection. The expanding and establishing of this great express business at Nashville, Memphis, Vicksburg, Louisville, and New Orleans, and many other cities and towns, proved to be a herculean task requiring much arduous travel, often in stage-coaches by day and night, over rough roads, through swamp and forest, in summer's heat and winter's cold. It goes without saying that in securing efficient service, properly locating offices, appointing qualified agents, and earning the confidence and patronage of an exacting public, there was demanded a discriminating judgment, prompt decision, skill, and tact of the highest order. It was a tremendous strain on mind and body, and that too upon one not yet used to a Southern climate. It must be remembered also that the express business of the South forty years ago was in its infancy; the great Adams Express Company was still in its swaddling clothes, and required the greatest care and skill to nurse it into maturity, strength, and power, especially in the peculiar condition of the country at the time when a dreadful civil war raged throughout the land.

Few men would have ventured on such a hazardous undertaking, and fewer still would have conducted it to such a successful completion.

To the cool, clear head, the calm, quiet spirit, the persistent energy and dominant will of Henry B. Plant, is due the success of this great achievement. The Southern Express Company and the Texas Express together do a business now extending over twenty-four thousand four hundred and twelve miles of railway, have lines in fifteen States, employ six thousand eight hundred and eight men, use one thousand four hundred and sixty-three horses and eight hundred and eighty-six wagons. Of both these companies, Mr. Plant is the honored and efficient president, and were we to attempt to estimate the amount and value of the goods handled by these great organizations we feel sure the figures would be beyond the credulity of our readers.

This comes down to the year 1861, the beginning of the civil war, when the Adams Express Company, believing that it would be hazardous for Northern citizens to hold property in the South, decided to dispose of their interests there. After unsuccessful negotiations with other parties resident in the South, the company sold and transferred their entire interest in the express line to Henry B. Plant. He formed a corporation under the laws of the State of Georgia, taking in all the shareholders of the Adams Express

Company who were then residents of the States south of the Potomac and Ohio rivers.

The company thus formed, known now as the Southern Express Company, at once elected Mr. Plant as its president, and this honorable and responsible position he still holds. A central office was established at Augusta, Georgia.

Mrs. Plant's health now began to give way. Their little boy Morton was with relatives in the North. She saw that troubles many and great were coming upon the country. Her disease returned, consumption laid its cold hand upon her, and on February 28, 1861, this faithful wife and loving mother was taken from a world of strife, with its tumults of war and fratricidal conflicts, to the home of rest, peace, and eternal blessedness. The remains were interred in Augusta, but afterwards were removed to the family plot in the cemetery at Branford, the place of her birth and where her early years had been spent.

CHAPTER VI.

<small>Relations to the Confederate Government—Jefferson Davis Gives him Charge of Confederate Funds—Mr. Plant Buys a Slave, who afterward Nursed him through a Severe Sickness—Impaired Health—Goes to Bermuda, New York, Canada, and Europe—Second Marriage.</small>

THE seat of the Confederate Government at this time was Montgomery, Alabama, and the express company, just organized by Mr. Plant, was appointed by that government collector of tariff upon all goods consigned by the express company, and was also given the custody of all funds of the Confederacy that were to be transferred from one place to another. The express company filled this latter office until the dissolution of the Confederacy.

In consequence of this responsibility, officers and agents of the company were either relieved from military service, or detailed for the service of the express company. Its officers and agents were also for the same reason exempted from jury duty in Southern States.

Shortly before the removal of the capital of the Confederacy from Montgomery to Richmond, it was deemed necessary by government officials to define citizenship, and consequently a proclamation was issued by President Davis, that specified a time in which all citizens of States not in the Confederacy should leave it, or failing to do so within the time specified, would become citizens of the Confederacy, and would be subject to all duties and requirements of citizenship in the said Confederacy.

"At that time I thought it was incumbent on me," said Mr. Plant, "that my duties and opinions should be understood by President Davis and his advisers. To that end I caused myself to be represented by counsel to Mr. Davis and his Cabinet, in order that my opinions and position might be clearly defined and known to the government, so that its wish might be expressed, as to whether I should continue to have charge of the express company without interference, or avail myself of the proclamation, and take my departure with other citizens of the State of New York.

"I wished to know whether by remaining I would be required to abandon the express and its obligations. It was a great satisfaction to me to learn from my counsel that the Cabinet were unanimous in this decision expressed by the President, that I should remain and continue to conduct the business of my company, he having full confidence in whatever I might do."

The substance of this interesting episode has been published before with some slight variations, but the above is from the most authoritative source, and may therefore be received as correct.

While living at Augusta, Georgia, a curious incident occurred which resulted in the purchase of a slave by Mr. Plant. When the express office was opened at this place, help was needed, a sort of man-of-all-work for the many requirements of the office. Dennis Dorsey, a colored man, was hired from his owner to act as porter, and in whatever capacity he might be required. One summer when Mr. Plant was about to go north, Dennis came to him and said that his master was going to sell him, and that he wanted Mr. Plant to buy him. "What does your master want for you?" asked Mr. Plant. "Fifteen hundred dollars," Dennis replied, "but it is too much, I am not worth so much. You can buy me when you come back, as there is little danger of my being sold at that price." But Dennis was sold in Mr. Plant's absence. When Mr. Plant returned, Dennis besought him to buy him from the trader at Mobile who then owned him. Mr. Plant bought him for eighteen hundred dollars, and brought him back to Augusta. In a short time after this Mr. Plant was stricken down with gastric fever, and Dennis proved a good and faithful nurse to him. Mrs. Plant was in her grave, and Mr. Plant lived alone at the hotel, so Dennis was gratified by the opportunity to return the kindness rendered to him by his generous purchaser.

Early in August, 1863, Mr. Plant returned from the mountains, whither he had gone during his convalescence. His health had been improved by the change, but he was still far from strong. Mr. Thomas H. Watts, attorney-general for the Southern Confederacy, had seen Mr. Plant's physician, who had advised a change of climate. Mr. Watts sent Mr. Plant a passport, with an order from President Davis authorizing him to pass through the Confederate lines at any point. In about a month after this he went to Wilmington, North Carolina, and embarked on the steamer *Hansa*, for the Bermudas. He remained there about a month, when he went by the steamer *Alpha* to Halifax, Nova Scotia, and thence to Montreal. There some friends from New York came to see him, and brought his son Morton from school to him. Mr. Plant then went to New Haven, Connecticut, to visit his mother, and in the fall took passage on the steamship *City of Edinburgh* for Liverpool.

He was now a stranger in a strange land; the weather was cold, and with impaired health his experience was rather depressing.

However, Mr. Plant has never been the man to despond, still less to despair, but to make the best even of discouraging circumstances. So he went to Paris, whose mercurial people seldom cry, and always laugh when they can. Here he heard of some friends who were staying in Rome, and whom he would like to meet, so he determined to go there. By the French Commissioner of Passports he was informed that his passport from the Confederacy could not be recognized, and he was summoned to appear at the commissioner's office. He at once presented himself to this official, answered many questions, and was informed that there was no way by which his passport could be accepted at present, but as he wished to visit Rome, then occupied by French troops, his case would be considered.

A few days afterwards he had the satisfaction of receiving a document which served as a passport, given in the name of the Empire of France, and in which he was described as a citizen of the United States of America, resident at Augusta, Georgia, and all officers, civil, military, and naval, were commanded to protect this stranger. He went to Rome *via* the Mediterranean Sea, and was received everywhere with great respect. He was about two weeks in France, several weeks in Rome, and from thence he went to Naples, Leghorn, Genoa, Milan, and Venice, which latter place was occupied by an Austrian army.

From Venice he went to Switzerland, visiting many

places in that picturesque land, and returned to Paris by way of the Rhine. He then passed his time between London and Paris until the autumn, when he returned to America by way of Canada. He afterwards went to New York, where he was staying when President Lincoln was assassinated. By the end of April he was back in Augusta, Georgia.

Mr. Plant's second tour in Europe was in 1873, on the occasion of his second marriage. He was then accompanied by his mother and his son, Morton Freeman, and on this occasion he made quite an extensive tour of the continent.

His third visit was in the year 1889, when he went to the Paris Exposition with an exhibit of Southern products. Soon after his arrival in Paris he was asked by General Franklin, representative and Commissioner-General of the United States, to accept the position of juror in Class Six, representing the United States. To this responsible position he was duly appointed by the proper authorities, and served with entire satisfaction to all concerned. He was the only English-speaking juror in that class, as Sir Douglas Galton was absent until near the close of the Exposition. From this Exposition the "Plant System" was awarded a large number of medals, which may be seen framed in that palace of art, wrongly named an hotel, at Tampa Bay. A diploma was given to Mr. Plant, in addition, and many other marks of esteem and courteous attention were freely tendered him.

Mr. Plant led a very busy life in Augusta. He lived with his wife at the hotel, and, when she was travelling in the North in the summer, he had his office, for convenience, on the same floor as his bedroom. It had been his habit to keep pad and pencil by his bedside, so that when there came to his mind a matter that called for attention he at once put it down on his memoranda. He was constantly receiving reports from his express offices all over the South. There came to him, for adjustment, many questions of management that were perplexing and urgent, so that he was often on the road, called away at short notice, north, south, or southwest. Complications, great, varied, and numerous, were superinduced by the civil war. The railroads were often seized by the contending armies, offices were raided, and confusion worse confounded heaped troubles thick and fast upon the president of the company, sufficient to have crushed a man of ordinary brain and nerve. But Mr. Plant was not the man to give way to difficulties,—only coolly to plan, determine, execute, and conquer.

The following communication in memorandum form, from one intimately acquainted with Mr. and Mrs. Plant while in Augusta, Georgia, will be found suggestive of the busy life he led, and will prove valuable in furnishing the dates when he lived in that city, and the location of his various residences while there. Moreover, its sequel sounds like the plot of a good novel.

"Mr. and Mrs. H. B. Plant became residents of Augusta, Georgia, in 1854. Captain W. and his wife moved to that city in 1855. Both families boarded at the Eagle and Phœnix Hotel, and thus became acquainted. The Eagle and Phœnix was on Broad Street, and is now believed to be the property of Mr. Plant. Mr. Plant was busy organizing and developing the express business, was continually on the road, and made frequent visits to the North. He moved to the Globe Hotel about the summer of 1856. Captain W. and his wife moved to the Trout House, in Atlanta, Georgia, early in 1858, and Mr. and Mrs. Plant joined them there and spent the summer months with them, while Mr. Plant still made Augusta his headquarters and was constantly on the road.

"On Mr. and Mrs. Plant's return to Augusta in the fall of 1858, they took residence at the Planter's Hotel, then kept by Mr. Robbins. In the spring of 1859, Mr. and Mrs. Plant, leaving their young son Morton, with Captain W. and his wife in Atlanta, visited New Orleans and remained there during Mardi Gras. Their stay, however, was much shortened by the demands made upon Mr. Plant's time and attention by the celebrated Maroney robbery. Mrs. Plant's health, which had been failing for some time, was rapidly growing worse. Mr. Plant's movements were thus handicapped, and his trips necessarily became shorter and more frequent. Captain W. and wife moved to Athens in April, 1861. Mrs. Plant intended to spend the spring and summer of 1862 with them, but their plans were broken up by her death, at the Planter's Hotel, Augusta, February 28, 1862.

"Mr. Plant visited Athens shortly after the funeral, and remained several weeks; from thence important business called him back to Augusta. Health began to fail him and he visited Athens again in the following year. It was at this time that his friends prevailed upon him to pay a visit to Europe in the hope that his strength would be restored to him.

"In illustration of the good memory which Mr. Plant possessed for a past kindness, the following interesting story is told. The narrator was sitting in his office talking with Mr. Plant, when the latter suddenly turned from him to a clerk to instruct him in the following words. 'While I remember it, I want you to write to Mrs. W. to say that her request that we take charge of her money is granted. We will take it and give her six per cent., this will give her —— dollars to pay for her board, and we will add to it —— dollars, which will keep her comfortably among her friends.'

"The amount added was very nearly one and a half times as large as the interest on the moderate amount of insurance which her deceased husband had placed on his life before he died.

"Then when all arrangements for this poor widow's comfort had been made with the treasurer, Mr. Plant, not supposing that I had ever heard of the woman, explained that long years ago, when his first wife was sick in Augusta, this now widowed woman was very kind to her and also to his son Morton who was then a very little child. This was thirty-six years ago, but it was as fresh in Mr. Plant's memory, and as near to his heart as if it had occurred only a few weeks ago. Little did this good woman think at the time she rendered this kindly service to a delicate wife, that thirty-six years hence it would be paid back to her with compound interest. It may be truly said that 'bread cast upon the waters shall return after many days.'"

The Southern Express Company rendered very valuable services to the men engaged on both sides during the Civil War, by carrying packages, boxes, and parcels of all descriptions free of charge,—medicines, and comforts of various character, that made the hard life of the soldier a little easier, and gladdened his heart with the evidences that he was remembered tenderly in his far-away home. This service was especially acceptable on the occasions of exchange of prisoners, when clothing and money were the special needs of the men.

The benediction of many a brave heart, now still in death, rests upon the kindly services of the Southern Express Company so generously given during the four years of the bloody struggle.

In evidence of Mr. Plant's popularity and the esteem in which he was held by his associates in business as early as 1861, it may be mentioned that on January 1st of that year, at Augusta, Ga., he was made the recipient of a magnificent testimonial in the form of a service of solid silver bearing the following inscription:

PRESENTED TO
H. B. PLANT
BY HIS ASSOCIATES IN THE ADAMS
SOUTHERN EXPRESS
AS A TESTIMONIAL OF THEIR
RESPECT AND ESTEEM
AUGUSTA, GA.,
JANUARY 1, 1861

In 1873, eleven years after the death of his first wife, Mr. Plant married Miss Margaret Josephine Loughman, the only daughter of Martin Loughman, of New York City. She is descended from an ancient and noble family, whose ancestral estate, eight miles long, in the Land of the Shamrock, is now occupied by Lord Dundrum. Mrs. Plant's great grandmother on her mother's side was Lady Mary Murphy, of Ballymore Castle, Ballymore. Her own mother was Miss Ellen O'Duyer, said to have been a woman of great beauty and to have been descended from the Kings of Munster.

The finest train of Pullman palace cars we ever saw was prominent among the beautiful exhibits at the Atlanta Exposition of last year (1896). Their exquisite upholstering and decoration owed their superlative finish to the refined taste of Mrs. Plant. The Tampa Bay Hotel, more like a palace of art, is indebted to this same lady for much of its elaborate furnishing and artistic adornment. The two hand-carved mantelpieces in the salon, the admiration of all visitors, as well as some of the fine cabinet-work in the gentlemen's reading-room, evinced her business capacity and fine sense of the fitness of beautiful furnishing that costs no more than the plain and commonplace. She has given much time and earnest effort to the selection, purchase, and direction of the upholstering and decorations of that finest of American-built steamships, *La Grande Duchesse*, just completed at Newport News.

The impress of her forcible character and refined taste can be detected in many places throughout the great system over which her husband so ably presides, but is known only to those who are admitted to the inner circles of its operations.

CHAPTER VII.

Education from Books, and from Experience—Keen Intuitions—Abreast of the Progress—Mr. Plant's After-Dinner Speech at Tampa Banquet Given him by Tampa Board of Trade, March, 18, 1886—Location of Tampa—In Territorial Days Had a Military Reservation—In 1884 Population about Seven Hundred—Its Cosmopolitan Population now—Many Cubans and Spaniards in Tampa—Tobacco Industry—Phosphate Abounds in this Part of the State—Much of it Shipped to the North and to Europe—Plant System Gives Impetus to the Prosperity of the Place—Its Progress the Last Five or Six Years.

TEXT-BOOKS are necessary instruments in a systematic course of instruction, especially in the period of school and college days, but their chief value lies, not so much in the actual knowledge which they impart as in the intellectual training which they give for the acquisition of knowledge in the future. Hence, as civilization advances and the schools of higher education increase, less dependence is placed on text-books, and more emphasis is laid upon lectures and laboratories by which the student is stimulated to original investigation and independent thought. The knowledge of current events which we derive from observation of human nature, and which gives us great opportunities to do good to ourselves and to others, is not acquired from books.

The books may have done good service in the previous mental discipline, but the actual knowledge, the practical experience in a professional or business career, has come to us in the course of solution of the problems of life. Mr. Plant is a striking illustration of this fact. He was never a bookish man, and lays no claim to classical erudition or scientific knowledge; yet he is fully alive to the progress of the human race. Few events of importance in the world escape his keen observation.

It was his quick insight and keen penetration which led him to see the opportunities and possibilities offered in the South, when others had passed them by unseen.

Mr. Plant has an intuitive knowledge, possessed by few men, of many things outside his immediate sphere of action. He spent several days going over the plans of *La Grande Duchesse* in minute detail before the contract for building her was signed, noting scores of corrections which the architect was more than gratified to make. His after-dinner speeches at Southern banquets have no spread-eagleism in them; no declamation, but calm, quiet, easy suggestion, as if talking to a few friends whom he loved and wanted to help, and better still, wanted them to help themselves. There is no alarm, but friendly admonition, wise counsel, valuable instruction, most kindly administered.

In March, 1886, the Tampa Board of Trade honored Mr. Plant with a splendid banquet, and warmly welcomed him and his friends to this once sleepy old hamlet, now kept awake by the steam whistles of the South Florida Railroad and those of the steamships sailing to the West Indies. In reply to a toast by General John B. Wall, Mr. Plant said:

"Some two years and a half ago I was escorted here by some of the gentlemen present, upon a wagon-line across the peninsula of Florida from Kissimmee City, with Mr. Haines, Mr. Ingraham, Mr. Elliott, and Mr. Allen. We had a day's journey to reach over the gap in the railway that was then being constructed, connecting Tampa with the St. John's River. It was an interesting trip. I think to the best of my recollection we passed not more than seven habitations on that journey, certainly not more than that while daylight lasted, and now we can make the trip from Kissimmee to Tampa in three or four hours and find cities on the way,—cities of enterprise, with a frugal and industrious population. Business has grown, and great progress has been made in this part of Florida, but no place has improved more than this town of Tampa. Tampa, it seems to us, had a chill, although the climate was good. A citizen told me on that visit that they did not value the land at anything, but that the air was worth one thousand dollars an acre. That gave the value of Tampa land at that time. All are aware what is the value of Tampa land at present. Very little I am told is for sale.

"That is what the railroad has done for Tampa. The gentlemen who are associated with me look with pleasure upon the progress that has been made in Tampa. We go back and look upon the progress that has been made by what is known as the Plant System, which commences at Charleston, reaches out to Chattahoochee, and terminates at Tampa. This system, which you probably know, we call under various names; it is part railway, part express company, part steamboat company, part steamship company, but it all has one object and is known as the Plant System. It has been successful in what it has undertaken so far. I think that success may be attributed to the harmony that prevails in the councils on the part of the officers of the railroads, of the steamships, of the steamboats, and express, that go to make up that system. There is no jealousy, but rather a rivalry to know which will do the most. And to that spirit, in every one connected with the system, to do all that is possible to advance its progress, is due the success of the Plant System.

"This is, I think, all that can now be said in

direct response to the toast, but I would like to say a few words of Tampa, of its possibilities and its opportunities. You are all aware that Tampa is but one port on the Gulf of Mexico from which a railroad extends to the interior. There are ports north of it and ports south of it; ports where railways extend to deep water. Some of them have the advantage of Tampa. It is useless to mention the names, for you all know them; you are familiar with the advantages of all these ports. I will not give the reason why they have not advanced. It may be because they have not all had the railway backing that Tampa has had; they have not had a united line of railways leading to them and extending from them. Tampa has just started, it seems to me, in its progress towards prosperity, and the prosperity that it must receive if it receives the backing that commerce would dictate to it. The wants of commerce are large; they are exacting, and Tampa has many rivals. There are many cities that aspire to it and to grow as these cities see that Tampa is growing at the present time. They will do it, if it is possible, by putting on steamship lines, by putting on railway lines, by extending them to get some of the business at least, that is now drawing towards Tampa, and it is for the people of Tampa to determine for themselves to what extent they shall share it.

"As I have stated, it is important to Tampa's interests to see that all obstructions to commerce are removed; in other words, that commerce and trade shall be unimpeded both to and through Tampa. You all recollect that last year there was a great Exposition in a neighboring city of the Gulf—New Orleans,—where millions of money were expended to draw the attention of the countries south of us, notably the West Indies and South America. This, that their attention might be drawn to the United States, and especially the southern part of the United States, for trade, and, as I said, millions of money were expended on making that Exposition and maintaining it all the winter for the purpose of showing the people of the West India Islands what could be done. That Exposition was gotten up not for benevolence, but for the purpose of inviting trade. Now we are doing all we can to encourage that trade by opening up mail communication between the United States and those very countries that so much money was spent to encourage the trade from.

"We are running steamships three times each week, and I think that every gentleman in this hall should raise his voice to the authorities at Washington and endeavor to persuade them to send the mails of the entire United States (I mean the mails of the entire United States, the South and West as well as the

East), by the quickest route whereby they can reach those countries of which I have spoken. By that route the mails can reach the whole of the West India Islands, the whole of the west coast of South America, in better time and more frequently, with the present source of communication than by any other line. And notwithstanding that line was put on on the 1st of January, our postal authorities at Washington hardly seem alive to that fact, and, as I said before, I think that the gentlemen of Tampa should raise a united voice that the Post-Office Department may be waked up to know there is a route via Tampa that is the quickest for the entire countries south of us. I do not know that I can say any more. I have responded to the toast 'Our Honored Guests,' and said very little about them. I feel somewhat in the position that Mr. Ward probably felt when he was advertised to deliver a lecture on 'Twins.' He occupied his entire evening on the introduction, and left the speech on the 'Twins' out altogether."

The following account of the growth of Tampa is taken from the New York *Daily Tribune* of November 17, 1891. It illustrates the large share which Mr. Plant has had in this growth, and the way in which he has closely identified himself with its history.

"Over on the west coast of Florida in Hillsborough

County, or less than two hundred miles north of the southern end of the State, is an old, old town, which, in the territorial days of Florida, when the Government first established a military reservation here, was a small settlement that grew into a village and was called Tampa. Owing to its extreme isolation, its growth was slow, and, in 1884, there were not more than one or two shops, and a population of a little less than seven hundred. A year later the southern terminus of the Plant System of railroads was established at Tampa, and since then the growth of the place has been phenomenal. As Postmaster Cooper, one of Tampa's wide-awake citizens and a newspaper editor, says: 'Henry B. Plant may be said to have been the founder of Tampa, and people of enterprise, industry, and capital from every State in the Union, and Cuba, have flocked here and built upon the foundation, until to-day Tampa rivals the best cities in the State. The South Florida Railroad is one of the best equipped railways in the South, extending from Port Tampa to Sanford, a distance of 124 miles.'

"The South Florida Road runs through the most fertile and most prosperous part of the State and has done more than any other agency to develop South Florida. And while it is true that the railroad gave to Tampa her first onward impetus, and has done, and is yet doing, much toward the development of the place, yet there are other agencies which have done much to help along the great work. The most prominent of these is the cigar-making industry, which was first established here three years ago. It is second to none as an important factor in Tampa's substantial prosperity and commercial success. Tampa has also profited by the immense deposits of phosphate, which is shipped from here, not only by rail all over the country, but by water direct to Europe. There is a large grinding mill here, and a meeting of representatives of phosphate interests was held recently, and a movement started to put up the necessary tanks and machinery for making the acids and other materials for the manufacture of superphosphate. When factories of this sort are put up it will no longer be necessary to send the phosphate to Europe to be acidulated.

"I went over to the palatial Tampa Bay Hotel, an enterprise of Mr. Plant, and the completion and furnishing of which, preparatory to its opening in two or three weeks, Mr. Plant has been personally supervising. I found him and a portion of his family at breakfast in his private car, in which he was to start north in the afternoon for a brief stay before coming down here for the winter. Mr. Plant is always approachable, genial in his manner, ready to talk about people and their prosperity, but not of himself or his. No one can accuse him of egotism. He said nothing of his massive hotel until I drew him out. I said: 'Mr. Plant, I learn that no one knows better than you of the beginning and the progress of Tampa and its probable future. In fact, they say that you are the father of Tampa; tell me about it, please.'

"'Well,' said the genial railroad president, 'when I first drove across the country from Sanford, for we are nearly west of that point, and there was no other way of getting here by land, I found Tampa slumbering as it had been for years. This was eight years ago. It seemed to me that all South Florida needed for a successful future was a little spirit and energy, which could be fostered by transportation facilities. There were one or two small shops and a population of about seven hundred in Tampa. I made a careful survey of the situation, calculated upon its prospects and concluded to take advantage of the opportunity, and we who made early investments have proved the faith in our own judgment. Tampa was really unknown to the commercial world until the South Florida Railroad introduced her there. This was in 1885, and it brought to the town a new life, and breathed into it all the elements of push, progress, and success. Tampa at once began to spread itself, and ever since has been fairly bounding along the road to greatness. It has now a population of about ten thousand, and is rapidly increasing.

Hundreds upon hundreds of thousands of dollars have been invested in business, and instead of a few scattered and unpainted storehouses, there are now many magnificent brick blocks, handsome private residences, cosey cottages, large warehouses, mammoth wholesale establishments, busy workshops, comfortable hotels, two newspapers, a phosphate mill, cigar factories, first-class banking facilities, telegraph and telephone communications, two electric-light establishments, ice factories, a complete system of waterworks, eight lines of steamships and steamboats giving communication to Key West and Havana, Mobile, places on the Manatee River, etc.'

"Mr. Plant's hotel, upon which he has spent about $2,000,000 on the building and grounds and $500,000 for the furnishing, and which is nearly ready for the opening, is in the centre of a sixteen-acre plot of ground just north of the city bridge. The architecture is Moorish, patterned after the palaces in Spain, and minarets and domes tower above the great five-story building, each one of which is surmounted with a crescent, which is lighted by electricity at night. The main building is 511 feet in length, and varies in width from 50 to 150 feet. A wide hall, on either side of which are bedrooms, single and in suites, runs the entire length of the building to the dining-room at the southern end. The exterior walls are of darkened brick, with buff and red brick arches and stone dressings. The cornices are of stone and iron; the piazza columns are of steel, supported on pieces of cut stone.

"The main entrances are through three pairs of double doors, flanked by sixteen polished granite columns, supporting Moorish arches, over which balconies open from the gallery around the rotunda to the second floor. The principal staircase is of stone, and the horseshoe arch and the crescent and the star meet the eye at every turn—the electric lights in the dining-hall, the music-hall, the drawing-room, the reception-room, the reading-room, and the office being arranged after these patterns. The drawing-room is a casket of beautiful and antique things, embracing fine contrasts. There are a sofa and two chairs which were once the property of Marie Antoinette; a set of four superb gilt chairs which once belonged to Louis Philippe; two antique Spanish cabinets, and between ten high, wide windows appear Spanish, French, and Japanese cabinets, both old and quaint. Old carved Dutch chairs, rare onyx chairs, and queer seats of other kinds are scattered along the hall. Among the large collection of oil paintings, water-colors, and engravings, are portraits and old pictures of Spanish castles and fortresses.

"A large rustic gate for carriages and two for pedestrians lead into the grounds on the northern side. These gates are made of cabbage-palmetto trunks, the mid-ribs being of the leaves worked into a quaint and rustic design. On either side of the great gate stand giant cabbage-palmettoes, thirty and forty feet high, set in groups of five and seven, the Moorish numbers. A number of large live-oaks, one a tree of great breadth and beauty, remain on the grounds. Near the centre of the lawn a fort has been built of white stone, having two embrasures. In it are mounted two old cannon that were spiked on the reservation of Tampa during the Civil War. The grounds front on the Hillsborough River and overlook the city, Fort Brooke and Tampa Bay, and are filled with fruit-trees, roses and flowers.

"The streets of Tampa are not what they will be, but a great improvement has been going on in the last year; and when all the thoroughfares are paved, macadamized or otherwise hardened, they will be attractive drives. The roads on the west side of the river are naturally hard and smooth, giving fine drives in various directions. The water supply is obtained from one of the largest springs of water in the State, and is abundant for all purposes, and ample factories provide ice from distilled water. Until the session of Congress of 1889, Tampa was in the Key West customs district, and the custom-house business was looked after by a deputy appointed by the Collector of Customs at Key West.

But when Congress passed a bill making Tampa a regular port of entry, a collector and a full corps of assistants were appointed. To give an idea of the growth of Tampa, it is only necessary to compare the customs returns for 1885, when, under a deputy-collector, the receipts were only $75, with the report of last year, which showed receipts considerably above $100,000.

"For a long time builders had suffered great inconvenience and delay because there were no brickmaking works. It was not believed that good brick could be made in Tampa, and all orders for this necessary building material had to be sent away from home. But in 1888, one of the enterprising citizens, who had found a bed of good clay just north of the city, began to manufacture bricks. The result is that builders are now furnished with home-made bricks almost as fast as they need them. It was stated to me that as much as $300,000 had been expended in the erection of brick buildings during the last year. One of the new public buildings is the City Hall and Court House. It is 50 by 100 feet on the sides and is two and a half stories high.

"Tampa's population may certainly be called cosmopolitan, comprising people from every quarter of the globe; but three classes preponderate so largely as to warrant distinction,—the American, the Cuban white people, and the African or colored people. There is no difference worthy of note between the first mentioned in Tampa and those of other sections of the United States. They have all the push and enterprise characteristic of the American people, and are the peer of any in social life.

"There are between three and four thousand Cubans in Tampa, and some Spaniards, too, but there is an intense prejudice on the part of the Spaniards against the Cubans, and as the latter feel the same dislike for the Spaniards, conflicts between the two sometimes occur, and if it were not for the good police administration might prove serious in some instances. The Cubans are many of them propertyholders and are identified closely with the city's growth. They are reported as moral, temperate, energetic and quite desirable citizens; and, are almost without exception, engaged in cigar-making and kindred industries. They are also an amusement-loving people, have several clubs and societies, an opera-house, a band and a newspaper. The Cuban settlement is in the Fourth Ward, called Ybor City, after Martinez Ybor, the pioneer cigar manufacturer in Tampa. Only four years ago this part of the city was an unimproved and uncultivated forest; now it is an active, bustling, wealthy town within itself, and, to add to its interest, Postmaster Cooper recently established a branch station, as he has also in the settlement of the colored people, for the accommodation of those who live far from the general post-office.

"Twelve cigar factories are located in Ybor City, and there nearly all of the cigar-makers live. The largest factories are those of Ybor & Co., Sanchez, Haya & Co., Lozano, Pendas & Co., R. Monne & Bro., and E. Pons & Co. These five factories manufactured 33,950,575 cigars last year, the output of the Ybors alone being 15,030,700. The total number manufactured in the thirty factories in Key West was 77,251,374. More than $30,000 is paid out to the 1500 or 2000 cigar-makers in Ybor City every Saturday night, one-fourth of which is paid out at Ybor's factory; and about $150,000 has been expended here in the past six years upon improvements. This cigar-making industry has contributed materially to the development and growth of Tampa during the last five years, and it promises much greater benefit in the future. It was in October, 1885, that Martinez Ybor & Co., who began manufacturing in Havana in 1854, and afterward put up a large factory in Key West, came to Tampa to investigate the resources and advantages offered for cigar-making. They soon afterward purchased forty acres of land in the Fourth Ward, cleared it of the pines, wild-oats and gophers, and built a factory, a large boarding-house or hotel, and several small cottages for the workmen whom they brought from Key West and Havana. The venture proved a success from the start and improvements were added. The original factory, a wooden structure, is now the opera house, and a large brick factory has succeeded the first one, where the daily output of the 450 cigar-makers employed is 40,000 to 50,000 cigars. Then came Sanchez & Haya, Emilio Pons, and others, and all declare that they are doing an excellent business.

"'The required condition of the climate of Tampa for good cigars is said to be fully equal to that of Key West or Havana,' said one of the manufacturers who has had factories in both places. 'This has been proven by an actual and thorough test. Another advantage comes from the superior transportation facilities of the South Florida Railroad, which gets freight quickly to New York.'

"The colored people of Tampa are declared to be in a better general condition than they are in any other part of the South. They are also represented to be a generous, quiet and inoffensive class of citizens. They are also far more industrious than those in some other sections of the South, working almost every day, and the 2000 negro population have a settlement of their own, midway between Tampa proper and Ybor City, which would be a credit to any community. Many of the houses, like the streets, run in irregular lines, but the homes and the shops have a tidy and orderly appearance as though not neglected, and at night everything about them is quiet and peaceful, only the songs and the moderate conversations and the musical laughter being heard. Very few of these people live in rented apartments, but nearly all own their little cottage homes. They have many excellent churches, schools taught by colored teachers, and nearly every home has a small library. Then, too, or with very few exceptions, the colored people command the respect of the whites.

"Port Tampa, which is the port from which the Plant Steamship Line sails for Havana and other places, is about ten miles below here. One of its attractions is 'The Inn,' a great hotel built in colonial style, beside the South Florida Railroad, over the water and about 2000 feet from the shore. It is both a summer and winter resort for tourists and Floridians. Another attraction is the fishing, either for bass from the wharf or boats, or for the tarpon, or, 'Silver King,' at Pine Island. The third attraction is Picnic Island, the name itself telling its purpose."

Notwithstanding the general depression of the country during the last five years, the growth of Tampa has gone forward with a rapidity unsurpassed in any five years of its history. The entire city has increased in population from seven thousand to twenty-eight thousand during the past decade and is still growing steadily. Property is as valuable on the main business street of Tampa as it is in New York City above Central Park. The city has a Board of Trade, a Board of Health, schools, academy and churches of all Christian denominations. Few, if any, cities in Florida have a more promising future before them than Tampa.

CHAPTER VIII.

Florida Mr. Plant's Hobby—Banquet at Ocala—Mr. Plant's Speech—Sail on Lakes Harrison and Griffin—Banquet at Leesburg—Visit to Eustis—Cheering Words to a Young Editor—Make the best of the Frost—It may be a Blessing in Disguise—Must Cultivate other Fruits, (and Cereals) besides Oranges—Importance of Honesty—Sense of Justice—Consideration for the Workmen—Unconscious Moulding-Power over Associates and Employees—Letter of Honorable Rufus B. Bullock.

MR. PLANT'S associates say of him: "Oh, Florida is one of the President's pets." Anything touching the prosperity of Florida is sure to get a sympathetic hearing from him at all times. He loves the Land of Flowers and has spent many pleasant days in it at all seasons of the year. Nor does it fall to the lot of every man to receive such high appreciation for the good he has done and such esteem and affection as Mr. Plant receives from these warm-hearted, whole-souled Southern people. Mr. Plant having recently included Ocala in his railroad and hotel system, a fact which promises much for the future progress of this enterprising town and section of Western Florida, the people wished to express their grateful appreciation of the man whom all the South delights to honor. So, in the winter of 1896, they tendered to him a grand banquet to which he and his friends and associates in office were welcomed. Nothing was left undone by these good people to make the occasion pleasant.

The feast was held in the Ocala Hotel which came into the possession of Mr. Plant during 1896, and was opened that season as one of the Plant System Hotels. The house was elaborately decorated with Southern ferns and flowers. A reception was first held in the parlor, then about seventy ladies and gentlemen sat down to a sumptuous dinner, enlivened by sweet music, and good cheer. Many beautiful tributes of esteem and friendship were eloquently presented to the guest of the evening, who had been requested by the committee of arrangements to speak to the toast, "The Plant System." The following account taken from the Atlanta *Constitution*, is a fairly good report of his speech, which held the audience spellbound from beginning to end. He said: "I am gratified and pleased beyond measure to be with you to-night on an occasion of social enjoyment to exchange compliments and greetings with the undaunted citizens of Ocala and revel in the bounteous hospitality of this proud and prosperous little city. Words count for but little in the effort to express my sincere appreciation of such evidences of cordiality as have been shown this night to me and to my friends and associates in business. Surely the very presence of so many of your community's worthy citizens, your city's leading business and professional men, who have rendered the further compliment of bringing with them their charming wives and daughters, would of itself inspire any man, who is not insensible to the impulse of gratitude, with a feeling of gratification and deep appreciation for the compliment it conveys. It pleases me to see so many of the ladies of Ocala here to-night, for their charming presence lends beauty to the brilliant scene and makes all the more enchanting this hour of pleasure and promise.

"I feel that it is good to be here. I am always glad to mingle in social intercourse with my good friends of Florida, for I warrant you that nothing is more comforting than to know that in all my endeavors to aid them in the upbuilding of their favored section I have their hearty good-will and unstinted co-operation. In congratulation upon the continued prosperity of Ocala, despite the recent chilling frosts, which seemed well-nigh to sweep away your beautiful orange groves and blight the interests of your agricultural community, I wish to say that it is pleasing to me to observe the undaunted pluck and courage of your irrepressible and invincible people, who, never swerving from the duties of citizenship, have set about the arduous task of building up again the agricultural and industrial interests of this region of Florida, with a newness of life and a heartier zest. Such determined effort will surely be crowned with unbounded success and prosperity in the end. There is no reason why Ocala should not be a prosperous city. Your climate is excellent; your water is pure and wholesome; your lands are fertile and prolific, and your people are joined with a unity of ambition and a unity of aim for the upbuilding of every interest alike.

"I have been asked to speak to you of what is known as the 'Plant System.' Not this mere physical system of the man—for that speaks for itself. But the system of railways and steamships and other interests which have been built up as all other industries are built up in the great march of American progress and industrial development. In touching upon the plans and scope of the Plant System, I believe I will be credited with perfect sincerity when I say in the very outset, that if some of the conditions of which we now have knowledge had been known in the beginning, much of this system would not exist to-day. I have reference to such conditions as have in late years arisen and confronted corporations in the nature of an obstacle and an obstruction. As you all perhaps know, there has been a great change in the plans and methods of railroad construction during the last decade or two. In the old days railroads were built for the most part by the people of means along the proposed route, and they were for the most part short lines. People did not set out in the earlier days to build long lines of railways. As years rolled by, however, there sprang up among the people of some sections an unexplained feeling of hostility to corporations— a sort of antagonism to capital—which has worked its way like a devouring worm into the politics of the nation, and which, in recent years, has well nigh sapped the lifeblood from many of the leading railway systems of the country, by plunging them into such a complicated pool of injurious legislation as to land them on the dangerous shores of bankruptcy. Just at the time when such a spirit of antagonism was at its zenith there came a change in the methods of operating railway lines. Instead of the short lines, several of the roads began to be joined together for a longer line, thus reducing the expenses of operation and at the same time giving better facilities of travel and of shipment. It was found that the railroads could not live if operated on the short-line basis, for competition grew so great it became necessary to link this road and that to form a through line binding the commerce of one section to that of another in rapid transit at reduced expenditure. This came as a necessity born of the situation, for the railroads were being bankrupted on the old plan and were sold out by receivers for their original owners to the men of capital, and they saw the absolute necessity of a more economical basis of operation. Taxes were high, competition was great and everything served evidence that the old plan would no longer prove feasible.

"Just why there should be any hostility to such a plan of railway management among the people who are, after all, the ones benefited most by the increased facilities that are given them, is not made clear to me, but such a spirit did prevail, and does prevail to-day in some sections to such an extent that men, blinded to the interests of the people of their sections, are continually stabbing at the very heart of the railway corporations and crying out that they need to be watched by legislative censors, and of this notion the railway commission was born. My friends, I know but little of the motives that prompt such legislation against railroads, but I do know that some very serious mistakes have been made. It has been said that the king can do no wrong, but it has with equal truth been said that the king can make mistakes. In the State of Georgia, this persistent spirit of hostility to railroads, this organized effort of legislative restriction, has within the past few years thrown nearly every railroad in the State into the hands of a receiver. The result has been a gradual reorganization of these properties by the men of capital in the East, and a new plan of operation at reduced expenditure through consolidation. What else could have resulted?

"The interests of the people and the railroads are certainly not conflicting interests. They are common interests and should go hand in hand and heart to heart in the great work of building up this country. The one should not be made an obstacle for the other. I cannot see how the Plant System of railways and steamships could be other than a pillar in the structure of the industrial world of this Republic, interested in all that tends to the promotion of the general interests of the people. Of what avail would railroad construction be to the owner if it were intended to be run in hostility to the business interests of the people of the country it traversed? What would a railroad be worth if not supported by a healthful business community in perfect harmony? On the contrary, what would any country be without the railroads?

"It is true that the people of this section have suffered heavy loss lately through some unexplained stroke of Providence, by which the orange groves of Florida were laid low by the withering touch of the hand of dread winter, and it is furthermore true that the phosphate interests have been injured by an over-production, but that is a matter that rests with the fates, to be worked out in their own good season. Misfortunes sometimes prove to be but blessings in disguise, and it rests not with mortals to gainsay the wisdom of that edict which comes from an Omniscient Providence. In all your losses on the farms and in the phosphate mines, bear in mind that the railroads are suffering a kindred loss, for the blow was as keenly felt by them as by you.

"Let us move together while the hand of adversity weighs heavily upon us, just as we have always tried to do when we were more prosperous. Let us take no part in the systematic effort that some are making, to persecute the railway enterprises of Florida at such a time as this, for such persecutors are blinded to their country's interests. If there was ever a time when the people and the railroads ought to work in perfect harmony that time is at hand. I believe labor ought to be protected in a reasonable and rightful degree, but I also believe that capital ought to be protected against the unrighteous onslaughts of those who know not what they do.

"In conclusion, my good friends of Ocala, I beg to thank you again for your generous reception tonight. I believe there is much in the spirit that rules here that bespeaks the dawn of brighter and better days for the people of this region."

The following day a special train took Mr. Plant and his party to Leesburg, where arrangements had been made by the people of that beautiful little town to give Mr. Plant and his friends another ovation of most healthful pleasure and exquisite enjoyment. The Mayor and leading citizens of the place met the party at the railroad station and welcomed them with marked cordiality to their best hospitality and friendship. At the close of a day's most delightful sailing up Lakes Harrison and Griffin, and many carriage rides on the shores of those beautiful lakes, situated as they are in some of Florida's most picturesque scenery, the party sat down to a banquet in the hotel given by the Leesburg Board of Trade. "It was truly a feast of reason and flow of soul," for nothing could have been in better taste or evinced more genuine esteem and friendship for the guest of the occasion than was shown there.

On the next day a special train took Mr. Plant and his party to Eustis. At the station all the prominent people in town were gathered to welcome him. Carriages were in waiting to take him and his friends through the beautiful little town. It was with visible emotion that he looked upon the withered, lifeless orange trees bared by the terrible frost of the preceding winter, a drear and desolate scene as compared with the bloom and beauty of other days. Mr. Plant, however, was never given to fruitless murmuring. To a young editor in the carriage with him he said : "No, we must make the best of even the adverse situation. It might be worse. You must publish words of cheer and hope to your people, and do all that you can to help them over this trying time. Suggest to them the planting of other crops, the rearing of other fruits. It will not do to be altogether dependent on oranges. The soil is capable of raising many other things besides oranges, and it may be that this calamity will become a blessing in disguise." So he ministered good cheer and practical instruction to the people, who felt that he loved them, and who were very responsive to his encouraging words.

I doubt not these people uttered the true sentiments of their deep feeling when they said as they bade him good-bye : "Mr. Plant, you have done us all a great deal of good, we shall never forget you for this visit you have made us. It will be a pleasant memory to us always, and if you and your friends have enjoyed your visit half as much as we have enjoyed having you, then is our happiness increased a hundred fold." Never have we witnessed anything more beautiful and tenderly impressive than the kindly interest which Mr. Plant's visit called out among these people. His every want was anticipated, luncheons, rare and delicious, were carefully stored away on boat and train and brought out at the right time. After sail or ride in train and carriage in this most appetizing atmosphere had made the party hungry as prairie wolves, then a sumptuous repast was served and enjoyed to the full. Rooms, and rest and care in hotel, cars, or boats were provided with a skill and tact that made one think of the Plant System.

Honesty is the foundation and keystone of every noble character. It is the quality that must pervade the whole nature. Nothing can take its place or atone for its absence, nor can there be a perfect manhood where it is not the warp and woof of the whole man. "Honesty is the best policy" says the policy man, but he who is honest only from policy and not from principle, is not an honest man, but a knave, if not a fool as well. Genius, scholarship, wit, humor, brilliancy are worse than worthless when they do not rest on a foundation of honesty. Never was a greater tribute paid to man than when President Lincoln's neighbors dubbed him "Honest Abe." Nor did poet ever rise to higher flights of truth than when Scotia's Bard wrote "An honest man's the noblest work of God." "To be honest, as this world goes, is to be one man picked out of ten thousand," says Shakespeare. In the history of the human race men of all ranks have ever paid the highest tributes to honesty and accorded to it the first place in human character. It is this quality, combined with his great energy, which has enabled Mr. Plant to carry his undertakings to so successful an end.

One of his associates in business for long years said : " Mr. Plant does not rashly promise but when he does, performance is sure, cost what it may. Were I having a business transaction with Mr. Plant for any amount, and knew that he would live to fulfil his engagement I would ask neither bond nor written contract. His word would be just as good to me as any security that could be drawn by the best legal authority in the land." "I should name honesty as the dominant principle of Mr. Plant's character," said another.

It has been naïvely said that no "man is a gentleman to his valet," but the testimonies here quoted are from men of long and most intimate acquaintance, and might be multiplied by hundreds of those who were once in his employ as well as by those still connected with the great System over which Mr. Plant presides. Careful scrutiny and good judgment have characterized all Mr. Plant's dealings with his fellow-men, but crooked ways and mean advantage never. He has rendered to his generation an invaluable service in that he has demonstrated to it that honesty is the best *principle* and the surest way to the greatest success. And he has done this in departments of commerce proverbial for their unjust and unfair methods of dealing.

He has a wonderful amount of unconscious power which moulds those who come within its influence. Hence his associates have remained long with him even when tempted by other positions. The following extracts from a letter of ex-Governor R. B. Bullock will be found of interest in this connection.
" Rev. Dr. Geo. H. Smyth.
  " Reverend and Dear Sir :—
    "Replying now to your esteemed favor of March 17th, would say that Mr. Henry B. Plant came to this city in 1854, representing the Adams and other express interests, which were then being extended through this section of the country; and he continued to make this city his headquarters in that connection until '69 or '70, when he made his home in New York. There are no 'incidents' within my knowledge connected with Mr. Plant's life here, which would be of special interest to incorporate in a biography. He developed then the same persistent, conservative and industrious perseverance in planning for and directing the interests in his charge, which have since developed into the important and widespread interests over which he now presides.
    " Naturally, in the development and establishment of the business in his hands in those early days, it became necessary for him to select proper men to fill the various positions connected therewith and it is a

notable fact, by experience shown, that the selections so made by him, were wise and judicious, and one of the marked features of his executive action has been the kindly exercise of unlimited and undisputed authority. There is no recollection of his having displayed impatience or irritable temper, even under very vexatious circumstances. His manner was always friendly, frank and appreciative, so that the disposition of the men subject to his control, was always found to be actuated by a desire to accomplish all that was possible for the interest of the institution over which Mr. Plant presided, sufficiently encouraged and cheered by the hope of his approbation. So close an eye did he keep upon the services rendered by the most insignificant employee, that no service well rendered failed to receive his personal endorsement and approval.

"By reason of his evenly balanced judgment and temper, his relations with the chief officers of railroad and steamship companies over and by which express service was transacted, and with bank officials—who were then our chief patrons—were always of the kindliest character, and he always enjoyed their perfect confidence and highest respect.

"In fact, all of the characteristics, which have made his later life the magnificent success which the country appreciates, were developed and maintained throughout his early business experience.

"There is nothing new or peculiar about the facts to which I have referred, because they are well known and appreciated by hundreds of men now in the service, who have been continuously with it since its organization.

"Very respectfully and truly,
"RUFUS B. BULLOCK."

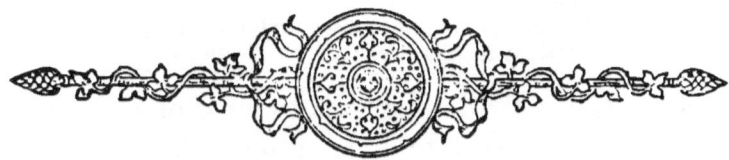

CHAPTER IX.

Mr. Plant's Industry and Power to Endure Continuous Strain—Labor of Examining and Answering his Enormous Mail—Letter from Japan—Mail Delivered Regularly to him at Home and Abroad—His Private Car, its Style, Structure, Hospitality, and Cheering Presence—Numerous Calls—The Secret of his Endurance—The Esteem and Love of the Southern Express Company for its President—Mr. Plant Enjoys Social Life—He is a Great Lover of almost all Kinds of Music—Mr. Plant a Medical Benefactor—Some of the Progress Made in the Healing Art—Bishop of Winchester's High Estimate of the Value of Health—Dr. Long's Opinion of the Gulf Coast as a Health Restorer—Unrecognized Medicines in Restoring Lost Health—Nervousness among the American People—The Soothing and Strengthening Effect of Florida Climate—Mr. Plant's Part in Facilitating Travel and Providing Comfortable Accommodations for the Invalid.

MR. PLANT'S industry and power of endurance are a marvel to those around him in office work. Over five hundred letters a week received is no unusual thing. These are read to him by his private secretary, and answered under his direction or dictation. They come from the three different departments of the Plant System, which extends over many thousands of miles, by land and by sea, and in its Express department forwards goods over a mileage greater than the circumference of the globe.

Some of these letters require deliberation, skill, care, and sound judgment in replying to the many complex questions of such a large and important business as the Plant System covers. Others are less complicated and more easily disposed of, while many are of a social character, from Mr. Plant's numerous friends scattered, I might say, over the world. One day while sitting in his office at Tampa Bay Hotel, he said: "I had a very pleasant letter this morning from Japan. Some lady missionaries there write me of an excursion I once gave them in Florida, which afforded them much enjoyment and of which they write in enthusiastic appreciation though it occurred many years ago, and I had forgotten all about it."

This large mail is a matter of daily occurrence. No day in the whole week is free from its arrival. If he travels, as he often does in his own elegant private car, his mail is delivered at important stations all along the road. Being in constant communication with all departments of the System by telegraph, telephone, or messenger, his mail is forwarded to him promptly at all railroad stations named for its delivery, is examined and replied to as readily as if in his main office in New York City, for he has an office, desk, and all needed facilities in his car for sending out telegrams, letters, or messages from the different stations by the way. His car is a model of convenience, comfort, and elegance in all its appointments. It is finished in richly carved mahogany, upholstered and curtained in rich blue velvet, with numerous windows and mirrors of heavy French plate glass. It is numbered "100," and known all over the South. Its entrance at any station causes sunshine to break on every face, and the old colored men who come, bucket in hand, to wash and polish it where it happens to remain over a night or a day at the station, are fairly beaming when they greet "Massa Plant" and are always paid back in their own coin with United States currency added. Every old "uncle" at the railroad stations in the Cotton States knows "Car 100," and asks no better holiday than to "shine her."

To return to the enormous office work of the President of this great system of transfer and traffic, it is a marvel how he has stood it all these years. It is no unusual thing for him at Tampa to spend two hours in hard work in examining his mail before breakfast, then till luncheon, with perhaps an hour's intermission, and then work until late in the afternoon. His numerous calls from all sorts and classes of people, are a constant strain upon brain and nerve, not to say heart at times. The secret of this endurance of long and fatiguing work, is found in the fact that to a sound constitution, inherited from a hardy, thrifty ancestry, Mr. Plant has added a temperate life and great moderation in the use of stimulants. While a man of quick intuition and keen sensibility, he has shown the most wonderful self-control in the most trying circumstances. When others would be agitated and wholly thrown off their balance Mr. Plant would remain calm, quiet, cool, and clear-headed to a degree that stilled the tempest all around, and effected an amicable adjustment of matters most important as they were most complicated and difficult of settlement. This self-control is joined with great fertility of resources, great charity for the peculiarities of men, and withal a kindliness of nature, a disposition not to hurt any one, that have enabled him to render services to his associates and to his country that may not now be told, and perhaps will never be known until the great day when the "cup of cold water" shall be rewarded. Mr. Plant is never in a hurry, much less is he ever flurried, chafed, or worried about anything. All he does is done deliberately, systematically, easily, and once done it seldom or never has to be gone over again. "Make the best of everything," is his motto.

A gentleman occupying a prominent position in the express department of the Plant System writes:

"It affords me great pleasure to acknowledge the esteem and love of the Southern Express Company's employees, known to me, for Mr. Plant, who has favored us so often with his kindness, liberality, and mercy even when we were at fault. My knowledge extends back about thirty years, having commenced with the Southern Express Company in North Carolina in 1866, and having worked in Tennessee, Alabama, Louisiana, Georgia, Kentucky, and Mississippi since that time, mingling very freely and socially with my fellow-employees. I have never heard one word of condemnation of Mr. Plant during all that time but, on the contrary, a hearty, free expression of respect and affection for the man who, by divine aid, had done so much for the whole South as well as the great number of employees in the Southern Express.

"Faithfully

"I. S. S. A."

In long years of intimate association with Mr. Plant I have never heard him utter a profane word or a bitter expression against any one.

"Greater is he that ruleth his spirit than he that taketh a city," said the wise man. Mr. Plant has told me himself that if he learned of any one made unhappy by anything he had ever done or said, or if any misunderstanding should arise, he could not rest until all was settled to mutual satisfaction, and that, too, just as speedily as possible. "Charity for all, malice toward none," briefly expresses the spirit, tone, and temper of this great and good man. Hence he has been saved the consuming force of friction and hatred which grind and wear out so many before their time. The young men now entering public life will find most valuable suggestion even in this brief record of a life so large, useful, and honored, through a period of our country's history the most intense as it has been the most important since the days of the Revolution and the formation of a free and independent republic.

His busy life has made him neither a recluse, a pessimist, nor a slave of the world. He has been a good deal in society—both as guest and host he has mingled freely with his fellow-men and enjoyed to the full the pleasures of friendly reciprocity.

Mr. Plant's love of music, in a man of his years and busy life, is remarkable. He says: "Music rests me, and helps me to sleep when I retire for the night, while I find it a great enjoyment in my waking hours. It is medicine to me." Hence he is often seen spending the last hours of the day in the music room of the Tampa Bay Hotel, enjoying with the guests the delightful music rendered with such exquisite taste by the skilled orchestra. Mr. Plant is familiar with the best of the modern operas as well as with the finest classical music of the past. Among his favorites are Haydn, Handel, and Mozart. He is also fond of popular ballads and songs, such as Moore's melodies and national patriotic songs. He says he enjoys even the hurdy-gurdy.

Mr. Plant might be termed a medical benefactor,—

a health restorer,—because of the results of his work for the South and the North as well. In no department of scientific advancement during the last half-century has progress been more marked than in the department of medicine. The healing art, in its lessening of pain and in the prevention and cure of disease, has made, and is daily making, the most wonderful discoveries. What a boon to suffering humanity was the discovery of ether by Dr. Charles T. Jackson, of Boston, in 1846, who found that by the inhaling of this anæsthetic the patient is rendered unconscious of pain. Vaccine inoculation, introduced by Dr. Jenner in 1799, has prevented the spread of that much dreaded disease, small-pox. The name of Dr. Koch will long be held in grateful remembrance for his earnest efforts to cure consumption, as will those of Pasteur to cure hydrophobia. The Southern States to-day have thousands of people in ordinary good health, many of them in excellent health, who, ten, twenty, or thirty years ago, were given up by their physcians as past recovery and soon to die. But thirty years ago the modes of travel to the South and the lack of adequate provision there for invalids were such as only a person in fair health could bear. Through Mr. Plant's efforts in large measure, both of these requisites for a sick man, or a delicate woman, have reached a state of perfection difficult to improve.

At the banquet given to Mr. Plant at Leesburg, Florida, in the winter of 1896, one of the speakers referring to what Mr. Plant had done for the North as well as for the South, said: "In the 'Dixie' land he has made the desert to bloom like the rose, changed waste places into fertile fields, the swamps into a sanitarium, the sand heap into a Champs Élysées, the Hillsborough into a Seine, and reproduced the palace of Versailles on the banks of Tampa Bay, and away up in freezing, shivering New England and Canada, when the doctor had written his last recipe and the druggist had emptied his last bottle and the undertaker was at the front door, our friend has placed the patient in a wheeled palace, and signalled, 'On to Richmond,' not to die, but to live; and old Virginia has smiled on the dying man, North Carolina has fairly laughed aloud, South Carolina has taken him into her warm embrace, and Florida has thrown flowers not on his coffin but on the resurrected Lazarus, and the family have invited their friends, not to a funeral, but to a feast. The Plant System ships have ploughed the Gulf of Mexico and spanned the Caribbean Sea, and have brought health and happiness to many homes over which bereavement and sorrow were hovering like the black angel of death."

The Bishop of Winchester once said: "The first thing is good health, and the second is to keep it, and the third to protect it. Then arises the question, where shall we go?" It is not known that the noted physician had ever seen the Bishop's question when he wrote: " Were I sent abroad to search for a haven of rest for tired man, where new life would come with every sun, and slumber full of sleep with every night, I would select the Gulf Coast of Florida. It is the kindest spot, the most perfect paradise; more beautiful it could not be made, still, calm and eloquent in every feature." This was said by Dr. Long, an army physician in charge at Fort Brook, Tampa. The power of the fine arts over the mind, and of the mind over the body, are demonstrated facts. The most frequent and depressing of ailments among Americans is nervousness in various forms, and in different stages of progress, from morbid sensitiveness to utter prostration. In many cases medicine merely aggravates it. Its chief symptoms are irritability and wretchedness, often ending in suicide. Healing must come largely through the mind in rest, peace, comfort, and pleasant occupation.

While the mind in this condition cannot bear strain, neither can it be idle. Idleness induces morbidness and misery. Physical comfort must not be neglected, but there must be wholesome, nourishing food, pure air, and proper exercise. Hence, the value of the well-equipped and elegantly finished Pullman palace car, and the well-built steamer designed for comfort and safety, furnished and finished in a style that delights the eye and ministers to the enjoyment of every faculty. Hence the luxuriant hotel, with all its home comforts, its artistic adornments, and its princely entertainment, beauty for the eye, music for the ear, feasting the æsthetic while feeding the materialistic nature of man. All this enjoyment, while a soft, balmy air is breathed beneath a clear, blue sky, and while the invalid is bathed in the bright, warm sunshine of a southern clime, induces repose, peace, content, happiness, and health. The spirit loses its irritability, the mind regains its elasticity, sleep refreshes the tired brain, food nourishes the exhausted body, the whole man is renewed, and life that was not worth living has become an inspiration, a joy, an heroic and manly achievement.

It should be said here that up to the time that Mr. Plant established the steamship line between Tampa and Havana, there had been no regular communication between those two ports during the quarantine season. There were some irregular opportunities of transfer when passengers were detained for days to be investigated, fumigated, and harassed by quarantine regulations. Mr. Plant held that ships could be built and managed that would make communication as safe in summer as in winter, and he has proved the correctness of his theory. In ten years of regular service, the steamer

Mascotte has never had a case of yellow fever. Through Mr. Plant's suggestions, the Tampa Board of Health has established rules and regulations for travel to the West Indian ports which make it perfectly safe at all seasons of the year, so far as contagion from disease is concerned.

How much Mr. Plant has done to bring this blessed change to thousands, many beautiful tributes testify in the public press of our times. The expressions of enjoyment in the following letters could be extended almost indefinitely. In the Saint Augustine *News* of March, 1895, an enthusiastic correspondent writes: " It was early in the present century that this man of brains and bounty appeared on the great stage, and began a career scarce equalled by any in the annals of American financiers, and it is to him that Florida owes a debt of gratitude, deeper than to any other man—and this man is H. B. Plant. Favored indeed is Florida, not only in climate, scenery, and fruit, but with the munificence of these mighty-hearted millionaires, who have Alladin-like metamorphosed the sunny peninsula into a veritable fairyland. I had the pleasure of meeting Mr. H. B. Plant, who has transmogrified Tampa, and ribboned Florida with his railroad system. As usual with men of great minds and means, he is wholly unpretentious, as much so as his humblest employee. He is anything but fastidious; yet he is a clean-cut man of the world, of vast business capacity, a keen, penetrating financier, and altogether lovable in his domestic life. His shipping interests extend from Halifax to Boston, his express and rail lines from New York to Tampa and New Orleans, and his connecting vessels run from Cuba and all Gulf of Mexico ports. Mr. Plant's homes are the family place in Branford, Connecticut, a palace on Fifth Avenue, New York, and the Tampa Bay Hotel in winter. Mr. Plant's family consists of a son who will succeed to his great responsibility and estate."

Writing from Cuba in January 1888, "J. C. B." says in his " Notes ":

"In the language of an intelligent observer, writing from Havana early in the present month, it would be difficult to find any other interesting foreign land, when its accessibility is considered, so worthy the attention of American travellers as Cuba. To the average thought of one who has not visited it, it seems far and repellent. It is neither of these.

"The improved special fast facilities furnished by the Pennsylvania Railroad, the Atlantic Coast line, the Plant system of railways, and its new, swift, and superb steamships, carry you from the American to the Cuban metropolis in three days.

"While the north shore of the island has three important harbors—Havana, Mantanzas, and Cardenas—the former is incomparably the finest and most spacious; the city, to the west of the gleaming bay, is a rare study in Moorish, Saxon, and Doric architecture. The scene has been thus pen-pictured:

"'On the east side, where the close jaws of the harbor open, and clambering up the mountain side where frown the landward outworks of Moro Castle, is Casa Bianca, with its queer villas and structures, each one standing out in this wonderful daylight of the tropics in such distinctness, and with such a strange seeming of approaching and growing proportions, that, in your fancy, the houses individually become great pillared temples. In and over and through this dreamful spot, away up the side of the mountain, thread and run such indescribable wealth of vegetation that, as you look again and again, the clustered, shining houses seem like great white grapes bursting through a glorious wealth of vines and leaves.

"'Beyond Casa Bianca the bay debouches to the east. Here is a veritable valley of rest. Every half a mile is a little cluster of homes set in a marvellous wealth of rose and bloom. Beyond this valley are seen pretty villages, each with its half-ruined church, whose only suggestion of use or occupation is had in the din of never-ceasing chimes; and still beyond these are uplands which almost reach the dignity of mountains, upon whose far and receding serrated heights an occasional cocoa tree or royal palm looms lonely as a ghostly sentinel upon some mediæval tower.

"'Farther to the south lie the great Santa Catalina warehouses, where the saccharine source of Cuba's wealth is stored in huge hogsheads, or rests dark as lakes of pitch in tremendous vats. Behind these is Regia, the lesser Havana, across the harbor, with its churches, its quaint old markets, its cockpits, its ceaseless fandangoes and its bull pen. Over beyond this, set like a gleaming nest in the crest of the mountains, a glimpse is caught of Guanabacoa, full of beautiful villas, beautiful gardens and fountains, and in the olden times the then oldest Indian village of which Cuban legends tell. Beyond Regia to the south, and upon the shores of the bay, is the ferry and railroad station, whence thousands reach the outlying villas, or leave the capital for the various seaports of the northern coast; and right here, night and day, is as busy and interesting a spot for the study of manner and character as may be found in all Cuba. At this station is seen a famous statue to Edouard Fesser, founder of the Havana warehouse system. The entire southern portion of the bay, where some day the barren shore line will be lined with great warehouses and docks, is filled with old hulls of sunken steamers and ships, conveying the keenest sense of desolation, and the shore here rises to uplands bare as Sahara, until, skirting to the right, the bold mountain, Jesu del Monte, is seen; and then come the great outlying forts extending far around to the sea. Between you and these, if still aboard-ship, you see Havana's domes and minarets, and, to all intents, you are anchored in a sceneful harbor of old Spain.'

"This schedule of the quick mail service performed by the elegant steamers, *Mascotte* and *Olivette*, of the Plant line, in connection with the railway system heretofore mentioned between Tampa and Key West, in the east, affords but a few brief hours of rest in the harbor at Havana. Upon the first appearance of the *Olivette*, fresh from her conspicuous performances in distancing the fleet of steamers which accompanied the racing yachts of the international regatta, the writer had the good fortune to be among the invited guests who paid a visit to this magnificent vessel, which is justly the pride of her distinguished owner, Mr. H. B. Plant, the President and Managing Director of the Plant System of railways and steamships."

CHAPTER X.

Reason for Submitting Press Sketches of Mr. Plant—*Descriptive America*, December, 1886—*City Items*, December, 1886—*Railroad Topics*—*Home Journal*, New York, March, 1896—F. G. De Fontain in same Journal—Ocala *Evening Times* June, 1896—*Express Gazette*.

IN the following chapter are given a few press notices of Mr. Plant and his work in the South, because they contain reliable information of some of that work which we have left to them to chronicle, and because they are public expressions of the appreciation of that work and of the justly high esteem, and friendly regard in which the worker is held by the people among whom and for whom he has spent the best part of his life. Instead of a brief chapter, a volume of such complimentary sketches might be presented, written in even stronger language than is here used and by masters in the art of writing. But these few will suffice to show the deep interest of the people in the life and work of their friend and benefactor, Mr. H. B. Plant.

The following extract is taken from the *Florida* number of *Descriptive America*.

RAILROAD AND EXPRESS PRESIDENT.

"In our *Wisconsin* number we gave the life-history of one man who, beginning as a farmer's son, had, by his energy, ability, and integrity, come to occupy a position of great power, wealth, and usefulness, and we emphasized the point, that, while he had been wonderfully successful, his highest claim to our admiration, lay in the fact that, whenever the opportunity offered, he had sought the prosperity of the nation, the state, or the city of his adoption, and had made his own gain and increasing wealth subordinate to the public weal. In this number we have some similar characters, who, if their wealth does not equal that of the great banker and railroad king, have at least followed his good example.

"Such men are always modest, their achievements seem to them very small, compared with what they might and should have done, and they shrink from publicity with genuine dread. One of these men is the subject of our present sketch, Mr. H. B. Plant.

"Mr. Plant is of pure Puritan stock; his earliest American ancestors left England about 1640, and if they were not among the little company who came with John Davenport to Quinnipiac, afterward called New Haven, they followed very soon after. They settled in Branford, Connecticut, a town lying between New Haven and Guilford, at which place some of Davenport's most eminent men soon established themselves. The Plants of Branford were a good family, and they have always borne a high reputation through the eight or nine generations which have elapsed since they first established themselves in Branford. They were intelligent, thoughtful farmers, industrious, sound thinkers, orthodox in faith, and leading those quiet country lives, of which the old New England towns presented so many examples. The village minister was a man greatly reverenced by all his people, and if a youth of more than ordinary promise could be instructed under his direction, it was something to be proud of.

"To one of these Branford families, the representative Plant family in the town, several children were born in the earlier decades of the present century; one of them, H. B. PLANT, gladdening their hearts in October, 1819. He must have been a boy of considerable promise, for after the usual course of study in the District Schools, not at that time of a very high grade, he spent several terms in the Branford Academy, then under the oversight of the Branford pastor, Rev. Timothy P. Gillett, a man of high scholarship and great aptitude for teaching. Whether he had any aspirations for a collegiate course, we do not know; but he did not rest content, till he had completed his course of study with John E. Lovell, of New Haven, the founder of the Lancasterian system of instruction in America, and, at that time, the most celebrated teacher in the country.

"His school days over, Mr. Plant soon found employment on the steamboat line plying between New Haven and New York. Very soon, one of the first express lines ever established in this country, known as Beecher's New York and New Haven Express, was started, and young Plant became interested in it, and from that time to the present has always been largely engaged in the express business. His first important interest in it was with Adams Express. In 1853, he went to the South, and established expresses upon the southern railroads, as a branch enterprise of Adams Express. In 1861, he organized the Southern Express Co., and became its president, and has continued so to the present time. He is also president of the Texas Express Co. In 1853, he visited Florida for the first time, for the benefit of the health of an invalid wife. There was no means of communication with Jacksonville, except by steamers up the St. John's. The place was small and the accommodations meagre, but the fine climate and mild and balmy air were the means of prolonging her life many years, and from that time he made yearly visits thither. During these visits the place grew, and he saw the necessity for railway communication with that and many other points in Florida; but he devoted most of his attention to his extensive express business, until 1879, though owning large blocks of railroad stocks, particularly in the Georgia and Florida Railways. In 1879, with some friends, he purchased the Atlantic and Gulf Railroad of Georgia, and subsequently organized the Savannah, Florida, and Western Railroad, of which he became president. Soon afterwards he extended this railroad to the Chattahoochee River, and he also constructed a new line from Way Cross to Jacksonville.

"The Savannah and Charleston Railroad (now the Charleston and Savannah), had been in the courts for many years, but, in 1880, Mr. Plant purchased and thoroughly rebuilt it; his purpose being to perfect the connections between Florida, Charleston, and the North.

"The immense labor connected with the management of these railways, and of the vast business connected with the expresses, led Mr. Plant and his associates to organize the Plant Investment Co., to control these railways, and also to manage and extend, in the interest of its stockholders, the Florida Southern and the South Florida Railway. The former road was extended by the Investment Company to Tampa, and to Bartow, and they are now building it to Pemberton Ferry, where it will be joined by the South Florida line thus making connection *via* Gainesville with South Florida, and *via* Tampa for Key West and the West India Islands.

"In connection with these railroads, we may well answer the question which is of special importance to us in this *Florida* number.

"What has Mr. Plant done for Florida? We answer in general, that he has rendered the culture of the orange and of the other perishable products of the State profitable, has greatly facilitated the occupation of the best lands of the State, opened the way for the settlement of the lands of Southern Florida, given free and ready access to the Gulf ports, and thence to Mobile, New Orleans, and Galveston, and established a regular, frequent, and prompt steamboat service on the St. John's River.

"How has he done this? When he had purchased and rebuilt the Charleston and Savannah Railroad, access to the interior of Florida was difficult and almost impracticable except by wagon road. There was irregular and fitful navigation of the St. John's River, but the steamboats ran when they had sufficient freight, and only then. There had been some railroads built (especially those of the Yulee system) but the country was undeveloped, and as the orange groves required from five to ten years of growth before they came into profitable bearing, meanwhile the railways were suffering for want of freight and were unprofitable. Mr. Plant was convinced that although a more rapid development was in progress, there would still be delay before the railroads he proposed to build would prove paying investments. He therefore determined to avail himself of the land grants already made, and to keep them in repair.

"The orange product would not bear jolting over wagon roads, or being stacked up on the wharves waiting for the uncertain coming of the steamers. His first move was to build a railway direct from Way Cross, Ga., to Jacksonville, thus bringing his Georgia roads into immediate communication with a port on the St. John's River. He then established a steamboat line on that river which was regular, prompt, efficient, and carried freight at low rates. Meantime a road had been constructed from Jacksonville to Palatka, making connection with St. Augustine *via* Tocoi; this road is now being extended to cross the river a few miles above Palatka and thence by way of De Land and other places, re-crossing the St. John's a short distance north of Lake Monroe; thence proceeding to Sanford where it will form a connection with the South Florida, thus opening up the fine highlands west of the St. John's and those east of that river to a ready market, and giving choice of a river or rail transportation at several points. The Legislature having granted a charter for a railway connecting Palatka with Lake City by way of Gainesville and thence down the peninsula it was taken in hand by capitalists from Boston, and connection made by rail between Gainesville, Palatka, and Leesburg.

"With this company Mr. Plant made arrangements for the construction of the road from Gainesville west to a connection with the Southern extension of the Savannah, Florida and Western Railroad which has been constructed and is now in operation.

"A branch will soon be built to connect it with Lake City.

"By reference to our map, it will be seen that these roads traverse all the counties of the interior, down to the Everglades, and open them to settlement and to profitable orange culture and the production of sugar, cotton, and rice. These roads have brought actual settlers by scores of thousands to occupy these rich and fertile lands, the finest in the State, and other railway companies, stimulated by their example and encouragement, have constructed roads connecting with these. By the charters of bankrupt railroads which they have bought, the Plant Investment Company is entitled to a large amount of lands from the State, 10,000 acres to the mile, in most cases, as well as later grants on their newly constructed roads; but the State has not yet the lands to deed to them, except to a small amount, though eventually it may have.

"Mr. Plant is a man of fine and commanding appearance, dignified and quiet, yet genial in manners, and of the most genuine modesty and gentleness in his intercourse with others. No judge of character could fail to observe, however, that he is a man of remarkable executive ability and sound judgment, or that he has a greater amount of reserve power than most business men possess. His associates, and those with whom he is brought into business relations, all speak of him in terms of the highest admiration and esteem."

The *City Item* for December 4, 1886, says:

"Mr. Henry B. Plant is a very admirable type of that class of successful men of enterprise who owe their prosperity to broad business views, large public spirit, and commanding integrity of character joined to solid capacity. Born in Branford, Conn., his entrance upon active life was in connection with transportation on the New Haven steamboat line, and his subsequent career has been identified with similar enterprises. Ultimately entering the service of Adams Express Company, he was instrumental in extending its business throughout the Southern States, and finally, with others, purchased its lines, and formed the Southern Express Company, of which he became president. This position he still holds, having by his energy and enterprise greatly enlarged and extended the business of the company.

In 1853, when the delightful climate, attractiveness and fertility of Florida were as yet but poorly appreciated, Mr. Plant recognized the possibilities which that State opened up, and an opportunity being presented for the extention of transportation facilities by the sale of the Savannah and Charleston Railway, and the Atlantic and Gulf Railway, those properties were purchased and reconstructed by him, the name of the former being changed to the Charleston and Savannah, and the latter to the Savannah, Florida, and Western Railway. This last he extended to the Chattahoochee River, to Jacksonville and Gainesville, in Florida. Subsequently he constructed the road between Way Cross, Georgia, and Jacksonville, and Live Oak and Gainesville, and also placed steamship lines on the Chattahoochee and St. John's Rivers, connecting the railroad at Jacksonville with Sanford on Lake Monroe, and building the South Florida Railway thence to Bartow and Tampa, establishing steamboat communication to the Manatee River and other points on Tampa Bay. More recently he has established a steamboat line between Tampa, Key West, and Havana. This service was increased on the 1st inst. to tri-weekly trips, under special contract with the Post-office Department. By this route, in connection with the railroad from Tampa, the line from New York to Havana is only three days, thus enabling the invalid or pleasure seeker of the metropolis to exchange the rigors of our winter climate for the delicious temperature of Cuba, with an ease and under conditions of travel which must make this line increasingly popular with the lapse of years. The *Mascotte,* now running on this route, is one of the most handsome and complete steamships built, its appointments being in every respect really luxurious, while in point of seaworthiness it is everything that the most expert mechanism could make it. Its staterooms are dainty boudoirs, while its saloon is as exquisitely fitted up as any drawing-room. A second vessel, now building for the line, will be equally attractive in all its interior arrangements. Mr. Plant, while a thorough man of business, and deeply immersed in material pursuits, has never lost the courtliness of manner and genial whole-heartedness which are Nature's choicest gifts to her favorites; and among all who know him he ranks as the loyal friend and elegant gentleman."

Railroad Topics says:

"In this day of vast individual fortunes, it is no special compliment to say of a man that he is rich. If the public takes any interest in his wealth, there is generally more concern manifested in the manner in which he made his money, than in the mere fact that he has it. But conspicuous success and marked prominence do, and will always, command attention and challenge admiration. The spirit of the American people is to applaud achievement and honor distinction wherever they are observed, and when found combined in one man, they make him a popular object of praise and an interesting subject for biographical sketch. Such a case we have in the person of Mr. Henry B. Plant, whose record we attempt to outline in the following brief story:

"Mr. Plant was born at Branford, Conn., in October, 1819, and is consequently now in the seventieth year of his age. It is indeed a pleasure to contemplate the record of a man who has fulfilled the sacred tradition of his allotted time, and stamped that rounded life with innumerable evidences of steadily growing strength, constantly increasing usefulness, continually widening reputation, and vastly expanding possessions. The personal history of H. B. Plant, if shorn of all details, would stand complete in that one paragraph.

"He has thus far lived to excellent purpose, and in the run of that existence has accomplished in fullest measure all that is comprehended in the descriptive suggestion.

"If we wrote not another line, we would feel that we had made a practical analysis of his life and set forth the salient truths of it. But when a man has attained Mr. Plant's prominence, and compassed achievements such as his, people are interested in the details of his career, and naturally inquire as to his distinguishing characteristics. In deference to that reasonable curiosity, and likewise for the pleasure that there is in it to ourselves, we gladly make this sketch of him.

"It is nothing remarkable to say that he was born poor. Most men who have ever amounted to much were. Hence in that particular he is not exceptional. Neither would we be satisfied simply to class him with that great multitude, popularly termed, "self made men." He does belong in that catagory, but is so far above the average, that we incline to think of that descriptive fact more as an accident than as a cardinal virtue.

"The first account we have of him is only a meagre record of his school days. He never went to college, but had to content his ambitious young spirit with a good academic course, supplemented by a brief term of finishing study under a thoroughly competent tutor. This, however, was only a theoretical disadvantage, from the fact that the termination of his school days was no interruption to his mental acquirements. He was born with an ambition for knowledge, and does not to this day feel himself too old, or too wise, to learn.

"Mr. Plant's first experience in business, was when, a mere boy, he secured employment on one of that line of steamboats, then running between New Haven and New York. Although very young, he appreciated even then that the only way to learn any business thoroughly was by beginning at the bottom. Accordingly he took his first lessons in steamboat life in a humble position. It was not long, however, before, by faithfulness and efficiency, he lifted himself into higher and more responsible places. That first and prompt promotion was the initial sign of what his life would be, and from then till now, he has steadily marched onward and upward, overcoming obstacles and mastering difficulties with heroic energy, and winning success in the various lines of his broadening operations with positive brilliancy.

"While employed by the New York and New Haven Steamboat Company, one of the first express lines ever established in this country was inaugurated between New Haven and New York, and the enterprise at once fascinated young Plant. He bent every energy toward the acquirement of a small interest in the new express company, and in reasonable time accomplished his purpose. From that day to this, express business has been his best love throughout the wide range of his material interests. His first important connection in that line was with the Adams Express Company about 1847. In that corporation he became a leading spirit and holds such position to-day. His special pet, however, among the various express systems with which he is identified is the Southern Express Company which he established in 1862. This child of his wisdom has grown to be a giant, and is to-day one of the richest, most influential, and ably managed corporations in this country. It traverses all the Southern States, and is, for all practical purposes, permanently established on nearly every important railroad system in the South.

"Of late years Mr. Plant has been giving much of his attention to the acquisition of railroad properties, and in admirable continuance of his previous record, he has crowned this undertaking with splendid success. He is virtually master and largely owner of the Savannah, Florida, and Western Railway, and likewise of the Charleston and Savannah Railway. This gives him a direct and popular line from Charleston, South Carolina, to Jacksonville, Florida. He has also made various branches from his main line, penetrating the principal districts of Florida, and by this wise railroad building has done far more than can be computed or told, toward that marvellous development of Florida which has been accomplished within the last ten years. Mr. Plant was truly a pioneer in this praiseworthy work, and there is probably no man who deserves more than he does the grateful acknowledgements of the Florida people, as well as the hearty gratitude of the countless thousands who have gone from all other sections of the country to enjoy the healing benefits of that curative climate, and the sweet restfulness of that floral dreamland.

"The Plant Investment Co., of which Mr. H. B. Plant is the head, and in which he has associated with him several sagacious millionaires, is a powerful corporation which was organized for co-operative investment in valuable southern railroad properties and advantageous control of the same. This company is managed with exceptional ability, and by its vast acquisitions and extensions, has become a great power in the railroad world, and is rapidly accumulating for its stockholders untold wealth. This Investment Company is practically controlled by Mr. Plant, and its entire policy is shaped by his judgment. One of his latest enterprises, under the auspices of the Investment Company, is the establishment of a fast line of steamers from Tampa, Florida, to Cuba. At Tampa, Mr. Plant has extended one of his railroads out to deep water, and thereby made it an excellent port for even heavy draught ships. The whole of Florida bears the impress of his energy, enterprise, and wisdom.

"Mr. Plant's home is New York City, where he has a palatial residence on Fifth avenue, and luxurious business quarters at No. 12 West 23d street. Whenever a man amasses a fortune he naturally drifts into Wall Street, the financial centre of America. Mr. Plant is a conspicuous exception to this rule. He rarely treads the narrow golden street leading from Trinity Church to East River. There is no speculative element in his nature. He is conservative to the last degree, and works on no plan that is not founded on reason and justified by a positive trend from cause to effect. He has all the vigor and alertness usually to be found in a man of fifty years of age. He is keenly alive to all the possibilities of affairs that come under his observation, and quick to determine any question that is presented to him.

"He is a thoughtful man and extremely reserved. It is necessary to know him well to appreciate the excellent fairness of his mind, and the kindness of his heart. He is ostentatious in nothing, but under all circumstances conducts himself with modest dignity and irresistible reserve force. He is emphatically what might be called an extractive man. That is, he has an inexplicable faculty for drawing any one out, without ever appearing inquisitive, or leading on by talking much himself. If he has one characteristic stronger than all others, it is his wonderful genius for keeping his own counsel. He never lacks cordiality of manner, but is always gracious and genial. Another forceful point of his character, is that inexhaustible patience which has enabled him to live undisturbed in the faith that 'all things come to him who knows how to wait.'

"He thoroughly systematizes every department of his life, and keeps his house in such perfect order that if he should shake the harness off and quit work to-morrow, all those far-reaching plans which have had their foundations laid under his wise direction, would by his faithful followers be worked out to rounded completeness and finished perfection.

"And thus by the mighty working of his master brain he has achieved success, won renown, accumulated an immense fortune, done great good, and made for himself an undisputed place among the leaders of this day. And besides all these victories, he has set on foot gigantic plans that may not fully mature for many years to come, but in those very plans he has laid the corner-stone of a great monument to his worthy memory, and those who come after him, if faithful to their trust, will build on as wisely as he has planned, until the capstone of his imperishable memorial is fitted in its place, by the final accomplishment of each and every purpose of his well-spent life."

The Home Journal says:

"Henry B. Plant, president of the Plant System of hotels, railways, and steamship lines, is one of the men of to-day, whose work will influence the future. He controls twelve different railway corporations with a mileage of 1941, and 5506 employees; is president of the Southern and the Texas Express Companies, employing 6808 men; president of steamship lines, covering the coasts of the Gulf, going to Cuba and Jamaica, and skirting the coasts of the North, running to Cape Breton and the maritime provinces; founder of the most palatial winter resort in America, the Tampa Bay Hotel, and owner of five other beautiful resorts within the State. To Mr. Plant may be accredited the development, if not the real discovery, of the grand West or Gulf Coast of Florida. He is an American, and is seventy-seven years old; a man of tireless energy, wonderful ability, and remarkable industry. His career is marked by honesty, uprightness, straightforwardness, and business-like dealings. These qualities, together with a broad intelligence and keen perception, have brought him success. Withal, he is modest and unassuming, and has no pride but that which he takes in good works."

From the Ocala *Evening Star*, June 22, 1896:

"H. B. Plant, the railroad king, has again stepped into our midst and proposes to add to the new improvements of our city a large and elegant passenger depot.

"Notwithstanding the fact that he has done much already to advance the prosperity of the beautiful perpetual summer land of flowers and sunshine, he is still, at the present time, losing no opportunity to add to the beauty and upbuilding of the State of Florida.

"If every railroad running into our State would feel as much interest in her welfare as does the Plant System, but a few years would elapse before this section would be the most prosperous in the Union.

"Thousands upon thousands of dollars are spent every year by the officials of this road in the improvement and erection of property within our borders.

"H. B. Plant is indeed a friend to Florida, and if other roads would spend as much money in our State as he does, there would not be such a cry for free silver, as there would be plenty in circulation, and every one, from laborer to governor, would have his share.

"While Mr. Plant is somewhat advanced in life, the *Star* hopes that his years may yet be many and his love for the sunny peninsula as great in coming years as in the past."

From the *Home Journal*, New York, March 11, 1896:

"If, comparatively a few years ago, one had ventured the prophecy that the time would arrive when we could leave New York at half-past nine one morning, and wake up at daylight the next morning in Charleston, a court of inquiry would have been called to pass upon his mental condition. Such, however, are the facts to-day.

"You leave Jersey City in a sleeper, supplied with all of the latest appointments for comfort; a courteous conductor takes your tickets, with which you have no further concern until you reach Charleston, when they are handed to you in an envelope. What a comfort not to have to be pulling out the everlasting ticket just in the midst of conversation or while reading an interesting magazine article!

"If the cars are not crowded, you feel a sort of proprietary right to roam around at pleasure, change your seat as often as you desire, and wash your face and your hands whenever they need it in the cosy little toilet-room. What a change from the old-fashioned water-cooler, where a cupful of water was wont to be poured over a pocket-handkerchief, and the face and hands wiped with it, leaving arabesque designs in black and white wherever it touched!

"Then, instead of rushing to a railroad eating-house in order to refresh the inner man, having to put up with 'railroad coffee,' and experiencing a nervous shock every time a whistle blows, your meals are taken at dainty little tables, in your own compartments, where polite and efficient waiters do your bidding.

"Instead of the tiresome, old-fashioned trip of two days and a night, the trip now is twenty hours.

Verily the twin powers of steam and electricity have wrought wonders in the conditions of life.

"The Plant System, to which the Atlantic Coast Line is 'a feeder,' has emphatically gridironed the South. To-day Mr. Henry B. Plant is the president of a railroad system that embraces twelve different corporations, and whose mileage extends to 1941, with a list of employees numbering 5506. He is also president of the Plant steamship and steamboat lines, covering the coasts of the Gulf, Cuba, and Jamaica, and skirting the coasts of the North, running from Boston along Nova Scotia to Cape Breton and Prince Edward Island. In addition to these interests, Mr. Plant is president of the Southern and Texas Express companies, which do a business as express forwarders over 24,412 miles of railway, and have lines in fifteen States, employing 6808 men and using 1463 horses and 886 wagons. Mr. Plant is seventy-six years of age. He needs no eulogy; his works speak for him. Although of Northern birth, he is as much beloved and respected at the South as if native-born.

"Thirty-six years ago, President Jefferson Davis, of the Southern Confederacy, demonstrated his confidence in, and admiration of Henry Bradley Plant by giving him a pass entitling him to move hither and thither at will through army headquarters, or wherever he pleased, in the interest of the Adams

Express Company, which he then represented, although Mr. Plant declared that he did not sympathize with the political movement which sought to rend the States.

"The Tampa Bay Hotel, Port Tampa Inn, and the Seminole, Winter Park, Florida, are monuments of Mr. Plant's enterprise and a portion of the System. From one of these palatial hotels one can catch a fish on the back porch and pluck a lemon to dress it with from the front porch. In Charleston the name of Henry B. Plant is a synonym for success, and a name which many a young man mentions with veneration, as one to which he owes a lasting debt of gratitude."

The May number of the *Express Gazette*, Cincinnati, Ohio, has this appreciative paragraph:

"The editor of the *Advertiser*, Key West, Florida, pays the following eloquent tribute of praise to Mr. H. B. Plant, President of the Plant System of Railroads and the Southern Express Company:

"'Mr. H. B. Plant, the president, the founder, and the controlling spirit of the great Plant System, is held in high estimate by the citizens of this island. He found it, years ago, isolated and remote from the great centres of commerce, and his partiality to us soon changed a semi-occasional connection with the mainland, by vessels of inferior character, into a tri-weekly communication by the finest coastwise steamers in the Southern waters. Brought in ready touch with the marts of trade, factories sprang into existence, commerce grew, and a city with millions of revenue supplanted a fishing hamlet. Through his enterprise we are enabled to write our history in a line—a village, a city, a metropolis—and all this in a decade.

"'The debt of gratitude which Key West owes to Mr. Plant is beyond estimate. Indeed, so accustomed are we to the conveniences at hand, that we are prone to fail in appreciation of what we have, in our greed for more. That Mr. Plant has been and is still our best friend cannot be questioned in the light of past experience; and while we cordially welcome and hail with delight the coming of other transportation, our city should never be forgetful of the man who was our friend when we had no other.'"

CHAPTER XI.

<small>Mr. Plant's Close and Constant Contact with the Great System as Seen in the Following Letters—Letter Written on Board the Steamer *Comal*—Letters on Trip to Jamaica, West Indies, March 15, 1893, and Published in the *Home Journal*.</small>

MR. PLANT keeps himself constantly informed of the workings of the whole System over which he presides, by daily communication with every part of it. The head of each department writes to the president every day, or telegraphs, or does both if necessary, and in return, Mr. Plant, through his secretary, replies daily to each communication received. So close does he keep to the workings of the System that wherever he travels in the country his mail is regularly delivered to him at points arranged for the purpose, and it is as promptly answered from his private car as if he were at his own office in New York City. Nor are all these letters which pass between the president and his associates about hard business; they are often social, familiar greetings, and interchanges of friendly intercourse. The following extract from a letter, written by Mr. Plant when traveling to Galveston, Texas, is an illustration of this:

NOTES OF THE VOYAGE.

"Left wharf on Steamer *Comal*, Saturday, July 22, 1893, 4 P.M., wind southwest. Passed Sandy Hook about 5.30, found sea smooth; well off the coast, shore houses vaguely seen in the distance.

"*Sunday, 23d.*—Had a still and comfortable moonlight night; smooth seas; wind southwest; off Cape Charles, twelve o'clock. About one o'clock wind all died away. The sea perfectly smooth until 2.30, when a light breeze came in from the southeast, which lasted until sunset, then died away and came out again from the west about six o'clock. Passed Body Island Light with light breeze. No sea.

"8.10 P.M.—Hatteras Light fairly abreast—ten sailing vessels and one steamer in sight. Weather being fine, captain concluded to cross the Gulf Stream and run down on the east side and along the Bahama Banks. We have now been out twenty-eight hours, and I have felt very well. No annoyance from the stomach so far in any particular.

"12 *o'clock noon, Monday, 24th.*—We are bowling along in the Gulf Stream with a good breeze from the west—smooth sea. Had a fairly good sleep. Room being on the port side and the wind from the west made it rather warm. At noon to-day the temperature of the water is eighty degrees and the air is eighty-two degrees, which is not so bad as might be.

We are now well off Charleston and about abreast of the Bermudas.

"*Tuesday, 25th.*—The wind continued from the west until about four o'clock, when it ceased, and from that until nine we had a dead calm and a smooth glassy sea. Now at ten o'clock a light breeze comes in from the east, and we have prospect of a comfortable day.

"Yesterday P.M. we had crossed and were entirely east of the Gulf Stream and there was no wind, of course, in still water. While in the Stream we had a current of about three knots against us. Our course is now bringing us again near the stream, which we shall cross in the course of the day and will probably pass Jupiter before bedtime, say, nine o'clock. We are having a delightful voyage so far, and I seem to be doing quite well.

"P.M.—The southwest wind has died out and we have a gentle breeze from the east; this gives promise of the northeast trades for to-night, which will be quite acceptable and will put me on the windward side of the ship; have been on the lee side so far.

"5 P.M.—Have not seen a sail to-day, and am having a very restful time.

"9.30 P.M.—Have been with the captain since dinner, and for the last half hour on the lookout for Jupiter Light. The lead informs us that we are too far off the coast to enable us to see the Light just yet.

"9.50 P.M.—Now we just have a glimpse of the Light from the bridge, and as 'All's well,' I will to my couch for the night. The winds are favoring those on the port side, having swung around to the northeast, giving a promise of the southeast trades for to-morrow; so good-night.

"*Wednesday* A.M.—Had a splendid shower this A.M. just after daylight, and right after the northeast wind died out and was soon followed by the good southeast trade, and now (10.30) we are sailing along just outside the reefs, having passed Cape Florida early this A.M. During the night we have passed Palm Beach (Lake Worth).

"10.30 A.M.—We are now directly abreast of Carysfort Light, and a more pleasant day to be at sea could not be desired. While at breakfast we passed near the wreck of the English steamer *Earl King*. She went on the reef about a year and a half ago; nothing now in sight but a portion of what looks to be the bow—a good beacon to warn others from this dangerous reef. She is reported to have been an old ship loaded with cement and other cheap freight, bound for New Orleans, and well insured.

"The indications are that we shall arrive at Key West about seven o'clock this P.M. and in time to meet the *Mascotte* on her return from Havana. As we have but a small freight for Key West, we shall not be long detained there, and shall expect to arrive in Galveston early Saturday night. Temperature of air at one o'clock 81¾ degrees; water 83 degrees.

"*Wednesday* P.M—Passed Aligator Light one o'clock; this will bring us to Key West about eight o'clock, and enable me to place this on *Mascotte* without much to spare, and probably place us ashore at Galveston Sunday morning, and as you may not be in Darien Sunday, you will only receive the message at office on Monday A.M. Send to Mrs. Plant at Branford on arrival, so she may receive the information same day. Would like to have you make at least a synopsis of the daily notes to Mr. O'B., that you may send to him should he be absent. We are now well up with American Shoal Light; next we shall have Sombrero, and then Sand Key and Key West. We are likely to fall in with the *Mascotte*.

"We are jogging along very pleasantly with wind well on the port quarter and temperature quite comfortable."

The following letter from Mr. Plant, published in the *Home Journal*, New York, March 15, 1893, speaks for itself. It shows its author to be at home on shipboard, and as much at his ease as in his own parlor; while carefully noting all points of interest and enjoying to the full all that was enjoyable.

On Board S. S. "Halifax."
Sunday, Feb. 26, '93.

"We sailed from Port Tampa on Thursday, February 16th, and after a delightfully smooth and pleasant trip arrived at Nassau, N. P., on Saturday morning. A number of our party were entertained by the Honorable Sir Ambrose Shea, governor of the island; others of us preferred to pass the few hours in riding and driving, seeing something of the beauties of the place. We returned to the steamer in the afternoon and got under way, passing out of the harbor through the "Hole in the Wall," as it is called. We steamed down over the banks, passing along the eastern shore of the island, and leaving Cape Mayce on our starboard, until away over to port were seen the highlands of Hayti.

"All the way from Port Tampa to Jamaica, the weather was simply delightful, and the sea as smooth as the waters of our Seneca Lake. We arrived at the wharf at Kingston at seven o'clock Tuesday morning. Our excursionists all went to the Myrtle Bank Hotel, where choice accommodations were provided. We received a call from the Consul-General of the United States, Mr. Dent, and also visits from other important people of the city of Kingston. In the afternoon we received an invitation, conveyed to the party through our conductor, Mr. A. E. Dick, a hotel man well known in New York, to attend a garden party given by Lady Blake at King's House. Lady Blake is the wife of Sir Henry Blake, the governor of the island. We found a large crowd of people, a gracious welcome, exquisite music and bountiful refreshment. Only think of it—an out-of-door reception on the twenty-first day of February!

"In the evening we were surprised to learn that a grand ball would be given in our honor by the citizens of Kingston. It proved a very brilliant affair. The beautiful costumes of the ladies formed a striking contrast to the military costumes of the officers of the British West Indian Squadron; there were eight ships in the harbor.

"We were called very early in the morning, coffee and fruit being served in our rooms, and took carriages to the Western Railway station, whence we started by rail for Bog Walk, on the Rio Cobre River. We arrived at half-past ten. After leaving the train our attention was called to a group of negro men and women who were engaged in loading bananas into a car for transportation to the city of Kingston and thence to the United States.

"At Rio Cobre, we enjoyed one of the most beautiful drives that your correspondent has ever experienced, down the valley of the Rio Cobre, a most beautiful sheet of water, and after a ride of two hours, reaching Spanish Town, one of the principal cities on the island of Jamaica. It was at Spanish

Town that a son of Christopher Columbus settled when he came to the island of Jamaica. We were entertained by the proprietor of the Rio Cobre Hotel, where we remained until the afternoon, when we again took train for our headquarters at Myrtle Bank, in Kingston.

"Early the following morning we were called, fruit and coffee were again served in our rooms, and we started at six o'clock for a drive of twenty-five miles over and across the beautiful mountain ranges and towards the north coast of the island. At ten o'clock we arrived at the Castleton Gardens, a beautiful spot owned and sustained by the government as a garden of acclimation. Here are found the grandest of all tropical palms. At the hotel connected with the gardens we partook of a royal breakfast, into which entered many different kinds of fruit. After a stop of two hours we resumed our journey over the mountains, and in the distance we obtained a good view of the lovely Annotta bay.

"En route, we visited a sugar estate where we saw the conversion of sugar-cane into Jamaica rum of the first quality. Most of the labor is performed by Malays, brought from the valley of the Ganges in India, who while here are compelled to labor in competition with the negroes. The men are paid at the rate of one shilling and six pence per day, while the women receive only one shilling per day. I can assure you, from the manner in which they work, it is evident that they earned every penny they received. By the way, the coachman who drove us, informed me that his wages were ten shillings per week of seven days' continuous work and he has to board himself out of that pittance.

"On the afternoon of this day, Friday, we were well off the coast of Jamaica, homeward bound. Now as I write, Sunday morning, we are approaching Egmont Key, which is situated at the entrance of Tampa Bay. Soon we shall be docked, and soon thereafter at that haven which has been so often described but to which no writer to my mind has done justice—the Tampa Bay Hotel."

CHAPTER XII.

MANAGEMENT OF THE GREAT PLANT SYSTEM WORTHY OF ADMIRATION AND IMITATION.

THERE is perhaps no greater source of waste in our country than that of labor strikes, which have become of frequent occurrence during the last two decades. There is great waste of material from the destructive violence of infuriated mobs. In 1877, the great railway strikes of the Baltimore and Ohio Railroad, and the Pennsylvania and Erie Systems, resulted in the destruction of sixteen hundred cars, one hundred and twenty-six locomotives, and five million dollars worth of property. A report made in 1895 by the United States Commissioner of Labor (covering a period of twelve years and six months, that is, from January 1, 1881, to June 30, 1894) on strikes in the United States, gives the following suggestive statistics. We read that the number of strikes was 14,390, affecting 69,167 establishments. The number of employees thrown out of work was 3,714,406. Loss of wages during this period to the striking workmen amounted to $163,-

807,866. From lockouts the loss was $26,685,516. The losses to employers from the same cause were, from strikes $82,590,386, and from lockouts $12,235,451. The losses to employees and employers amount to the enormous sum of $285,319,219. And this is only a part of the losses, for it does not take into account the cost of police, detectives, and soldiers, required to protect persons and property. In one strike eight thousand of the latter force alone were needed to subdue riots, and save life and property. What estimate can be made of the damage to commerce, the disorganization of labor, the demoralization of the laborers, the families broken up and scattered, the hate and bitterness engendered? The corporation, therefore, that can co-operate peacefully with its working force adds much wealth and moral progress to the nation, as well as legitimate profits to its own treasury, and comfort, well-being, and happiness to its employees. There is mutual advantage on both sides, and far reaching and beneficial influence on all sides. There must be justice and consideration for the workman from the employer, and there must always be justice and appreciation from the workman to the man who gives him work,—mutual interest, benefit, and advantage. It is greatly to the credit of the Plant System, that the public has never suffered inconvenience in travel from strikes among its large working force, that the men have not suffered in person or estate, and that the company has been saved losses and crosses from this hydra-headed monster, "Conflict between labor and capital." That these evils have been avoided, is due to the head of this great System, due to his sense of justice, to his personal knowledge of, and friendly interest in such a large number of the employees, and to a large-hearted consideration for the weaknesses of human nature. Mr. Plant was one day riding in a baggage car, when he saw an expressman turn wrong side up a box that had been marked "Glass." He called attention to the fact. "That box," said he to the man, "is marked 'Glass' and should be kept 'glass' side up as marked." "Oh I know it is marked 'Glass,' but I never pay any attention to that," said the expressman. Mr. Plant said no more. When the man and the superintendent of the express office were alone together, the superintendent said to the man, "Do you know who that gentleman was who spoke to you about the box marked 'Glass'?"—"No."—"Well, that was Mr. Plant, the president of the express company."—"Oh my! that means my dismissal sure."—"Yes, I think it does; I shall have to dismiss you"; and he said, later, to Mr. Plant, "I shall dismiss that man of course." "No," said the president. "Don't discharge him; call him to your office and impress it upon him that that is not the way this company does its business, and he won't forget it." The man has been long a faithful and efficient employee of the company. Mr. Plant's name does not figure as often as do some others in lists of large donations to churches and charities of deserving character, though they have not been passed by without recognition, and kind and generous treatment of the deserving men in his employ have never been wanting. While travelling with Mr. Plant to Atlanta, one of the heads of a department reported to him that an old gentleman who held an honored and important position in the System was greatly broken down with nervous prostration. "Send him to his home to remain until he is well, and remit his salary all the same." It was remarked by a bystander that he thought that that was very kind of the president. "Oh," was the answer, "that is only a regular occurrence to those of us who have been with President Plant as long as I have."

Those who have read the blood curdling accounts of some of the strikes that have occurred within the past ten years, and have experienced some of the inconveniences and dangers resulting from them, will contrast such accounts with what was seen on "Plant Day" at the Atlanta Exposition, and on all other days throughout the South as well, and will feel that the account of that day was worthy of a place in the record of the noble life we are endeavoring to preserve as an example to public men and as a lesson and inspiration for coming generations. We let the associates and employees of the Plant System tell their own story. It was printed in a beautiful pamphlet as a souvenir of the day, and was specially designed for those whose devotion to duty prevented them from sharing, in person, the pleasures of that memorable day. With the exception of a few paragraphs of biographical matter contained in other sections of the volume, or merely of temporary interest, the account is published in full in a later chapter.

It is as creditable to the men who have stood around their president most faithfully in his arduous labors, as it is honorable to him who has led them on to noble achievement, and deserved success. Mr. Plant's methods of management are worthy of highest commendation, and would repay careful study in like conditions. If any man were to discover a plan for extinguishing fire that would to save the country $285,390,219, in the course of a dozen years, the insurance companies would purchase his patent for a large sum of money, and the country would raise monuments to his honor. Mr. Plant's method is even better; it is on the philosophical principle of prevention. It prevents the kindling of the flames, and while it may not be absolutely fire-proof, it has stood a long and severe test. We honor him and his loyal associates and employees for the more than peaceful course they have left on record. We say "more than peaceful" for it has been a course of mutual concessions, personal interest, and friendly association, as the following chapters will show. Nor is the view taken in these chapters narrowed to special and individual cases. It is as broad as the South linked to the North, and covers the whole United States; for no part of our country can be advanced without every other part sharing in the uplift.

It would not be surprising if the best part of Mr. Plant's work should fail to be recognized. People see the material progress of a State, the things that can be measured, weighed, and valued at a price; the subtle forces that produce the material are often overlooked. The intellectual, moral, patriotic, and philanthropic spirit that moves the man and diffuses itself throughout the State or nation is not the first thing that arrests attention. Yet this unrecognized force is the great uplifting power of a people in all that is best and noblest in their onward march of progress. It is now an axiom that the North and South did not know and understand each other previous to the late war; that if they had understood each other, a war such as the revolt of the Southern States would never have occurred, would, in fact, have been impossible. The facilities afforded for travel and the superior hotel accommodations which have been provided by, and have resulted from, the Plant System, have brought North and South together in mutual interest and friendly accord to such an extent that a war can never again take place, for these two sections of our country are so interlaced, interdependent, and identified in interest, and withal in such friendly association, that the misunderstandings of the past can never again arise. It is a fact of history, that in proportion as nations, races, and religions come closer to each other, the causes of conflict are, to the same degree, lessened. A homely illustration of this fact is contained in the story of the Irishman who was walking along the Strand in London one morning, when through the fog he discovered a monster from which, at first, he was going to run away; then, grasping his shillelah, he came close up to the monster intending to kill the "baste," when "lo and behold," said Pat, "it was me brother John!" So it often comes to pass that the monster in the distance to be annihilated, in closer proximity is a brother to be loved.

CHAPTER XIII.

Plant Day at the Cotton States and International Exposition of 1895 at Atlanta, Georgia—Preparations for its Celebration—Impressive Observance of Mr. Plant's Birthday at the Aragon Hotel—Mr. Plant's Remarks in Acknowledging Presentation of Gifts.

THE Atlanta Cotton States and International Exposition was created through the zeal and enterprise of a number of the patriotic citizens of the city of Atlanta and of the State of Georgia, and, on the 18th day of September, 1895, when its doors were opened to the world, naught but words of admiration and praise could be spoken for the men, who, through the devotion of their energies, time and money, had made it in every way a success.

There are already extant records of the speeches of the prominent men who, from the Auditorium platform in the Exposition grounds, addressed the public on that day and proclaimed to the world the reasons which actuated the creation of this Exposition, not only for the advancement of the mercantile interests of the southern section of the country, but as well for the education of its people.

While it is, therefore, futile to reproduce here

the history of the Exposition, it might be well to say that as far back as December, 1894, Mr. H. B. Plant was called upon by a committee of gentlemen representing the Cotton States and International Exposition Company and urged to make an exhibit at the Exposition. In recognition of his acquiescence, and the erection of a building by the Plant System of Railways and Steamship Lines, in which was placed a most creditable exhibit from the sections of South Carolina, Georgia, Alabama, and Florida traversed by the Plant System of Railways, the Exposition Company determined that a day should be set apart, to be known as " Plant System Day," and as the founder and president of the System, Mr. Henry B. Plant, was to celebrate the seventy-sixth anniversary of his birth on October 27, 1895, it was decided that in his honor the two events should be commemorated as a unit. This plan was impracticable, as the 27th fell on Sunday, but that the celebration should be as closely connected as possible, the day following, October 28th, was named by the Committee and announced to the public as " Plant System Day " at the Cotton States and International Exposition.

From the time of this announcement until the day of the festivities, preparations were made to make the occasion in all ways enjoyable. Mr. Plant, accompanied by his family, arrived in Atlanta on

Saturday, and on the succeeding morning, the seventy-sixth anniversary of his birth, was greeted by the following article, written by Mr. Clark Howell, and published in the *Constitution*. It served as an index to a time replete with pleasure, and as a welcome to Mr. H. B. Plant, President, and to the Plant System in Atlanta, Georgia, October 27 and 28, 1895.

From the Atlanta *Constitution*, October 27, 1895.

"No more important day will be celebrated during the present Cotton States and International Exposition than to-morrow, which has been set aside in honor of Mr. Henry B. Plant, the head of the great Plant railway and steamship lines. The importance of the day will spring not only from the successful life of which Mr. Plant is an example, but from the fact that above any other man living he represents the great industrial revolution which has come over the face of the Southern States, and which marks the success of free over slave labor.

.   .   .   .   .

"To-day Mr. Plant might be called an international developer. Of this, however, the story of his life will be the best witness. To-morrow he will have completed his seventy-sixth year, forty-one of which have been spent in the South, during which time the twin powers of steam and electricity have wrought wonders in the conditions of life. To-day he is the president of a railway system which embraces twelve different corporations, and whose mileage extends to 1941, with a list of employees numbering 5506. He is also president of the Plant steamship and steamboat lines, the one covering the coasts of the Gulf and going to Cuba and Jamaica, the other skirting the coasts of the North, running from Boston and along Nova Scotia to Cape Breton and the maritime provinces of Canada. In addition to these interests, he is still president of the Southern and the Texas Express Companies, which do a business as express forwarders over 24,412 miles of railway; have lines in fifteen States, employing 6,808 men, and using 1,463 horses and 886 wagons. As a complement to the handling of railroads, and the sailing of ships, and the expressing of freightage, Mr. Plant has erected four winter resort hotels in Florida, one of which, the great Tampa Bay Hotel, is probably the largest winter resort hotel of its kind on the continent. It will thus be seen that this great man, who is to be the toast at the Exposition to-morrow, does service under three flags, those of America, England, and Spain.

"Such developments as these are enough to make his life history of interest to the old and of profit to the young, as showing the vast possibilities which our country affords, and the immense rewards which come to industry, tact, and intelligence.

.   .   .   .   .   .

"The coming of Mr. Plant to the Southern States really marked the opening of Florida to the people of this country as a winter resort. It was in 1853, the year of Mr. Plant's arrival, that he visited Florida for the sake of his invalid wife, when access could only be had by steamboat, by the St. John's River. The mild climate of that State prolonged Mrs. Plant's life for years. He saw the necessity of railroads in the State, and it was in this way that he began buying stock in various Florida and Georgia railroads, though he did not engage in any railroad enterprise as a manager until 1879. In that year Mr. Plant purchased the Atlantic and Gulf Railroad of Georgia, and subsequently reorganized the company as the Savannah, Florida, and Western Railway, of which he is still the head. The Savannah and Charleston Railway was next purchased in 1880, and the story of the completion of the Plant System—now extending to Charleston on the one side, to Montgomery, Alabama, on the other, covering Florida and forming a perfect network—would be to repeat the story of railroad development in that entire section.

"In these enterprises it was the purpose of Mr.

Plant and his associates to extend and add to the various properties, and they believed this could best be accomplished under a single organization with ample powers. With this object in view, several of his associates being residents of Connecticut, the birth-place of Mr. Plant, a charter was obtained in 1882 from the legislature of that State, and the Plant Investment Company organized. Mr. Plant became president, and remained such to the present time. Among his associates were W. T. Walters and B. F. Newcomer, of Baltimore; E. B. Haskell, of Boston; Henry M. Flagler and Morris K. Jessup, of New York, and Lorenzo Blackstone, Henry Sanford, Lynde Harrison, H. P. Hoadley, and G. H. Tilley, of Connecticut. Since the formation of the Plant Investment Company, several properties have been acquired by purchase. In 1885, they bought the South Florida Railroad, at the time running only between Sanford and Kissimmee, which was changed from narrow to broad gauge, with an extension of the line to Port Tampa, Florida, which is the port of entry for the West India fast mail steamers (Plant Steamship Line) between Port Tampa and Havana, Cuba. Subsequently the line was extended north from Lakeland to a connection with the Savannah, Florida, and Western Railway (Gainsville division) at High Springs, thus completing the line from Charleston, South Carolina, to Port Tampa, Florida.

Thereafter the company acquired, in 1887, the Brunswick and Western Railroad, between Brunswick and Albany, Georgia, via. Waycross, which road was rebuilt; in 1889, the Alabama Midland Railway, from Montgomery, Alabama, to Bainbridge, Georgia; and in 1892, the Silver Springs, Ocala, and Gulf Railroad, extending from Ocala to Homosassa and Inverness, Florida. In 1893, the Tampa and Thonotosassa Railroad was constructed, from Tampa to Thonotosassa, and the Winston and Bone Valley Railroad was purchased to accommodate the people of the phosphate mining districts. In 1894, the Abbeville Southern Railway, from Abbeville, Alabama, to a junction of the line of the Alabama Midland Railway, was built. The system has been extended in 1895 by the purchase of the Florida Southern Railway and the Sanford and St. Petersburg Railroad, both narrow gauge roads, and preparations are now being made to change them to standard gauge.

" In addition to the railway properties enumerated, Mr. Plant established two lines of steamboats: one, in 1880, to run between Sanford and Jacksonville, which was discontinued upon the completion of the railway between these two points; the other on the Chattahoochie River, known as the People's Line, plying between Columbus and Bainbridge, Georgia, and Apalachicola, Florida. In 1886, he established the Plant Steamship Line for regular service between Port Tampa, Key West, and Havana, Cuba, under contract with the United States Post Office Department, for the carriage of the Key West and Havana mails, and for occasional service between Port Tampa and the island of Jamaica, with regular service between Port Tampa and Mobile, and Port Tampa and points on the Manatee River.

"Subsequently the line of the Atlantic, Canada, and Plant Steamship Line, Limited, running between Boston and Halifax, was acquired by purchase, and chartered under the Dominion Government as the Canada, Atlantic, and Plant Steamship Company, Limited. In 1893, the North Atlantic Line of steamers was added to the line through purchase, and the route between Boston, Cape Breton, and Prince Edward Island is now operated by the company of which he is at the head.

"The Plant Investment Company had widened the gauges of its various roads to the standard measure, has organized the fast mail steamships between Port Tampa and Havana, and has in many other ways developed the country and revolutionized the face of nature in that section. A reading of the names of the directors of the Plant Investment Company shows that through Mr. Plant other men, such as Mr. Flagler, have been led to investments in the Gulf States, which are of incalculable value, and which will perpetually influence the destiny of the South.

"Without entering into the statistical and prosaic relation of railroad names and technical details, it may be said Mr. Plant stands foremost as a developer, and that while honor is due him for the creation of so much wealth, for the integrity of his life, for the energy with which he has built up the country, yet it is as a public benefactor and as one who has contributed vastly to the possibility of such an Exposition being held in the South, that he will be spoken of to-morrow. When he came here, in 1854, he found the country wedded to a slave-labor system, which necessarily meant a purely agricultural condition, and under which it would be impossible to develop manufacturing and other corporative industries. Without having been connected in any way with the war or with the politics which preceded it or followed after it, yet he was the pioneer of that new business which the war made possible, and which marks the end of the old and the beginning of the new. His career is a remarkable example of what can be accomplished by untiring industry and indomitable will. The people of Georgia, Florida, South Carolina, and Alabama cheerfully acknowledge the great obligations under which they have been placed by the labors of this energetic and capable man.

"In recent years he has made his home in New York City, spending each summer in Branford, Connecticut. He is a member of the Union League Club and of the New England Society of New York, a man of commanding appearance, genial of nature, dignified and courteous of manner, and as modest as he is competent.

"Such a man needs no eulogy. His works speak for him. Such a people as those of the South need no incentive to recognize worth wherever they see it. Mr. Plant will be royally received to-morrow, and in the closing years of his life he may well rest satisfied that a people for whom he has done so much will not easily forget it, and that his name will be remembered as one of the men who have served their time and generation, and who deserve the laurel wreath of immortality.

"Forty-one years of his eventful life have been spent in the South; and his great fortune has been made in the South. How many important volumes of history are crowded into those forty-one years! Within that period this man of affairs has seen four million slaves emancipated; he has witnessed the greatest war of modern times; he has practically witnessed the birth of those twin powers—steam and electricity—whose combined forces have created new conditions of life; he has been an eye-witness to the tearing down and the upbuilding of States and the adjustment of the American people to a new environment. And yet, amid all this kaleidoscopic change, this quiet business man has gone on adding to his fortune in peace and in panic, in storm and in sunshine, and his potential force in Southern development will be fittingly recognized and crowned to-morrow, in a day set apart among the great days of the Exposition in his honor.

"What superb judgment and business sagacity make up the background of this picture! Mr. Plant has never sought or held office. His name is not on the roster of military heroes, nor is it emblazoned on the roll of those who have won renown in the evolution of statecraft. But in that great battle of rebuilding States and industrial life in the South he stands to-day pre-eminent. Behind him, and loyally supporting him, is a busy industrial army of 12,639 men, and, counting their families, an army of 60,000 people.

"The lessons of Mr. Plant's life are simple and should be an inspiration to young men throughout America. He has avoided politics and speculation; he has never bought nor built a railroad to sell; he has never wrecked a property in order to purchase it. He lives, and his companies live, within their income. He is scrupulously exact in keeping his engagements, and always acts within the limits of that truth, which he often quotes, 'It is easier to promise than it is to perform.'

"The lesson of his life, which the occasion justifies in emphasizing, is this: Faith in the South and her possibilities is the basis of his great fortune. When others have faltered he has gone on investing the earnings of his properties in the South. In his loyal friendship to the South, and his unwavering faith in her greatness and her coming glory, he has proven his faith by his work.

"Mr. Plant is one of those remarkable men who master all conditions and create environment. He is a builder—a creator. A whole State blossoms at the touch of his magic wand. Thousands and tens of thousands bless him that he uses and does not bury his talents. Long may he live—an example to all young men, an inspiration to investors, a true, a loyal, and a royal friend of the South."

Surrounded by many of his friends and associates, who had assembled to pay their respects, Mr. Plant's anniversary was most auspiciously ushered in by the foregoing remarks of a representative of the Atlanta people. But it yet needed the remembrance of the officers and employees of the Plant System of Railway and Steamship Lines and of the Southern Express Company to testify the admiration and esteem in which he was held by the men who served under him. This tribute on the part of the officers and employees was an unexpected pleasure to Mr. Plant. In referring to the event, the Atlanta *Constitution* published the following account of the presentations and of Mr. Plant's response:

From the Atlanta *Constitution*, October 28, 1895.

"Mr. H. B. Plant, President of the Plant System of Railway and Steamship Lines, was complimented yesterday as few great railroad kings have ever been complimented by the men who compose the vast army of workers under their direction.

"It was the seventy-sixth birthday of the well-known giant of the Southern railway world, and he was presented with rich and rare tokens of the love, honor and affection which his employees bear him.

"It was a happy day all round, and the Plant people fairly revelled in the privilege of paying such becoming tribute to the man who has done so much for the Southern States.

"As for Mr. Plant himself, he declared that it was certainly one of the happiest moments of his life, and the brightest, happiest birthday he ever enjoyed.

"At a quarter to ten o'clock Mr. Plant was notified that a number of prominent officials of his various systems of transportation lines were waiting to see him at his private parlors at the Aragon.

"He met them, and was informed that they wanted to join with him in the name of every employee of the lines to exchange the congratulations and compliments of the season of his birthday. Mr. Plant at once summoned his family and friends, who are with him here, and soon Mrs. Plant, Mrs. M. A. Wood, Dr. G. Durrant, Rev. Dr. Smythe, and Vice-President M. F. Plant were in the parlor. There were also present the following friends and associates in the railway and express business:

"R. G. Erwin, Vice-President and General Counsel, Plant System; M. J. O'Brien, Vice-President and General Manager, Southern Express Company; D. F. Jack, Assistant to the President; B. Dunham, General Superintendent, Plant System of Railways; J. W. Fitzgerald, Superintendent, Plant Steamship Line; B. W. Wrenn, Passenger Traffic Manager, Plant System; F. B. Papy, General Freight Agent, Plant System; Hon. F. G. duBignon, General Counsel; T. W. Leary, Assistant General Manager, Southern Express Company; G. H. Tilley, Secretary and Treasurer, Southern Express Company; F. Q. Brown, President, Florida Southern Railway; Hon. S. G. McLendon, Counsel, Plant System of Railways; O. M. Sadler, Superintendent Southern Express Company, Piedmont Division; H. C. Fisher, Superintendent Southern Division, Southern Express; C. T. Campbell, Superintendent Southern Express Company, Central Division; W. W. Hulbert, Superintendent Georgia Division, Southern Express Company; Mark J. O'Brien, Assistant Superintendent Southern Express Company, Central

Division; F. DeC. Sullivan, New York; E. M. Williams, New York; W. S. Chisholm, member of the firm of Erwin, DuBignon, & Chisholm, Attorneys for the Plant System of Railroads, Savannah.

"The room was a scene of rare beauty, there being on every side a huge bank of flowers, fragrantly speaking the affectionate salute of the employees of Mr. Plant and members of his family. On one side was a beautiful vase of American Beauty roses, sent from the main office of the Plant System in New York, by the employees there.

"Appropriate inscriptions were embroidered in letters of gold on the ribbons of red, white, and blue tied about the long stems of the roses. On the other side was a bank of carnations, chrysanthemums, lilies, and roses from H. B. Plant, Jr. This pleased Mr. Plant greatly, coming from a little son of Mr. M. F. Plant, a grandson of the distinguished railroad magnate.

"On a pretty table in the centre was a huge and gorgeous silver cup—a loving-cup—which was presented to Mr. Plant by Mr. S. G. McLendon, on behalf of the employees of the railway department of his great System. It is a most beautiful and elaborate solid silver cup, and will hold two gallons of champagne. It is, perhaps, the finest and most artistic piece of work ever made by the Gorham Manufacturing Company, of New York. The idea conveyed in the loving-cup is a most beautiful one. The cup has two large handles, and around the festal board is turned from hand to hand, each guest taking a quaff, the cup being held by two persons. The cup never touches the board until it has made the round of the guests.

"This cup, presented by the Plant Railway System employees, is handsomely engraved, and bears on one side this inscription: 'The Railway Employees of the Plant System to H. B. Plant, President.' On the reverse side is the date, 'October 27, 1895.'

"In presenting this beautiful token, Mr. S. G. McLendon, attorney for the Plant System at Thomasville, read the following testimonial on behalf of the employees:

"'Mr. Plant:—The employees of the Plant System of Railways extend to you their sincere and heartfelt congratulations upon this, your birthday.

"'As a slight token of their affectionate and loyal regard, they present you this loving-cup, filled with their best wishes for your continued health and strength. It was no idle fancy which prompted the selection of this modest testimonial; its name aptly marks the impulse which prompted the gift, and which it but inadequately measures by its size.

"'The author of a great railway system, such as that which bears your name, must be to all mankind a genuine benefactor; but to you belongs, in truth, an honor and distinction far more precious.

"'To promote the well-being of one fellow-man, to upbuild the material interests of great and growing States, and to see new life, hope, and promise rise up with smiling face and outstretched, laden hands, is indeed enough to fulfill the measure of any ordinary ambition; but when to the gratification which springs from such a consciousness is added the knowledge that those who labored with and under you in these great enterprises, whose part it was to follow and obey, are each and all as loyal and devoted to you personally as you have been, through many years and trials, to the great interests confided to your care, satisfaction must ripen into that contentment which only comes when the "softer green of our better selves" is in the ascendant.

"'It is the earnest prayer of the employees that for many, many years yet to come your life and activity may be spared to the great properties which owe their existence and prosperity to your foresight and sagacity, and as the seasons come and go, they crave for themselves no higher privilege than to refill this cup with renewed affection and esteem.

"'For the employees of the Plant System of Railways.

"'B. DUNHAM,
"'General Superintendent.'

"The employees of the steamship lines of the Plant System sent a handsome and perfect combination compass, barometer, and thermometer as a fitting birthday present to Mr. Plant. Hon. Fleming du Bignon, General Counsel for the Plant System, read the following letter in making the presentation on behalf of the men who manage this branch of Mr. Plant's vast business:

"'ATLANTA, GEORGIA, October 27, 1895.

"'Mr. H. B. PLANT, PRESIDENT.—Dear Sir: The love and confidence of associates, neighbors and friends are to be valued more than silver and gold. In this life the point set to bound one's career ought to be the esteem of his fellow-men. For such an honor good men strive in all the protean forms of earthly contest. To gain this reward, to touch the dust-covered goal with a glowing chariot wheel, is worthy of the loftiest ambition. No human being can possess any greater glory than the estimation of the people among whom he lives.

"'Acting upon the principle that labor conquers all things, and that time will bring its own rewards, you struck out for yourself into the great ocean of busy life around you and struggled heroically with its billows. You were strong and worthy, and your fellow-men were not slow in making the discovery. Your unbounded faith in the future of this marvellous section, coupled with your genius and intelligent direction, have advanced the several States into which your enterprises now extend into commanding positions of commercial superiority. Your ships have not drifted like dead sea-weeds upon the tops of sleepy waves, but, laden with the rich treasures of this and other climes, have travelled the wide seas over as a public benefaction. The mind of man cannot measure, nor can the tongue of man describe, the practical good your energies have accomplished. The Plant System, consisting of many thousands of miles of telegraph, express, railway, and steamship lines, founded by your genius, is a monument to your memory more lasting than brass and more enduring than marble.

"'Concealing quick feelings under an appearance of reserve, you have never deemed it a weakness to give sway to the influence of loving and sympathetic emotions. Your benevolences, therefore, have made life beautiful to many people. Associated with you for so long a time, it is natural that we, the employees of the Plant Steamship Line, should feel a filial pride in the success of your varied and various undertakings. We are proud of the history you have made. We come to-day, therefore, to bring you our greetings, to manifest our love and admiration, and to express the hope that your useful and distinguished life may be spared many years to your country, family, and friends.

"'As an evidence of our affection and respect, we herewith present you, as a fitting birthday gift, this compass, commonly used for directing and ascertaining the course of ships over a waste of waters. This compass is fitted with a magnetic needle which points ever to the north, enabling the tempest-tossed mariner to hold his way over the stormy sea when there is neither cape nor headland, sun, moon, nor stars, nor any mark in the heavens or on the earth to tell him when or where or how to steer.

"'We pray that the star of destiny, like this mysterious needle, will ever guide and help you to keep an unfaltering step along the dangerous crags and treacherous precipices which beset the pathway of every man, and that your life may be long and useful "in the land that the Lord, thy God, giveth thee."

"'Truly yours,
"'J. W. FITZGERALD.

"'On behalf of the employees of the Plant Steamship Line.'

"The Southern Express men presented their president with a handsome marine glass.

"The following testimonial, read by T. W. Leary, Assistant General Manager of the Southern Express Company, which was organized by Mr. Plant in

1853, explains the sentiment conveyed with the gift:

"'ATLANTA, GEORGIA, October 27, 1895.

"'MR. H. B. PLANT, President Southern Express Company.—Dear Sir: The employees of the Southern Express Company extend to you on this anniversary of your birthday cordial greetings, fraught with sentiments of highest respect and esteem, inspired by the kindly courtesy and impartial consideration which have ever marked your intercourse with them.

"'Regarding you not alone as an official superior, but also as a personal friend, sensible to their welfare and the true relationship of the employer and the employee, exemplified by your long career in friendly association with those with whom you have called around you in the conduct of the company's affairs, they are glad to avail themselves of this auspicious occasion to manifest the interest it inspires within them by an offering in token of their appreciation and good will.

"'It is, therefore, the privilege and pleasure of the undersigned, in behalf of the employees of the Southern Express Company, to present to you the accompanying testimonial, coupled with heartfelt wishes that as things viewed through its lenses are brought clearer and closer to vision, so with each succeeding return of the day this glass commemorates, may you see the nearer fruition of the unremitting labor of years devoted to the upbuilding of those important enterprises with the history of which your name is indissolubly connected.

"'Commending this souvenir to your acceptance with the united hope of those from whom it comes that continued health, strength, and success may be granted you in the future, we are, yours faithfully,

"'F. L. Cooper,
"'W. A. Dewees,
"'W. M. Shoemaker,
"'Committee.'

"After the above letters were read, Mr. Plant addressed those present in substance as follows:

"'Gentlemen of the Plant System of Railroads and Steamship Lines and of the Southern Express Company, and my Friends: I thank you sincerely for the beautiful presents which you have given me on this the anniversary of my birth, and for the loving words of congratulation which accompany them.

"'While it reached my ears that there was to be some observance of the occasion, I am wholly unprepared for the magnificence of the gifts and the demonstration of fidelity and affection with which they are accompanied, and I am, therefore, unable to do justice to myself in expressing to you the appreciation I feel. I speak from a full heart, and can more than fill this beautiful loving-cup with affection and esteem for you, and for the employees whose feelings towards me are manifested not only by this testimonial, but as well by their constant and untiring devotion to the trusts confided to them through many years. To them, in a large measure, is due such success as has crowned my efforts in railway construction and management, and I now take pleasure in making this acknowledgment, and in assuring them of my continued confidence in them and of my gratitude to them; without their unflagging efforts no measure of success could have been achieved. I look to them all with the full assurance that the future, with their assistance, will result in still greater accomplishments in our railway enterprises.

"'This compass, the gift of the employees of the Plant Steamship Line, brings to my mind the thought that, whatever may have been my mistakes in life, I have always had one aim, which, like the needle, though oscillating and varying at times in some slight degree, pointed ever to one end, and that was to endeavor to do what was right and just.

"'Our steamships were the children of my later years, and they, with the faithful employees who operate them, are, and shall continue to be, very near to my heart.

"'The gift of the employees of the Southern Express Company brings to my mind pictures of the past. The express business was my first love, and I see here present those who were with me in troublous times, and bore with me the heat and burden of the fight. Their affection and loyalty have sustained me in many an anxious moment, and the knowledge that I had around me those upon whom I could count in every peril has enabled me to achieve some measure of success. To extend to them my thanks for all that they have been to me and done for me would be idle. They know how I feel towards them, and I am sure I know how they feel towards me.

"'I wish to say to you all that I am more apt to express my feelings in acts than in words; many of the employees of our several companies have been with me so long that they have become as members of my family. I feel towards all the employees that in a business sense they are members of my family and I want them to feel that they bear this relation to me.

"'I see with us to-day one to whom I feel I owe much; I refer to Dr. G. Durrant, of New York. I had a severe attack of illness last May, but did not know until long after it was over how near to death I was. To his untiring and faithful attention, both as a good friend and as a skilled physician, I owe my recovery, perhaps my life, and it gives me pleasure to take this occasion to express my confidence in him and my thanks to him.

"'These beautiful flowers on my left came to me from my little grandson, and I bespeak in his behalf from you all the love and affection which you have shown to me, and express the hope that in days to come, when I am no more with you, he may be one of yourselves and a co-worker in the enterprises which all the employees of our companies sustain by their energies and their work.

"'These flowers on my right come from those at our New York office, some of whom cannot be with us to-day in person, but who are with us in spirit and love and testify their memory of the occasion by this beautiful remembrance.

"'Mr. and Mrs. Frank Q. Brown, of Boston, have presented me with this cane, which I appreciate very highly, but will hope that I may not need to have immediate use for it, though if that time should come it will be a staff upon which I will gladly lean. Mr. Brown is now one of us, and though he has but lately come among us, I am sure you will all welcome the President of the Florida Southern Railway in our ranks.' [Applause.]

"It was the happiest of seasons for Mr. Plant, and his face beamed brightly with the light of profound gladness.

"All day there was a stream of distinguished

callers, who congratulated him on the day with good wishes for many returns. Letters and telegrams and cablegrams were read, all bearing the hearty congratulations of friends and employees."

CHAPTER XIV.

Tampa Bay Hotel, One of the Modern Wonders of the World—Its Architecture, Furniture, Works of Art, Decorations, Tapestries, Paintings, Inlaid Table and Three Ebony and Gold Cabinets from the Tuileries, a Sofa and Two Chairs once Owned by Marie Antoinette—The Dream of De Soto Realized—A Palace of Art for the Delight and Joy of Those who are in Health, and an Elysium for the Sad and Sorrowful.

THE following account of the Tampa Bay Hotel, from the pen of W. C. Prime, is taken from the New York *Journal of Commerce:*

"The most charming book in all the world of literature is the collection of tales known to common fame as the *Arabian Nights.* Their charm consists in the total freedom from all restraints of verities, of either probabilities or possibilities. Events occur in dreamlike succession, and transformations take place with such delicious swiftness and ease that, if you read the story as you should, with forgetfulness of self, and without any of the folly of critical judgment, you are removed into another world than this —a world of refreshing liberty, wherein thought has no bounds and imagination flows in glorious revelry.

"That which the unknown Saracen story-teller created in words and fancies, this late nineteenth century seeks to create in reality, by the aid of wealth and steam and electricity. It does not succeed. But it comes so near to success that we may wonder and admire, and for a moment at a time we can forget that the result is artificial, not natural, and that it is a miracle of human invention which dazzles and astonishes our senses. All this by way of introduction to my letter. . . .

"The scene changed suddenly. The train emerged into a blaze of electric light. By this blaze of light you could see, high in the air and stretching a thousand feet to right and left, bright domes and minarets, appearing and disappearing with all the swiftness of magic. It was bewildering. A few steps lead into the blinding light of the grand hall of the new hotel, a wilderness of all that is gorgeous in works of modern art. Rich furniture in gold and ebony, velvets, tapestries, grand vases of porcelain, massive figures in pottery, bronzes in groups, small and of life size, oil-paintings, works of masters, etchings, engravings, carvings, in short, countless examples of the most costly and superb art productions of the age, under a flood of light from a hundred electric bands; all this bursting on the gaze of the traveller at the end of his journey, it forms what may well be considered a modern artificial approximation to one of the transformations in dreams of the Saracens.

"It is not to be denied that this Tampa Bay Hotel is one of the modern wonders of the world. It is a product of the times. It illustrates the age, the demands of the people, what they enjoy, and what they are willing to pay for. I have no space to enter into a description of it. It would require a guide-book for a full description. 'It is splendid, but it is incongruous,' said a friend. 'Why should it be incongruous?' was my reply. 'It is a hotel, not a private house.' There is, nevertheless, a sufficiency of uniformity in the building and decorations, while the general principle of the furnishing is in harlequin style, which is most pleasing to the mass of visitors. Each work of art (of which there are hundreds and hundreds) is chosen by some one who has exercised taste of high order. The objects are good, each worthy of examination. The many large tapestries are costly, and are fine works. The paintings are of extraordinary rank. There is no more striking feature of the furniture than the table porcelains. These are exquisite works of ceramic art. The plates are of infinite variety. You may have your beef on a very charming bit of French porcelain, your salad on a reproduction of an old Vienna plate of semi-Saracenic pattern, your ice on one of the little plates designed by Moritz Fischer, and copied elsewhere, your coffee in a very perfect repetition of one of Wedgewood's simple and lovely bordered cups. In fact, there is no end to the variety of these lovely porcelains. And just here I may add, that the cooking and the service are unexceptionable. The table is of the very best class, and equal to that of any hotel in the world. This, too, is miraculous, in a new house at this remote point.

"I may sum up a sketch of the hotel in a few words. There is nothing cheap, nothing inferior in it. Money has been freely expended in the purchase of the most costly objects, in all departments of art, for furniture and decorations; good taste has been exercised in the selection of these objects, and they are brought together in lavish profusion. The building is vast in extent. The grounds around it have been rescued from savage nature and reduced to order and beauty. The river is in front and Tampa lies across the river, which is narrowed to less than three hundred feet wide. Some hundred palmetto trees have been transplanted to form a grove near the river. Orange blossoms in neighboring orchards fill the air with their odor. Pineapples grow in luxuriance. To one who knew this spot as I knew it years ago, the gorgeous hotel and its surroundings may well seem the creation of a dream."

Mr. Henry G. Parker, in the Boston *Saturday Evening Gazette*, writes:

"It was reserved for the sagacious and enterprising railroad and steamboat magnate, Mr. H. B. Plant, to reap the honor of erecting in tropical Florida the most attractive, most original, and most beautiful hotel in the South, if not in the whole country; and it is a hotel of which the whole world needs to be advised. It has one vase, which is the admiration and wonder of all who behold it, in the grand office rotunda, where ladies and gentlemen congregate at all hours of the day and evening. The entire estate, including land and building, cost two millions of dollars, and the furniture and fittings half a million more. No one who does not see it and dwell in it for at least a day, can form the faintest idea of the comprehensiveness of its purpose, the breadth of its plan, the ideal refinement of its comforts, the noble scale of its luxuries. Nothing offends the eye or the taste at any point, and while the first view of the hotel exteriorly is impressive, the effect produced by a first glance on entering its broad and inviting portals is one of astonishment and delight.

"The architecture of the Tampa Bay Hotel is Moorish, patterned after the palaces in Spain. The horseshoe and crescent are everywhere visible in its design, and minarets and domes tower above the great building, which is five stories high above the basement.

The house is constructed of Atlanta red brick with rolled steel beams, and brick partitions, floors, and ceilings, and so is absolutely fire-proof.

"Numerous flights of stone steps lead up by easy ascent to the long verandas that extend along each side of the structure. These piazzas vary in width from sixteen to twenty-six feet. The length of the main building is 511 feet, but with the solarium and dining-room, which are connected with it, the house affords a continuous walk of twelve hundred feet, and the walk around it on the outside is exactly one mile. On the building there are thirteen minarets and domes, each surmounted with a gilt crescent, making in all a complete lunar year. The hotel contains, nearly five hundred rooms.

"The drawing-room, in perfect taste throughout, is a museum of beautiful things, embracing fine contrasts, rich harmonies, and pleasant innovations that render it indeed 'a joy forever.' Here there is an inlaid table which once graced the Tuileries, as did also three ebony and gold cabinets. On the table is a rare bit of sculpture, *The Sleeping Beauty*, in Carrara marble. There are a sofa and two chairs that were owned by Marie Antoinette. A set of four chairs may be seen that belonged to Louis Philippe. Then there are numerous French and Japanese cabinets, and above each is suspended a dazzling crystal mirror. All these and hundreds of other wonderful things were personally secured in Europe by Mr. Plant and his accomplished wife, while Boston, New York, and Grand Rapids have been drawn upon for what is best in their specialties in useful and ornamental furniture.

"The dining-room is octagon in shape, lighted from above, and is decorated with costly and elegant tapestries and Japanese screens. Its tables and nicely upholstered chairs are the very acme of comfort, and the whole apartment is tempting, aside from the unsurpassed excellence of the cuisine. The waiters are well groomed and well trained, having gained their knowledge and their courtesy in the leading hotels and clubs of New York. The *chef* is Joseph P. Campazzi, celebrated all over this country. He has fourteen first-class assistants, besides a dozen others, in his kitchen, which is the largest, most thoroughly equipped and most convenient to be found in the United States. He has arranged his departments for the care of meats, game, and fish on a plan of his own, which is worthy the attention and examination of every *chef* in the land. His ice-box contains between four and five tons, and he provides also for The Inn (also Mr. Plant's property), at Tampa Port, and for the Havana steamers of the Plant Line. Meats are shipped in a refrigerator car from New York, while game goes from Baltimore, and largely from the sportsmen in and about Tampa. Fish is to be found in great variety and abundance in Southern Florida, at very low prices, and red snapper, pompano, sheepshead, and shad, deliciously cooked, are always to be found upon the table. Giovanni Carretta, who for fifteen years enjoyed a remarkable fame in New York at Delmonico's and the Union Club, is the pastry-cook, and his deft hand has lost none of its wonted cunning. Rossi, from the Manhattan Club, is the baker.

"There are two hundred employees in the Tampa Bay Hotel, all of them carefully selected with a view to their special fitness for the places they fill. The chambers and suites are handsome and convenient proportionately with the public rooms. The carpets everywhere are harmonious in color, restful to the eye, and in the best of taste; more than thirty thousand yards of them have been laid.

"The music-room is a special feature. It is large, well ventilated, attractive in its circular form, simple in decoration, has a raised stage, and its acoustic properties are fine. Moreover, the band is superb. It consists of sixteen picked and skillful musicians, six of whom were taken from the Boston Symphony Orchestra. Their performances of classical music, as well as of the tuneful and delicious dance music, will stand the test of severe criticism, and not be found wanting. This important feature of entertainment is to be maintained at any cost, and it affords a great deal of pleasure to all who visit the Tampa Bay Hotel.

"Tampa is of interest historically, being the place where Ferdinand De Soto landed, May 25, 1539. From there he started on his search for the mines of wealth supposed to exist in the New World, which resulted in the discovery of the Mississippi River. There also Navarez, having obtained a grant of Florida from Charles V. of Spain, landed with a large force, April 16, 1528. Tampa is on the Gulf coast of Florida, 240 miles from Jacksonville. There are two trains daily, with Pullman cars, from Jacksonville and St. Augustine to Tampa, passing through Palatka, Sanford, and Winter Park, both having direct connection with all Eastern and Western cities, and one being a through train from New York. Its rapid growth during the past seven years, from eight hundred inhabitants to as many thousands, has been brought about by the Plant System having completed the South Florida Railroad to Tampa for the purpose of developing it commercially. The climate is perfect, and it is the only city in Florida with all the advantages of both inland and coast without the inconvenience of either; the only city that affords all the delights of a sportsman's life to hunter and fisher, yachtsmen and horsemen, along with first-class business facilities in all directions. No malaria ever infects the delicious air, and the water is as soft as lavender. It is the place of places for invalids, and a lapse of two years will see Tampa the most important business city in its State. We are writing, not for the interest of the Tampa Bay Hotel alone, fine as it is, but to impart information and to convey suggestions that may be valuable to many of our readers. By no means fail to go as far as Tampa if you visit Florida in this tempestuous winter."

AT TAMPA BAY.

"Was it not some old reportorial ruse played upon the credulity of the ancients that made the story of Aladdin's wonderful lamp to live in literature and come down to us through the ages to make us listen with open ears, gape with open mouth, and wonder with open eyes at the wonders of it—and I wonder if that ancient reporter could prove in any way the foundation of his story of the lamp and the rubbing of it. Aye, there's the rub—I think he could n't prove it. He might show the lamp, but no palace would rise up at his rubbing, however hard. *But*, to-day, the vision may be produced and the palace reared, and yet no lamp to rub. I would lead to a land where balmy breezes blow and sigh among the pines, and make the feathery palm trees wave as nodding plumes. Coming out from under these, on a night when the moon is bright, to the banks of a beautiful river with banks fringed with ferns, look across its waters where the moon and stars are reflected and so many, many lights that are on the river's other shore, there the palace is, a brighter than Aladdin's, and more beautiful. That's Tampa Bay. That your coming under these pines and palms may be in a palace car, produces no disillusion,—there's a palace at Tampa Bay.

"It might have been, in the long centuries agone, when his ship floated lazily and his barges glided noiselessly over the waters to the fern-fringed banks of Tampa's river, that that ancient and original tourist, on the same mission bent as those of to-day, in search of the fount of perpetual youth, might have looked, disheartened, on the tangled forest and heard the moaning of the winds through the pines that brought no tidings of a land of life.

"I wonder if in his dreams that night, when his ship came in to Tampa Bay, this grand old Grandee was back in his castles in Spain, and sported in fantastic fandango with the dark-browed Señorita of fair Castile. Was his dream a prophetic vision that it seemed to be an Alhambra just there under the lee of his ship, or did some grander palace with Moorish minarets and silvered domes, glistening with more silvery brightness under the rays of a tropic moon, topped with golden crescents that could only come from the Orient to ornament its towers high above the pines, seem to be here in this far-off land—a dream passing all realization. And what a disappointing awakening awaited this ancient cavalier who sought the waters that would make him young again, for when the morning came, and the sun shone brightly, the knight must have trod the deck with restless impatience; the vision of last night carried him back to lordly Spain, the awakening brought him here again, and only a lofty pine stood in the place of the tallest tower, the swaying top was not a silver dome, and the mournful moaning in its boughs fell not as sweetly on his ear as the tinkling tingle of guitars and his dream-made mandolins. And I am sure, in haste he left a spot so disappointing, and perhaps to the tune of 'Over the Hills and Far Away,' marched to find the great Mississippi.

"I say, perhaps old De Soto dreamed all this when he landed here at Tampa, and if he did, behold 't was prophecy—for the swaying pines have toppled and in their places have risen higher the golden crescents of the Orient, and the silvered domes and Moorish minarets that ornament a palace, and here at Tampa Bay the Spaniard's dream has been realized two hundred years after.

"The tourist of to-day does not approach from the direction of his illustrious predecessor, but has the decided advantage, whether the coming be by night or day. If by day, the grandly magnificent picture comes suddenly upon the view as the train makes a turn and stops between the little town and the river. The foreground is the river, the middle distance, green sloping lawns dotted with flowers, around whose beds are winding walks that circle fountains and lead through groves of palms and oranges to the pines beyond, the same great pines that De Soto walked under in the struggle to get off his 'sea legs.' In the brightness of a semi-tropic sun the domes and crescents glisten intensely, and the massive pile grows to immensity. The broad galleries extend all along the front, the roof commencing above the third-story windows, slopes gently, so as not to obstruct the view, and at its outer edge drops in huge ornaments, in arched and hanging pendants ending in brackets at every column, and at the walls; the grateful shade inviting as on a summer's day.

"The lawn, carefully kept and green as one of Kentucky's own, has a miniature fort with mounted cannon and a flagstaff that floats the country's colors by day, and sports a crescent of electric fire at night. The fountains, the flowers, and tropic fruits growing here as if 't was their natural home, serve as ornaments. A dainty little boat-house at the bottom of the lawn is headquarters for all sorts of boats for rowing or sailing, as well as for naphtha and steam launches. The view from the cars comprises all this, as also from the bridge that spans the river from the hotel to the town. The intending guest need not leave the train here; after a short stop it will cross the river and come right to the galleries of the west entrance and stop under the shadow of the great hotel at Tampa Bay.

"If in the ecstacy of a first impression I likened this to a palace of Spain that Ponce de Leon might have dreamed of, I had no retraction to make when the second day of my visit came and I saw it with modern surroundings of railway and steamer—it is a palace still, and more of that than the hotel, and in its appointments more like a gentleman's residence on a scale exaggerated to positive magnificence—totally unlike any other, and it is no disparagement to any to say it is the most unique in the world—I was about to say of its kind—it has no kind; there is none other in similarity with it, and taken all in all is the finest in the world.

"I say this not without thought of what it means—the Ponce de Leon at St. Augustine may have cost more dollars to build, decorate, and furnish, and the name and fame of the Ponce de Leon has gone to the four quarters, and 't is not intended to compare invidiously. Here at Tampa Bay, the surroundings take one back through the centuries even before De Soto came, and this may have been the very spot where he landed.

"The horseshoe arches of the Moorish curve are everywhere, from the grand galleries to the rotunda doors, in the salon entrances and to the grand banquet hall, for it is nothing less, and every minaret is crescent crested, and passing under them leads to some old picture, antique, or cabinet that ornamented some palace hall before the land on which this one stands had been discovered,—and herein is the argument that this is the only one in the world. The others boast of their 'especially made' appointments, while these were made before the land was discovered.

"The rotunda is a grand assembly hall with its polished floors, rich carpets and hangings, antique vases and bric-a-brac, divans and luxurious lounges, as little like a hotel office as the 'east room' of the White House is like a railway station. The apartment is seventy-eight feet square and is thirty feet from the floor to the ceiling. The massive doors are of Spanish mahogany, highly polished, encasing heavy plates of bevelled glass, the frames are carved in designs of great beauty. Thirteen marble columns support a balcony that looks over from the second floor, around which is a carved rail, also in Spanish mahogany.

"The Moorish and Spanish styles which prevail in the architectural work do not always obtain in the decorations and furnishings—the divans in the rotunda were once in the Tuileries salons, and there is an original portrait in oil of Louis XIV. of France, also a clock of the same period. The paintings are varied in design, as they are in age and history, and every one, every antique and cabinet, has its history. On one wall is a beautiful canvas, the *Return from the Masquerade*, on another, *Wine, Woman, and Song*, these suggest the gay side of life, while some of the old faded examples of the school of long ago carry one back to the old masters. Two dwarfs in bronze that suggest the Black Forest legends guard the entrance to the hall of the grand salon, and near them are two Japanese vases, six feet high, which were exhibited at the Vienna exposition.

"Mirrors in antique frames rich in gilded carvings are on the walls, massive doors in bevelled glass lead to parlors, halls, libraries, and writing rooms, electric lights are imbedded in the ceilings and walls, and hang down in chandeliers. This is the rotunda. The business office occupies the smallest corner, as if it was of the smallest importance in a hall so replete with ornament and so devoted to comfort and luxury. The telegraph and ticket offices are also in the rotunda, and everything that pertains to the more prosaic business ideas—but they do not intrude upon the dreamy existence that obtains from the antique surroundings.

"The grand parlor is magnificent. Every nook and corner has some dainty bit to show a woman's hand has been here, and in all the grand apartment shows what might have been done by a princess in her own house. It was a woman's design that this divan should have growing flowers from its centre, and between the seat-arms, that roses and calla-lilies should mingle their perfume where beauty holds sway. Her idea that this cabinet, three hundred years old, should be brought from some castle in Seville or Salamanca to ornament this salon. It is an exquisite piece with inlaid woods, ebony, pearl, and ivory, with quaint little paintings under marvellously clear glass in the carved panels. The bronzes, gildings, and inlaid woods of the cabinets contrast with the white and gold of the surrounding decorations in pleasing effect. The white and gold of the upholstery and the hangings have their beauty enhanced by the shaded electric lights in ground glass, softly tinted, that are set in the arched dome above; the light falls on these cabinets, tables inlaid in a hundred woods and pearl and ivory, bric-a-brac and candelabra from every land. Paintings not from this shop or that, but from the old masters to salon celebrities of modern times. One is a portrait of Marguerite de Valois and another of the Duc de Savoy. On the mantels and cabinets are some beautiful, exquisitely chased ewers and drinking cups in silver, and busts of Elizabeth of England and Mary, Queen of Scots, in very rare silver bronze.

"There is marble statuary in exquisite designs

from the chisels of the best sculptors—some Sedan chairs with the eagle of France in their decorations.

"The drawing-room is a museum of beautiful things, embracing fine contrasts, rich harmonies, and pleasant innovations that render it indeed 'a joy forever.' Here, there is an inlaid table which once graced the Tuileries, as did also three ebony and gold cabinets. On the table is a rare bit of sculpture, 'The Sleeping Beauty,' in Carrara marble. There, are a sofa and two chairs that were owned by Marie Antoinette. A set of four chairs may be seen that belonged to Louis Philippe. Then there are numerous French and Japanese cabinets, and above each is suspended a dazzling crystal mirror.

"There are eight cabinets of antique pattern that have been brought from this or that province of old Spain, gathered in their travels by Mr. and Mrs. Plant, and *not*, as I have said, ordered from this factory or that, in the ordinary way of the modern hostelrie.

"The carpet—scarlet, with its black lions rampant, made in France—is a replica of one of Louis XIV., and covers the entire floor of this splendid salon, in which are chairs of gold and silk and plush of the same era—as there are also tapestries of incalculable values and richness that have hung in palaces before they came to this one. The writing and reading rooms just off the rotunda are furnished in the same unique manner—one which might be called 'the Louis XIV. room' has all its decorations and appointments of the era of that monarch; these are replicas, or in some cases originals.

"In the grand chambers the style is not less regal; in magnificence these surpass anything I have ever seen; no two of them are alike. They range in size from the grand suite of complete living apartments with parlors and libraries, to the chamber for two, with silken hangings of gros-grain watered silk, in white and delicate rose color; a canopied dressing-case, as dainty as the bride who may stand before it to attire her pretty self for the grand halls outside her door. The guest rooms on the floors above have every convenience known to modern inventive genius, including telephone connection with the office and through a 'central' to every other room in the house. A grand hall-way extends from south to north seven hundred feet, passing through the rotunda. Just south of the rotunda is the grand staircase, with its life-size bronzes, holding groups of electric lights, and near by are the elevators to the upper floors. The north hall passes from the rotunda by the grand parlors to the gracefully rounding curve of the solarium till it ends, where shall I say it ends?—in modern parlance at the dining-hall, but what might be the banquet-room of a Moorish king, with its lofty dome and arches that rest on fluted pillars.

"There is no more striking feature than the table porcelain. These are exquisite works of ceramic art. The plates are of infinite variety. You may have your beef on a very charming bit of French porcelain, your salad on a reproduction of an old Vienna plate of semi-Saracenic pattern, your ice on one of the little plates designed by Moritz Fischer and copied elsewhere, your coffee in a very perfect repetition of one of Wedgewood's simple and lovely bordered cups. In fact, there is no end to the variety of these lovely porcelains. And just here I may add that the cooking and the service are unexceptional. The table is of the very best class and equal to that of any hotel in the world.

"The room may not be faithfully described in its frescoes and its lights and pictures, any more than I could satiate your appetite by copying the menu here—it can't be done.

"Just at the end of this hall and very near the entrance to the dining-room is a grand orchestrion, which, with interchangeable rollers, plays the latest music, from the popular airs of the day to the classic productions of the great composers.

"Just off the rotunda is the music-room with its waxed floor for terpsichorean uses. There is a perfect stage suitable for concert, lecture, or tableau, there are foot-lights, and overhead, the electric fire gleams in a star and crescent group. The room is circular in form with broad galleries extending around it, so the company may sit in the open air and listen to the music or look in upon the dancers. These broad galleries extend on the west and east side, forming a grand promenade for the gay company such a place attracts.

"The interior scenes under the brilliant glow of the lights is entertaining, but I remember in more dreamy way a stroll by moonlight, down by the river under the palmettos. The moon shone bright and made a wide silver ribbon far up the broad river and across it, and here came to me the idea of Ponce de Leon's dream.

"The arched and towered façade, the silvered dome, again silvered by the moon's rays, lifted up more brightly against the star-lit sky, the crescented minarets, the electric-fired crescent on the color-staff, the lights from a hundred windows, the soft patter of the water in the fountains falling on the lily-pads, the perfume of the flowers, the splash of an oar and the half murmur of a love song from him who splashed the oar. Think you this is not an Alhambric picture? Then you have not read of the Alhambra nor seen Tampa Bay."

CHAPTER XV.

Programme of Plant Day Ceremonies—Ringing of the Liberty Bell—Presentation of Addresses to Mr. Plant in the great Auditorium—His Reply—Resolutions from the Different Departments of the System, from the Savannah Board of Trade, etc.—Mr. Morton F. Plant's Acknowledgments.

KNOWING that all employees would be unable to attend the celebration in Atlanta, President Plant requested the superintendents of the railways, steamship, and express interests to allow such men as could be spared from duty without detriment to the operative departments to be present, and also requested that special train service should be provided for their accommodation. This request of the president was so heartily carried out by the superintendents, and so willingly accepted by the employees, that three special trains of the Plant System, carrying several thousand employees, rolled into the Union Depot in Atlanta at an early hour Monday morning, October 28th. In order that all might be fully informed of the movements of their worthy president, and of the programme of the day, the following notice was published in the Atlanta *Constitution* of October 28, 1895:

"Mr. Plant will call on Governor Atkinson at 10 o'clock this morning.

"He will be at the Exposition grounds at 12 o'clock, when the Columbian bell will ring for the first time, in his honor.

"At 1 o'clock all the employees of the Plant System will assemble at the Auditorium on the grounds, at which time addresses will be delivered by President Collier, on behalf of the Exposition Company, and Mayor King, on behalf of the city of Atlanta. Mr. Plant will respond to these addresses.

"Music will be furnished by Innes's band, and, after Mr. Plant's speech, resolutions, congratulatory and otherwise, will be read on behalf of the employees of the system and commercial bodies.

"At 3 P.M. Mr. Plant will be at the Plant System Building, which is one of the most picturesque on the grounds. He will spend some time making a close inspection of the exhibit that has been placed there and which has attracted such attention all the while from visitors to the great fair.

"At 8 o'clock this evening a banquet will be tendered Mr. Plant at the Aragon."

Mr. Plant placed himself in the hands of his friends for the day, and carried out to the letter the programme as above set forth, in order that he might have opportunity of meeting the employees at the Exposition. Such of us who had the pleasure of being present and of personally congratulating the gentleman will be pleased, no doubt, to read the following account of the day's proceedings, and to those who were less fortunate it will be interesting to hear what the Atlanta *Constitution*, of the 29th of October, had to say of "Plant System Day at the Exposition."

"Eloquent indeed was the demonstration of affection and loyalty by the employees of the Plant System to their great chieftain, Henry B. Plant, yesterday at the celebration of Plant System Day at the Exposition.

"Never was there such an ovation to any living railroad magnate in the Southern States. The day was beautiful and bright and most auspicious, and the exercises in the auditorium at the Exposition grounds were profoundly interesting and impressive.

"Early in the morning Mr. Plant was driven to the Exposition grounds in a carriage, the rest of his party accompanying him in other carriages. They drove through the grounds, and at 12 o'clock sharp they stopped at the Columbian bell, near the Forestry Building, and, in accordance with the programme as arranged, the bell was rung many times over in honor of the great railroader. The bell was rung by Mr. and Mrs. H. B. Plant, assisted by Mrs. Wood, Mrs. B. W. Wrenn, Major O'Brien, and Mrs. Tilley.

"Those present at the ringing of the bell were:

Mrs. H. B. Plant, Mrs. W. A. Wood, Mrs. B. W. Wrenn, Mrs. George H. Tilley, Mrs. Porter King, Mr. H. B. Plant, Mr. R. G. Erwin, Mr. M. F. Plant, Dr. G. H. Smythe, Mr. G. H. Tilley, Major M. J. O'Brien, and Col. B. W. Wrenn.

"The party then drove through the grounds, and after a brief glimpse of the splendid Exposition from the carriages while passing, they went to the Auditorium, where the regular programme of the day was to be carried out.

"Long before they arrived at the auditorium the hall was fairly packed with the employees of the Plant System of Railroads and of the Southern Express Company, of which Mr. Plant is president. The distinguished party, consisting of Mr. Plant and his family and a number of friends, arrived at the eastern side of the auditorium and entered the vast hall through the doorway to the stage.

"At the first sight of them the vast multitude of people within gave a round of applause which lasted for a long time, and which was a becoming greeting from the several thousands of Mr. Plant's employees to him at such a season.

"When Mr. Plant and his companions were seated on the stage, the applause ceased and order was restored in the hall. On the platform, Mrs. H. B. Plant was seated on the left of Mr. Plant. There were also there Mrs. W. G. Wood, Mrs. G. H. Tilley,

Mrs. B. W. Wrenn, Mr. M. F. Plant, Mr. R. G. Erwin, Mr. M. J. O'Brien, Mr. S. G. McLendon, Mr. G. H. Tilley, Mr. A. A. Wiley, Mayor Porter King, Vice-President W. A. Hemphill, of the Exposition Company; Mr. W. F. Vandiver, Mr. Fleming G. du Bignon, Mr. W. C. Bibb, Judge Robert Falligant, Hon. W. B. Thompson, formerly Second Assistant Postmaster-General; Hon. W. H. Brawley, U. S. District Judge; Mr. F. Q. Brown, Mr. G. W. Adair, and others.

"After music by the Innes Band, Vice-President W. A. Hemphill, of the Exposition Company, acting as president in the absence of President Charles Collier, arose and addressed the vast audience on behalf of the Exposition Company, bidding them a cordial welcome to the fair.

"Mr. Hemphill said:

"'Mr. President, Ladies, and Gentlemen:—I have no doubt that the welcome that Mr. Collier was to have given you to-day would have been the most pleasant duty he would have had to perform since the opening of the Exposition, but he was suddenly called away, and wired me to welcome you.

"'This is an hour of thanks and congratulations. The Board thanks you for the interest you have taken in our Exposition. We thank you for the magnificent exhibit of the resources along your line that you have made at our Exposition, and for the competent people you have placed in charge of it. We thank you for your presence here to-day, and we are highly honored that so many distinguished people are here with us.

"'Mr. President, we congratulate you upon the magnificent system of railroads and steamships that you have builded up. Your life and example have been a great thing for the young men of this country to profit by [applause], showing them what it is possible for them to attain. We congratulate you, sir, upon your birthday, and we wish that you may live to observe many happy birthdays and that each one may be brighter than the one preceding it. [Applause.]

"'What an opportunity this Exposition has given to the States of this section! The State that has neglected to be represented here has missed the opportunity of its history. I am glad, sir, from your side, that Florida is represented here. Her grand resources of factory, of mines, of forest, of rivers, her fruits and flowers, are here to show our visiting friends from the North what a great country Florida is. [Applause.]

"'We thank you, sir, for being such a friend to the South. You have spent more money and developed more territory in this section than any other man in the Union. [Great applause.] We thank you and honor you for it, and we hope you will live to see the day when your railroad lines will extend all over this country [applause]; when your steamships will plow the Atlantic Ocean and reach the ports of Europe. We hope, sir, that you will live to see the building of the Nicaragua Canal; when your steamships shall go through that canal, and, crossing the Pacific Ocean, reach the ports of China, Japan, and Australia—all these lines pouring immigration and wealth into this section, making it the most powerful, most populous and richest section of this Union, and your System the greatest upon the face of the earth. [Continued applause.]

"'I now have the honor and pleasure of introducing to you Mayor King, who will welcome you for the city of Atlanta.'"

"Mayor Porter King was greeted with applause and spoke as follows :

"'Mr. President, Ladies, and Gentlemen :—On the part of the city of Atlanta it is to me a matter of peculiar pleasure and pride to welcome in our midst that broad-minded, grand, glorious, golden-hearted gentleman and the splendid men who come with him. [Great cheering and applause.]

"'I but re-echo the sentiment so beautifully expressed by Colonel Hemphill, who preceded me, that if Georgia, the South, and Atlanta owe aught to any man, it owes as much to Colonel Plant as to any one whose name I could call. I speak a truth which is perhaps not generally known, so modest is this gentleman, that to-day he is one of the largest real estate owners in the city of Atlanta. [Applause.] We think in that, he has shown the wisdom of his judgment.

"'I honor the head of this great System because of the policy that he has pursued—to build up himself, not by pulling down another, but by carrying others up with him. [Applause and cheers.] And not alone to him, but to this vast army of employees, who are themselves but representatives of the magnificent System of which he is at the head, I extend a cordial welcome. [Applause.] I am sure it is not in his heart to detract one bit from any progress, or any forward movement of the very lowest employee connected with his whole System. [Applause and cheers.] Rather than to grow up that way, I believe he would rather see his whole System wrecked.

"'We thank you for your presence here to-day. We thank you for the manificent exhibit which your System has placed upon these grounds. To you, one and all, Mr. President and gentlemen, we bid you welcome to Atlanta; all that she has is yours. We gladly turn it over to you.'" [Great and continued applause and cheering.]

"Colonel Hemphill proposed three cheers for President Plant. The cheers were given.

"Here the Innes Band gave a splendid rendition of the popular medley, 'Plantation Echoes,' including 'Way Down Upon the Suwanee River,' which was loudly cheered.

"Mr. Plant's Address was as follows:

"'Mr. President of the Cotton States and International Exposition Company, and the Honorable Mayor of the city of Atlanta:—In behalf of my associates and employees of the Plant System, and friends, gentlemen and ladies, whom I see around me and before me, I scarcely know how to thank you for this glorious welcome, this grand reception. I can but say that we are here to witness a very magnificent Exposition, quite beyond any conception of mine, and, I believe, of any of the gentlemen who have come here with me to-day, to examine and make a study of this monument to the enterprise and energies of the good people of the city of Atlanta and of the State of Georgia.

"'When I was called upon in Jacksonville, Florida, in December, 1894, by a committee of gentlemen of the Exposition Company, and requested by them to make an exhibit here of interesting products from the country bordering our lines of roads in South Carolina, Georgia, Alabama, and Florida, the four States that our rail lines traverse, I was backward to do so, for the reason that I feared we had nothing that would do credit to our line, our interests and our patrons; and had I known, sir, of the extent and the grandeur of this Exposition, I believe that I should have continued to hesitate.

"'It has been some years since I have visited Atlanta, and I was hardly prepared to see the growth, the tremendous growth, that I find has occurred in my absence. I see you are rapidly going forward; that you are becoming a metropolis. You represent, sir, the capital of one of the greatest States of the Union—the Empire State of the South. [Applause and cheers.]

"'You never need be backward to represent Atlanta; it appears to me that within a very short time, without saying anything to the detriment of any of the other cities in this country, that it will be called The City of the South. [Applause.] Other cities may advance, and do advance; many cities and many communities in the South advance rapidly; they advance in population and in wealth, but, sir, nothing have I seen in many years to admire like your city of Atlanta.

"'I hardly know what language to use that will fittingly present to you, sir, and to my audience, the opinions I hold in regard to this great Exposition. It is a surprise, it is a marvel, it is to me wonderful, and, sir, it proves what can be done by people acting in unison, united in their enterprise, united in their progress and their desires to benefit their people and their country, and united through their capital. Without this unity, and without the other qualifications that have made the representative men of Atlanta and of this Exposition what they are, this Exposition could never have been what it is. It is a visible proof of the importance of united action; it shows what may be accomplished through union. Without union none of us would be what we are to-day.

"'To my friends and associates, and to the officers and employees of the Plant System I desire to express my thanks for the numbers they show here to-day. I commend you all for your good judgment in embracing this opportunity afforded by the Cotton States and International Exposition Company, to come here and witness this great work that has been going on almost without our knowledge. We have all read in the newspapers about the Cotton States and International Exposition, but I believe that very few of us had any idea what we were to see and to meet here to-day. But we are here, most of us only for the day, and I hope that we will earnestly avail ourselves of all the time possible, not only for the gratification of our curiosity, but for our further education as well. Everything we see should be made useful to us; it is such an opportunity as some of us may never have again, and I therefore say to you all—while you are in Atlanta, emulate my example, and make this Exposition a study. [Cheers and applause.]

"'As I said before, I am pleased to see such a large representation here. It is very gratifying to me. It is gratifying to know that so many could be spared from their duties without disadvantage to the public whom we serve. You all know the general principles that have influenced us in the formation of the Plant System. It was to prepare the way to make as good means of communication as possible with the resources we had at hand. We have used of our means freely; not only myself, but my associates have not been sparing in this particular. We have expended capital and energy in the hope of some day reaping a benefit, which is proper. As you know, all men seek to benefit themselves; but there has been behind it, as the President of this great Exposition and the Honorable Mayor have to-day stated, a desire to do good to our fellow-man. [Applause.] We have at least been able to furnish good means of transportation, and I am pleased to say that it is appreciated by our patrons. I would, however, have you recollect that we are the servants of the people, who are our patrons, to the extent that we must treat their property, while in our possession, with all the care we would our own. We must be careful in our manners and our speech; we must see to it that no patron of the

Plant System ever comes to an officer or employee for information without getting it to the fullest. [Applause.]

"'We must also see that our connecting lines of railways receive proper treatment from us. Be sure that we cannot well serve the public unless we treat our allied lines fairly, justly, and properly; be sure of this. Be sure that we are not all for ourselves. We are public servants, and we must serve all well, and always recognize the rights of our patrons. We must never take a customer's money without giving him his money's worth. All this is very easy to say, but it is very difficult for human nature to carry it out, and we must, therefore, school ourselves in the effort to learn how best to serve our patrons, and at the same time be just to ourselves.

"'How are the railroads built? Where does the money come from that constructs and maintains them? It is through the union of men, and the combination of means and labor. This is how it is accomplished. [Applause.] There can be but little success in any effort to accomplish good, in this age, without union. This Exposition could not have been created and carried on, could not have presented the grandeur it does now, except through the combination of capital and the energy of men of enterprise. Look at the States that are represented here. We see not only many of the States of the United States, but also many foreign States as well. I find the Central American Republics are represented here; those unions that are dependent upon the voice of the people for their government are here. They are getting in line with us. They are here to co-operate with us of the South in this great work. Even our United States Government has made a large appropriation, and has sent down many of its people and many of its products to illustrate itself and its people. It is through union that success is attained. Look over this city to-day, I suppose it is so every day, we see floating from the house-tops, from the towers, and from the flagstaves, that emblem of Union, the Star Spangled Banner! [Great applause.] Long may it wave over us [applause], and we be fit and proper citizens to represent it in this "Land of the free and the home of the brave!"' [Long continued applause.]

"'We are going to have some resolutions read,' said Mr. Hemphill, 'and, Mr. President, I wish you would commission me a brakeman in order that I may vote with the boys.'

"' I do,' said Mr. Plant.

"In presenting the resolutions passed by the Commercial and Industrial Association of Montgomery, Alabama, Mr. W. C. Bibb, Jr., chairman of the committee appointed to convey them to Mr. Plant, said:

"'Mr. Chairman, Ladies, and Gentlemen: Among

the ancient Greeks and Romans the laurel was the symbol of triumph; the laurel wreath was second only to a kingly crown. Shafts of stone and marble and statues of bronze commemorated the deeds of demigods, kings, and conquering heroes. History teems with names and deeds of men who carved out a niche in the Temple of Fame with a bloody sword. To raze a fair city, invade, overwhelm, and destroy a smiling land, hew down and slaughter its inhabitants, or drag them in chains to slavery, were the only deeds by which Fame might be won.

"'In this fair land and enlightened age, he who makes two blades of grass to grow where was one before; who links new cities with the old by shining bands of steel; who masters the sea and brings the forces of nature subservient to the will, the comfort, and the uses of his fellow-man; who builds up, develops, and makes the land to abound in plenty, while thousands of happy men and women rise up and call him blessed—he it is for whom the laurel blooms, he it is who has builded for himself a monument more enduring than brass and more lasting than marble. We are gathered here to celebrate the natal day of such a man.

"'Sir, it is the pleasure of this committee, in behalf of the Commercial and Industrial Association, of the people of Montgomery, and of Alabama, to read in the presence of this audience and to present to you the resolutions I have in my hands, and to wish for you many happy returns of your birthday.

"' WHEREAS, The 28th day of October, 1895, has been set apart by the Cotton States and International Exposition Company, of Atlanta, Georgia, to do honor to H. B. Plant, the genius and controlling spirit of the two great Southern enterprises — the Southern Express Company and the Plant Investment Company; and

"' WHEREAS, We deem the time and occasion fit and opportune to unite with other Southerners in paying homage to one so richly endowed with merit and worth, yet so unpretentious; so eminently successful, yet unassuming; who has, by his latest achievement on land and sea, given to the three States of Alabama, Georgia, and Florida a system of railroads, steamships, and palatial hotels in the interest of commerce, travel, and internal development unsurpassed in the civilized world. Therefore, be it

"' *Resolved*, That we, the members of the Commercial and Industrial Association of the City of Montgomery, Alabama, by unanimous rising vote, do most heartily congratulate Mr. Plant upon his continued health and prosperity upon this his birthday; that we convey to him by these resolutions tidings that his name and fame are dear to us and to all Alabamians.

"'*Resolved*, That a copy of these resolutions be forwarded to Atlanta, Georgia, to be publicly read and presented to Mr. Plant on October 28, 1895.' [Applause and cheers.]

"Colonel Hemphill:—'I move these resolutions be adopted by a rising vote. All in favor of the re-resolutions will stand.' All present responded.

"On behalf of the Savannah Board of Trade, Judge Robert Falligant spoke as follows:

"'Mr. Chairman: I was spending with my family a season of quiet and rest amid the mountains of Georgia when we got news of this auspicious occasion. In former years I had the pleasure of serving under the great leader whose birthday we celebrate to-day, and I could not resist the temptation of being present and adding my voice to the universal acclaim, not only of Georgia, but of all Southern States. As I came in, these resolutions were presented to me to read and I was requested to make a few preliminary remarks. I really don't know what I can say on this occasion so replete with force and eloquence, both in speech and resolutions, but my heart is impelled to say something in this magnificent presence. I feel that not only Georgia is here, but the entire South and the entire country. [Applause.]

"'I am proud to see that Atlanta has touched the high-water mark of civilization in this illustrious display. I feel proud as a Georgian, and, as the representative of Savannah, I bid her godspeed in the magnificent tide of prosperity that awaits her. We have no envious feeling upon the coast, but trust that her future may be as limitless and as beautiful as the grand ocean that expands beyond her borders, the image of infinity.

"'I say this is an occasion for patriotic emotions, and we should all unite in doing honor to the citizen who has devoted himself to the public good. Let us honor the man who plants his high purposes in his native land, who knows no South, no East, no West, no North, but is an American, heart and soul.' [Great and continued applause and cheering.]

"Then the following was read:

"'ATLANTA, GEORGIA, October 28, 1895.

"'Mr. H. B. PLANT, Atlanta, Ga.—My dear Sir:—On behalf of the Savannah Board of Trade I congratulate you most heartily upon this auspicious occasion of your seventy-sixth birthday. You have, in the providence of infinite power, been permitted to dwell among your fellows beyond the allotted period of man, and it has also been your most favored privilege in that period to bring to completion undertakings of vast magnitude for the uplifting of the South especially, and for the whole country in general, which will stand a monument to your foresight, zeal and patriotic devotion to our common country long after the shaft or statues of marble or bronze have lost their significance as finger posts pointing to martial renown or the triumph of the forum. For your works, engraven upon the hearts of your generation with the stylus of commercial probity, will always be recalled with pleasant memory because free from the painful associations of sanguinary fields or the bitter words of fierce debates. May the mighty God, in His providence, as He spares you for the years to come, continue to bless you with bodily strength to pursue your active career of usefulness, until your eyes can look upon the full fruition of the great works in the interests of commerce, with which your name will ever be inseparably associated in fruitful memory through the multiplying cycles of time. With profound esteem, very truly and sincerely yours,

"'D. G. PURSE,
"'President Savannah Board of Trade.'

"The resolutions were adopted by a rising vote.

"The Plant System employees were represented by Hon. A. A. Wiley, who spoke as follows:

"'Mr. President, Mr. Plant, Ladies, and Gentlemen: These men who wear these badges to-day, whether they come from South Carolina, Florida, Georgia, or Alabama, are the employees of the Plant

System, consisting of telegraph, express, railway, and steamship lines. They number perhaps three thousand, but represent more than twelve thousand employees, and have come from the smoke and the dust of the workshop, from the railway car, from the locomotive, from express and law offices, to pay their tribute of respect, and to manifest their love for our distinguished chief, their admiration and appreciation of him. [Applause and cheers.]

"'This great day becomes a national day, because it is replete with mighty consequences to both North and South.

"'Here we may forget our business cares and worldly contests, for the soft hand of kindness, friendship, and hospitality smoothes down the ruffled brow. A quarter of a century ago, ruthless and unpitying war, with all the devastations that follow in its wake, swept with relentless fury over our fair and fruitful fields.

"'When that fratricidal struggle was ended and the soldiers who survived it returned to their desolated homes to find poverty and want at every door, Mr. Henry B. Plant, a Union man, who, notwithstanding his loyalty to the North, had been commissioned by President Davis, because of his honesty and integrity, to go at will everywhere throughout Dixie, was also true to the South. He recognized the fact that the war was over. He had confidence in the reserved energy, loyalty, devotion, and patriotism of the men who wore the gray. [Applause and cheers.]

"'He had faith in the magnificent possibilities of this land of golden summers. He knew that we would never again renew hostilities against the Union of our fathers; and he was right.

"'Mr. Plant began anew with us the battles of life. He poured out his wealth like water, to build up and beautify our waste places. He put activity and intelligent direction into the industrial life of the South; and his confidence was not misplaced. He has built grandly and well—wiser, perhaps, than he knew—and has rolled onward the car of progress and prosperity. The whole South has felt the touch of his magical hand, and recognized in him a potential factor in the advancement of commerce and civilization. To-day about fifty thousand people owe food, shelter, and raiment to his bounty and munificence. [Applause and cheers.]

"'He has carried happiness and plenty to many a fireside, and poured the sunshine of peace and gladness into many a weary heart. [Great cheering and applause.]

"'We, his servants and employees, have now assembled here, not only to do him honor on this, his birthday, but we desire to keep his name and memory forever fresh and green in our heart of hearts; and no more fitting method, it seems to me, can be devised, than by setting apart the 27th day of October, in each succeeding year, as a memorial day, to be commemorated by appropriate services and the planting of trees. With this object in view, I offer the following resolutions, and move their unanimous adoption by a rising vote:

"'WHEREAS, It is meet and proper that we, the employees of the Plant System, should in some appropriate manner observe the birthday of Mr. Plant, our worthy and honored President; therefore, be it

"'*Resolved*, 1. That the 27th of October in each and every year hereafter shall be set apart and observed and duly celebrated in honor of the life and character of Mr. H. B. Plant.

"'*Resolved*, 2. That on said 27th day of October, water-oak trees shall be planted at all station grounds and about all section houses on all the lines of the Plant System, this tree being the favorite of our much-loved chief.

"'*Resolved*, 3. That the general superintendent and the division superintendents are hereby created a permanent board, with the request that Mr. Plant's birthday be honored as herein set out.'

"These resolutions were adopted unanimously by a rising vote and with great enthusiasm.

"The Tampa (Florida) Band then furnished music.

"Mr. M. F. Plant addressed the crowds as follows:

"'Colonel Hemphill, Ladies and Gentlemen, and Members of our Family, the Plant System [Great cheering and applause]: I desire to thank you in behalf of my mother, of my wife, who is absent, and my boy, for the great compliment you have paid my father. [Great applause.] It is, indeed, a great treat to me to be here and to thank you for your kindness, not only to my father, but to the name of the System which, by your very careful, studious, and painstaking application to its business, you have built up. Gentlemen, I thank you.' [Great applause and cheers.]

"Mr. Hemphill announced that at 3 o'clock P. M. Mr. Plant would hold a reception in the Plant System Building.

"This reception was most pleasant. Mr. Plant sat beneath the tropical foliage of the Plant Building display and shook hands with all his employees, who passed him by the hundred. He was driven back to the Aragon Hotel late in the afternoon."

CHAPTER XVI.

Banquet at the Aragon Hotel Ends the Festivities of the Day—Sketch of the Southern Express Company—Distinguished Callers on President Plant during the Day—Many Telegrams and Letters of Congratulation Received—Many Press Notices of the Day, and many Tributes of Respect and Esteem for him who Called it forth.

"THE banquet at the Aragon last night," says the Atlanta *Constitution*, "given in honor of Mr. H. B. Plant, was a fitting climax to the day set apart for the celebration of the seventy-sixth birthday of that distinguished man.

"The occasion was one that must have been gratifying to the honored guest, in that he received the warmest assurances of the high esteem in which he is held by the people of the South from the eloquent representatives of many of the States. He was the toast of the evening, and he bore the distinguished honors with his characteristic demeanor.

"When Captain Evan P. Howell called upon the fifty prominent guests to rise and drink to the health of the guest of honor, Mr. Plant, there was an enthusiasm and love for the latter inspired in the heart of every man around the banquet tables, which found vent in the many eloquent speeches of tribute which followed. Upon Mr. Plant there was bestowed the highest encomiums of praise, admiration, and love, and he was made to feel the enthusiasm of the sentiment in the hearts of the speakers.

"The dinner in honor of Mr. Plant was given by the Exposition directors. It was the concluding honor bestowed upon the South's benefactor in connection with the great Plant System Day at the Exposition. About fifty guests assembled to do honor to the occasion, and among them were some of the best-known and most influential men of the country. The South was represented by distinguished men from many States.

"At the conclusion of the dinner, Captain Howell, who acted as toast-master, arose and proposed a toast to the distinguished guest of honor. At the request, every guest arose and drank to the health of Mr. Plant in silence.

"'I have been offered many toasts and received some honors,' said Mr. Plant, in response, 'but none has ever afforded me more pleasure than this. I feel that I am among friends to-night, and it is useless to assure you that I am deeply appreciative of this honor. I have had something to say to you already to-day, and am almost talked out. There is so much talent and so many men here to-night who can entertain you with a ventilation of the English language, and I am so hoarse that I will yield to them and not detain you. I thank you, Mr. Toast-master, and gentlemen.'

"Captain Howell, in introducing the speakers of the evening, took occasion to say many happy things about Mr. Plant and the guests around the tables. He was in his happiest vein, and with wit, wisdom, and story, he entertained the assemblage. Each effort of the toast-master was received with applause.

"'We are indebted to the distinguished gentleman we have gathered to-night to honor,' said Captain Howell, 'for one of the best exhibits at our great Exposition. His is an exhibit of which we should feel proud; one that reflects credit on his effort and the Exposition. He has shown us loyalty, fidelity, and love for the South by the work he has done for us. We are pleased and honored to have him among us, and to call him one of us. This Southland owes to him much of gratitude. He has benefited every section of the Southeast, and done work which will last as a monument to his fame for years to come.

"'We regret that our zealous president, Mr. Collier, is unable to be with us this evening to extend to Mr. Plant in person the welcome felt by the Exposition Company, but in that absence we have a man to speak for him who can do so fittingly.

We ask Mr. Alexander W. Smith to return to Mr. Plant the thanks of the Exposition Company for the splendid exhibit he has sent us and for the good work he has done, not only in our interest, but for the State and the entire South.'

"Mr. Smith paid a fitting tribute to the worth of Mr. Plant to the State of Georgia, the South, and to the Exposition. He thanked him on behalf of the Exposition Company for the complete and magnificent exhibit sent by Mr. Plant, and warmly congratulated him on his birthday, which gave occasion for such a great day as yesterday had been to the Exposition. Colonel George W. Adair was called upon and he made one of his best speeches. He entertained his hearers with stories and reminiscences of his boyhood and manhood days, referring to the time when he first met Mr. Plant. The speaker had assisted in forming the Southern Express Company, and he proposed to share the honors with Mr. Plant, for the evening at least.

"Among the other speakers were Colonel H. S. Haines, Colonel A. A. Wiley, of Alabama; Speaker Fleming, Major J. W. Thomas, of Nashville; Judge Falligant, of Savannah; Hon. Fleming du Bignon, of Savannah; Dr. Smyth, and several others. All of the speakers paid high tribute to Mr. Plant and his work for the South. He was eulogized in the language of highest praise, and declared to be a man worthy of all honors that could be bestowed upon a citizen.

"Some of the speakers referred to the esteem in which Mr. Plant is held by his twelve thousand employees, and laid stress on that fact as being the best evidence of the noble character of the man, one who treated all men with justice, moderation, and kindness. Mr. Plant was made to feel that the welcome extended him was sincere, and he left the banquet table honored as perhaps no other man will be honored during the Exposition period. To him was shown the appreciation of the Exposition Company of his work, by setting aside a special day in his honor, something that will not be accorded to any other individual.

"The banquet was one of the most elaborate of the season, and reflected credit on the committee in charge and Manager Dodge, of the Aragon, who supervised it in person."

With the banquet at the Aragon, tendered to President Plant by the directors of the Exposition Company and the citizens of Atlanta, the festivities directly incident to "Plant System Day" were brought to a close. This history, however, would be incomplete without reference to the Southern Express Company, to which Mr. Plant has been pleased to allude as his "first love." It numbers among its officers some of the men whom Mr. Plant had in mind when he said on Sunday morning, October 27th, "I see here present those who were with me in troublous times and bore with me the heat and burden of the fight," and this may be considered a fitting place to give a brief history of the company as published in the *Constitution* of October 29, 1895.

From the Atlanta *Constitution*, Tuesday, October 29, 1895:

"Among the thousands who gathered at the Exposition yesterday to do honor to Mr. Henry B. Plant, the great 'man of affairs,' the officers and employees of the Southern Express Company formed a notable group, the central and most prominent figure of which was Mr. M. J. O'Brien, the vice-president and general manager. It was fitting that this great enterprise should be represented by its most prominent officials and a large delegation of its employees on this day, for it was as an express company employee that Mr. Plant began life, and the history of the express business in the South is almost identical with Mr. Plant's great success. It was also appropriate that the representatives of the great army of Southern Express Company employees should be headed by the man whose master mind and admirable executive ability have contributed so largely to every success of the mammoth enterprise over which he presides with such marked distinction, for the history of the Southern

Express Company is not only the history of Mr. Plant but of Mr. O'Brien, since the latter gentleman has been closely identified with the express business of Mr. Plant for the past thirty-five years, and its achievements have largely been his own.

"HISTORY OF THE SOUTHERN EXPRESS COMPANY.

"On July 5, 1861, a charter was granted for the Southern Express Company for fourteen years, with H. B. Plant as President; R. B. Bullock, Superintendent of the Eastern Division; E. Hulbert, Superintendent of the Central, and D. P. Ellwood, Superintendent of the Western Division, who, however, shortly resigned, and was succeeded by A. B. Small, with James Shuter as Assistant Superintendent.

"As the Federal forces advanced into Dixie the Southern Express Company abandoned its lines, which were immediately utilized by the Adams Express Company. In fact, the Southern Express Company was operated under difficulties throughout those belligerent times, arising from the changing lines of armies, destructions of railroads, and from the conscription acts, until express employees were exempted from service in the army and navy.

"At the close of the war another source of danger presented itself. Gangs of disbanded soldiery and raiding parties, ever ready to appropriate portable property wherever it could be found, in many cases plundered the express offices, their horses being taken and nothing valuable left. But it's a long lane that has no turn. A reaction soon set in, and the marvellous prosperity of the 'Sunny South' has been only equalled by the growth and development of the Southern Express Company. To-day its service extends from Richmond, Louisville, and St. Louis on the North; Charleston and Savannah on the East; Springfield, Missouri, and Houston, Texas, on the West, and New Orleans, Mobile, and Tampa, Florida, on the South, reaching twelve States and embracing about three thousand agencies, with a through line to New York and direct communication with Cuba.

"In 1875, a renewal of the company's charter was applied for and granted, and, in 1886, the Georgia Legislature granted the company a charter for thirty years from December 21st of that year. The little concern organized at Augusta, Georgia, in 1861, has now become one of the strongest and most successful express companies in the United States.

"The *Constitution* to-day publishes excellent portraits of General Manager M. J. O'Brien, Assistant General Manager T. W. Leary, Traffic Manager C. L. Loop, and Superintendent W. W. Hulbert, all of whom have been intimately identified with the growth and development of the Southern Express Company.

"General Manager O'Brien began service with the Adams Express Company at Memphis, in 1859. He next served as way-bill clerk and then as messenger, being later promoted to the cashier's office at New Orleans. Evincing a remarkable aptitude for the express business, he was next appointed agent at Montgomery, Alabama, and, in rapid order, successively became President Plant's secretary, secretary of the Southern Express Company, general superintendent, general manager, and vice-president and general manager.

"Assistant General Manager Leary commenced as secretary to General Superintendent O'Brien and for years was his faithful lieutenant. Subsequently he was made assistant to the general manager and then appointed assistant general manager.

"Traffic Manager Loop began his express career as messenger in the Adams Express Company's service, and was particularly prominent in express operations during the war. He was for many years auditor and cashier of the western department of the Southern Express Company, and upon the consolidation of the eastern and western departments was made general auditor, succeeding from that position to his present office.

"Superintendent Hulbert began service as local

agent at West Point, Georgia, in 1858, and with the exception of four years, during which time he was in the war, has been continuously in the service of the Southern Express Company ever since.

"To give some idea of the magnitude of the Southern Express Company's business, it is only necessary to say that should their employees, with their families and others dependent for their living upon services rendered to this great enterprise, move to the State of Nevada, and the present population of that State should leave it, Nevada would have a much larger population than she has at present. In other words, the officers and employees of the Southern Express Company who are in Atlanta to-day represent a larger number of citizens of this country than do the two United States Senators who represent the State of Nevada in the upper House of Congress. Again, the amount of money invested in horses, wagons, etc., is simply fabulous, while their stationery bill for one year would make a man independently wealthy.

"The business of the company must necessarily be enormous to support and justify such an expense. It consists of forwarding freight, money, and valuables of all descriptions by the fastest passenger trains, in charge of special messengers. As forwarders of money, bonds, and valuables, they successfully compete with the government mail service. Absolute safety is guaranteed in all transactions, and in case of damage to, or loss of goods, the delay, almost inevitable in government red tape, is avoided.

"THE HANDSOME EXHIBIT.

" The Southern Express Company's office on the Exposition grounds makes one of the handsomest exhibits to be seen. It is not, however, altogether for show, but the express business in all its branches is conducted just as it is in the Atlanta office. The pretty, tasty little office is doing a thriving business, if one can judge from the crowds which are constantly about it. Mr. M. W. Wooding is in charge of the Exposition office, and yesterday happily sustained the reputation which he has earned of being a most delightful host. Mr. Wooding is an old Atlanta boy, and has been with the Southern Express Company for the past twelve years.

"Among the well-known gentlemen who called yesterday at the express office were: H. B. Plant, President, New York City, New York; M. J. O'Brien, Vice-President and General Manager, New York City, New York; M. F. Plant, Vice-President, New York City, New York; T. W. Leary, Assistant General Manager, Chattanooga, Tennessee; C. L. Loop, Traffic Manager, Chattanooga, Tennessee; G. H. Tilley, Secretary and Treasurer, New York; F. J. Virgin, Au-

ditor, Chattanooga, Tennessee; Superintendents—
H. Dempsey, Augusta, Georgia; C. T. Campbell,
Chattanooga, Tennessee; O. M. Sadler, Charlotte,
North Carolina; H. C. Fisher, Nashville, Tennessee; G. W. Agee, Memphis, Tennessee; W. J. Crosswell, Wilmington, North Carolina; C. L. Myers,
Jacksonville, Florida; V. Spalding, Roanoke, Virginia; C. A. Pardue, New Orleans, Louisiana; Assistant Superintendent Mark J. O'Brien, Chattanooga,
Tennessee; Route Agents—J. B. Hockaday, Greenville, South Carolina; K. C. Barrett, Florence, South
Carolina; S. R. Golibart, Suffolk, Virginia; P. B.
Wilkes, Monroe, North Carolina; J. Cronin, Waycross, Georgia; John Lovette, Atlanta, Georgia;
W. C. Agee, Memphis, Tennessee; Agents—F. L.
Cooper, Savannah, Georgia; W. A. Dewes, Chattanooga, Tennessee; W. M. Shoemaker, Montgomery,
Alabama; F. M. Folds, Messenger, Montgomery,
Alabama.

"It would not do to close this article without giving due meed of praise to Daniel Davis, the urbane colored boy who, under the direction of Mr. Wooding, dispensed 'the hospitalities of the house' in the most approved and satisfactory manner.

"Were we to record herein the numerous telegrams and letters of congratulation received by Mr. Plant from his many friends who were unable personally to be present in Atlanta, we would have to publish a second edition to retain a pamphlet form of this little volume. We must, therefore, content ourselves with saying to one and all who so thoughtfully remembered Mr. Plant on the occasion of his anniversary, that their kindly sentiments were highly appreciated by him, and to each and every one, through these columns, he returns his sincere thanks.

"To our newspaper friends, who so kindly espoused our cause, prior to, at the time of, and since the festivities in Atlanta, and who are always ready to deal kindly by us, we return our thanks. To them we would most heartily accord the space necessary in which to reprint all of the nice things they have said of us, but for the same reason as given in the foregoing paragraph, we must abbreviate. However, we feel that it is not just to them or to ourselves entirely to ignore all quotations from their columns, and with their permission we give below, in so far as our limited edition will permit, some of the many pleasant references made by our journalistic friends.

"Among the many telegrams of congratulation received by Mr. H. B. Plant, President of the Plant System, we give below two, together with copies of Mr. Plant's responses, which were omitted in our report of proceedings in yesterday's issue.

"'MONTGOMERY, ALABAMA, Oct. 28, 1895.
"'HENRY B. PLANT, Atlanta, Georgia:

"'Montgomery Division, No. 98, Order of Railway Conductors, tenders you its heartiest congratulations. It is the uniform hope of all its members that you may live to see many more years of such usefulness and happiness, and that your every wish may be realized.

"'JOHN C. ELLIOTT,
"'CHAS. J. READ,
"'*Committee.*'

"'ATLANTA, GEORGIA, Oct. 29, 1895.
"'JNO. C. ELLIOTT and CHAS. J. READ, Committee, No. 98, Order Railway Conductors, Montgomery, Alabama:

"'Of the many telegrams of congratulation I have received, none are appreciated more than the one from you, as representatives of the Order of Railway Conductors, and my best efforts in the future, as in the past, will be to deserve the commendation of all members of your order.

"'H. B. PLANT.'

"'TAMPA, FLORIDA, Oct. 27, 1895.
"'H. B. PLANT, Atlanta, Georgia:

"'Recognizing in you a friend of Tampa and of

Florida, our city congratulates you on this the anniversary of your birthday, and indulges the hope that you may live to celebrate many others and to reap the fruits of your labor and enterprise.

"'F. A. SALOMONSON, Mayor.'

"'ATLANTA, GEORGIA, Oct. 28, 1895.

"'F. A. SALOMONSON, Mayor:

"'I thank you personally, and through you the good people of Tampa and Florida, for your hearty congratulations and well wishes. I shall hope to celebrate many more anniversaries of my birthday, and as each milestone is passed I trust we may all look back and see that I have contributed in a measure to the interests of the good people of your State and city.

"'H. B. PLANT.'

"A REMARKABLE OVATION.

"President H. B. Plant, of the Plant System, was a happy man yesterday when he looked into three thousand smiling faces at the Exposition Auditorium and saw among them about one thousand five hundred of his faithful employees, who were assembled to celebrate his seventy-sixth birthday.

"It was a rare tribute to a great and a good man. Probably no railway president in the world could have commanded such an ovation.

"Mr. Plant was overwhelmed with graceful attentions from his employees, the Exposition directors, and our citizens generally. The day at the Exposition was a celebration in his honor, and at night the directors entertained him at a banquet.

"It goes without saying that this tribute is worth more to Mr. Plant than presents of silver and gold. It will touch his heart as nothing else could. That he may long hold his honored place among us is the earnest wish of all who know him.

"MR. PLANT AND THE NEGROES.

"In addition to what has been said of Mr. Plant and his great System, the negroes are grateful for what he has done for them. There are over two thousand negroes employed by Mr. Plant. A great number of them have accumulated homes, educated their children, and have nice bank accounts, and they all love him. He has contributed liberally to churches, school-houses, and other negro enterprises; in fact, he has built several institutions of learning for negroes. A number of negroes hold positions of trust, with good pay attached, as is not the case with any other system the size of his in the United States.

"May the years of Mr. Plant's usefulness in behalf of the South, colored and white, be many more."—Atlanta *Constitution*.

"HONORS TO MR. PLANT.

"Few men have done as much as Mr. H. B. Plant to develop the South, and the *Journal* joins heartily in the tributes which are being paid to him to-day.

"He has reached the age of seventy-six with a record which any man might envy, and we trust is good for many more years of usefulness. Mr. Plant is the head of great corporations which have been of incalculable value to the South. They have been so, not because they are rich and powerful, but because, under his direction, they have been conducted on broad and liberal lines. Mr. Plant's policy has been to build up. His career presents a splendid contrast to those of the railroad wreckers who have enriched themselves at the expense of thousands of individual victims and of great regions of the country.

"Mr. Plant has used his power nobly. He has made it beneficial to multitudes of his fellow-citizens, and has contributed immensely to the general development of the South. As the president of a great railroad system, of steamship lines, and of the Southern Express Company, and the Texas Express Company, Mr. Plant enjoys, not only the kind regards of a host of employees, but the respect and admiration of the public as well. The many evidences which he receives to-day of the good-will and esteem of his fellow-men must be exceedingly gratifying to him, but we are justified in saying that seldom have tributes been more richly deserved. We extend to Mr. Plant our cordial congratulations on his seventy-sixth birthday, and hope that we shall have the pleasure of seeing his honored and useful career continued for many years to come.

"Mrs. H. B. Plant, the wife of the distinguished president of the Plant System, is at the Aragon. She is a beautiful, cultured, travelled woman, and as such receives everywhere the most flattering social attentions. She will be the conspicuous social figure of this week, and several brilliant affairs will be given in her honor. Mrs. Plant is one of the New York Commissioners, and has proven her interest in Atlanta's Exposition in many satisfactory and assuring ways."—Atlanta *Journal*.

"A splendid banquet was tendered by the Southern Express Company to its superintendents, route agents, and agents attending the Cotton States and International Exposition, last evening in the Kimball House.

"The occasion was a most happy one.

"The banquet was held in honor of Plant Day— Mr. Plant being president of the Southern Express Company.

"Mr. T. W. Leary, the popular and genial assistant general manager of the Southern Express Company, presided and acted as toast-master. In this capacity he distinguished himself, and made some of the happiest hits of the evening. The speeches were of the happiest character, and befitted the occasion which they commemorated—the birthday of the venerable president of the express company, who has done so much towards the building up of this rich and powerful transportation company.

"Among those who spoke were the following:

"Mr. C. L. Loop, traffic manager of the Southern Express Company; Mr. H. Dempsey, superintendent; Mr. H. O. Fisher, superintendent; Mr. G. W. Agee, superintendent; Mr. V. E. McBee, general agent Seaboard Air Line; Mr. J. L. McCollum, superintendent Nashville, Chattanooga, and St. Louis Railway; Mr. F. H. Richardson, editor Atlanta *Journal;* Mr. C. S. Gadsden, superintendent of the Plant System.

"The entire occasion was marked by the greatest enthusiasm, and it will be long remembered by those present. The following is a list of the guests:

"J. S. B. Thompson, assistant general superintendent Southern Railway; V. E. McBee, general agent Seaboard Air Line; W. R. Beauprie, superintendent Southern Railway; J. L. McCollum, superintendent Nashville, Chattanooga, and St. Louis Railway; D. E. Maxwell, general manager Florida Central and Peninsular Railway; L. M. Weathers, Memphis, Tennessee; F. de C. Sullivan, E. M. Williams, George

E. Carter, New York; B. R. Swoope, Virginia; F. H. Richardson, Atlanta *Journal*, and G. W. Haines, H. A. Ford, C. O. Parker, C. S. Gadsden, W. B. Denham, Judge Brawley, of the Plant System; M. F. Echols, agent Southern Express Company, Atlanta, Georgia; W. A. Dewees, agent Southern Express Company, Chattanooga, Tennessee; F. L. Cooper, agent Southern Express Company, Savannah, Georgia, and H. M. McCulloch, W. E. McGill, G. A. Wilkinson, J. A. Cleary and F. M. Folds; C. L. Loop, traffic manager Southern Express Company; H. Dempsey, superintendent; H. C. Fisher, superintendent; C. T. Campbell, superintendent; O. M. Sadler, superintendent; W. J. Crosswell, superintendent; G. W. Agee, superintendent; C. L. Myers, superintendent; W. W. Hulbert, superintendent; V. Spalding, superintendent; C. A. Pardue, superintendent; J. C. Arnold, route agent; S. R. Golibart, route agent; P. B. Wilkes, route agent; W. C. Agee, route agent; J. Cronin, route agent; K. C. Barrett, route agent; John Lovette, route agent; H. E. Williamson, route agent; J. B. Hockaday, route agent; W. M. Shoemaker, agent Southern Express Company, Montgomery, Alabama.

"The Exposition was crowded to-day with the employees of the Plant System and the friends of Mr. H. B. Plant, the president of that System, for it was Plant Day.

"There is perhaps no more interesting figure in American business life to-day than H. B. Plant, and his employees have for him that feeling of love that is so rarely held by the employees of a great corporation for its head. As an evidence of that love and kindly feeling the employees gathered to-day to do him honor."—Atlanta *Journal*.

"The *Chronicle* publishes this morning an interesting sketch of Mr. Henry B. Plant, by Mr. Clark Howell. The writer has a most excellent subject for his theme, and he has handled it admirably. Than Mr. Henry B. Plant there is not a better man to be found anywhere. Starting from the plain people, unaided by the adventitious circumstances of birth or wealth, he has, step by step, ascended the ladder of fame and fortune, until he is now classed among the railroad magnates and the multi-millionaires of the country. He has been the architect of his own fortune, and he has done the work in the most artistic and substantial manner. His work for Florida and the South cannot be exaggerated. He has been one of the most potential factors in the upbuilding of this section, and he is still full of hope and faith in the present and future possibilities of the South. He knows thoroughly the advantages which we possess, and he is enthusiastic for their full utilization. Mr. Plant was for years a familiar figure in this community and a valued citizen of Augusta.

"Speaking of Mr. Plant yesterday, one of our prominent citizens observed that he had the remarkable gift of always selecting the right man for the right place. He is a capital judge of human nature. His life has been a most exemplary and laborious one. He is the personification of kindness and courtesy in his intercourse with his fellow-citizens, and his consideration for his employees is most marked.

"Monday was set apart by the Cotton States Exposition in honor of Mr. Plant. This recognition of his services to the South is well deserved. In his case it is an honor most worthily bestowed. At the age of seventy-six, Mr. Plant possesses a sound mind in a sound body. Long may he live to continue his good work for Florida and the South, and to wield his influence for good among his fellow-men."—Augusta *Chronicle.*

"The employees of the Plant System, who went to the Cotton States and International Exposition on the invitation of President Plant, returned yesterday very much gratified with their visit. And Mr. Plant was very greatly pleased to meet them at the Exposition. The occasion was the celebration of Mr. Plant's seventy-sixth birthday.

"Mr. Plant is still a very vigorous man. His mental faculties are as bright and keen as they ever were. He looks back on a long life of great activity and usefulness. He has built up a splendid monument to himself in the Plant Railway and Steamship System. All his life he has been a builder—never a wrecker. And the speech he delivered to his employees on Monday shows that he has a just appreciation of the relations he holds to the public.

"No man has contributed more to the building up of the South than Mr. Plant. The country tributary to his lines of railroad presents an appearance vastly different from what it did a quarter of a century ago. There are thousands of comfortable homes now where there was then only a wilderness. Plant Day was a feature of the Exposition, as the Plant System is a feature of the South."—Savannah *Morning News.*

"On this, the seventy-sixth anniversary of his birthday, we extend our wishes to Mr. H. B. Plant, the head of the great system of railways which bears his name. Long life and happiness to him."—The *Bulletin,* Savannah, Georgia.

"The ceremonies attending the anniversary of Mr. Plant's birthday yesterday in Atlanta were very imposing. There was a large crowd on hand, and Mr. Plant responded in a very feeling and appropriate

speech. There was a feeling and eloquent address by Judge Falligant. One of the gems of the occasion was the excellent letter of Capt. D. G. Purse."
—Savannah *Press*.

"To-day is a great one in Atlanta. The Plant System celebration of the birthday of its great founder is perhaps the most remarkable event of its kind that ever occurred in this country. It marks the beginning of a distinctive era in progress—when the men who are leaders in material progress are recognized and honored as public benefactors. While Florida is under vast obligations to statesmen of the past and present, to the heroes of several wars, to the pioneers who redeemed its lands to the plow and hoe—it is not too much to say that the present generation owes fully as much to the group of men who, having acquired large means elsewhere, are expending and investing them in developing the resources and advertising the resources of the State. And it is not overstating the case to say that to no one on this list belongs so much credit as to Henry B. Plant. He was the first, as he is to-day the leader, to see the good points of our soil and climate, and to bring them to the notice of the world. To him, and to his unwavering attachment to Florida, is due, to a preponderating extent, the surprising and persistent growth of the State. No pretense is made that he has done it all, but he led the way and set the pace, and it is a pleasure to the intelligent and fair-minded people of Florida to hold him in high esteem, and to testify to it. As long ago as 1853, Mr. Plant saw and appreciated Florida, and from that day to this he has been its unflinching friend. He has been the direct agency for the investment of many millions of dollars here, and the indirect cause of its duplication by others. He deserves the honors and compliments that are paid him, and more."—Tampa *Times*.

"The birthday of Henry B. Plant, head of the Plant Railway System and of the Southern Express Company, was yesterday celebrated in fine and appropriate style at the Atlanta Exposition. It was Plant System Day. Mr. Plant deserves such recognition. He has done much for the South, the section of his adoption. He has brought a great deal of capital and enterprise into the section, and built up important conveniences that have proven highly profitable to the Southern country and people. No one man has done more for the advancement of the South's material development. He was seventy-six yesterday, but looks twenty years younger, in spite of the big load of care and the big amount of work he has done in the last fifty years. Long may he live to enjoy the fruits and honors of his good works."
—*Daily Times*, Chattanooga.

"The west coast of Florida, Alabama, and the portions of the country around the Plant System in Georgia, sent thousands of people to the Atlanta Exposition for the celebration of Plant System Day at the Exposition. They have been coming on special trains since yesterday morning. To-day Mr. H. B. Plant celebrated his seventy-sixth birthday, and to-day is Plant System Day at the Exposition. Officials and employees from all the railway, steamship, and express lines controlled by Mr. Plant, and numbering nearly 5000 men, are here to celebrate the day. The public exercises occurred in the Auditorium, and the Plant System people were welcomed by Mayor King. Mr. Plant made a response to the welcome."—New Orleans *Times-Democrat*.

"The following invitation for last Monday the *Marine Journal* regretted very much not having been able to accept:

"'The Cotton States and International Exposition, Atlanta, Ga., having designated October 28, 1895, as Plant System Day, the officers and employees of the system will meet there to commemorate the birthday of their president, Mr. Henry B. Plant. You are invited to be present.'

"Advices from Atlanta since Monday announce that the event was a brilliant success, as befitted such an occasion. Mr. Plant was weighed down with congratulations, both personal, telegraphic, and

by mail, and presented himself in such an excellent
state of health and enjoyment that no one would
have imagined he had so far passed the regulation
threescore years and ten as the day commemorated.
Mr. Plant saw much that must have deeply gratified
him on the occasion, not only the result of his own
labor and enterprise, but in the encouraging presentation of things that give evidence of such a restored
measure of prosperity throughout the South as only
men like himself, who have worked so hard to accomplish such a happy state of affairs, can thoroughly
appreciate. The recognition of the Plant System in
such an auspicious manner by the management of
the Atlanta Exposition was a fitting testimonial to
the prominent part that the System is recognized to
hold in conducing to the well-being of the South,
not only from a commercial point of view, but from
the excellent reputation among the best classes of
people that must necessarily attach to the places
where the Plant hotels for winter tourists are situated. Thus the day became a fitting compliment to
the true worth of the founder and president of the
Plant System and an additional ray in the glory
with which his deeds crown him in the fulness of
his days. Long may he enjoy it."—*Marine Journal.*

"To-day the anniversary of the birth of Mr. H. B.
Plant, President of the Plant System of Railroads

and Steamships, the Southern Express Company and the Plant Investment Company, is being celebrated by the officers and attaches of these companies and friends of Mr. Plant at Atlanta—principally by the Plant System men.

"H. B. Plant is a remarkable man, and though well advanced in years, he is just as active in business to-day as he was a half-century ago. Thousands of his employees to-day assemble to pay tribute to his worth as a man; besides, thousands of acquaintances and admirers extend their heartiest congratulations.

"No better place or time for such celebration could be had than at the Atlanta Exposition, where is another, and the latest, monument to Mr. Plant's worth as a developer and as a man of enterprise and genius. The building and the exhibits there of the Plant System are similar to his good works all over the country, and every Floridian, South Carolinian, Georgian, and Alabamian must feel proud of these representatives of the products and enterprise of their States collected and displayed to such an advantage by the great System that benefits the States.

"The best men in Florida acknowledge H. B. Plant as one of the State's truest friends, and willingly in heart, if not in person, join in doing him honor on this, his seventy-sixth birthday, and all hope he may be spared many more years to the grateful people."—Jacksonville *Metropolis*.

"The reception given to the venerable president of the great Plant System of hotels in Florida on Monday, October 28, at Atlanta, was a deserved recognition of the work he has done in developing Florida and, indirectly, the whole South."—New York *Hotel Register*.

"As a rule, men of large interests are charmingly simple and unaffected in manner, and this is eminently true of H. B. Plant, President of the famous Plant System Railway and Steamship Lines, a millionaire, and the controlling power of three great hotels, the Tampa Bay, the Seminole at Winter Park, and the Inn at Port Tampa, all in Florida.

"Mr. Plant resides in New York much of the time, in an elegant home, but is also to be found a good deal in Florida, while he takes trips to Jamaica and other places where he has business to transact.

"Personally, he is a delightful conversationalist, and remarkably young for his years, which are not few. He is quite up to date in every way, and never lets a business chance go by him. The magnitude of his orders may be understood from the fact that he has recently given an order at Newport News for the largest coastwise steamer ever built,

440 feet in length, and having every comfort and modern arrangement for safety. He is deeply interested in the Cotton States and International Exposition, and has a building of his own at the grounds, with a comprehensive exhibit."—New Haven *Evening Register*.

"THE ATLANTA EXPOSITION.

"We hardly think the Northern Press has been as generous in its good offices to the Southern Exposition as it might. We have just returned from a visit to Atlanta, and were delighted with the beautiful landscape order of the grounds, the large and elegant buildings, and, above all, the wonderful exhibits they contained. The farm products will astonish our Northern visitors. Canned fruits and garden produce are varied, numerous, and luxuriant. The manufactures, especially of cotton, were very fine, and their machinery equal to the best in the country—was so pronounced by the Manufacturers' Committee from the New England States. The Art Building is a model of artistic taste and elegance. The Industrial Building, in which France, Germany, Italy, Spain, Portugal, and other nations are represented would require an entire day to explore. The minerals, fossils, photo plates, gold and silver ores, coal, salts, lime, and peculiar clays found in the Southern States, will repay close inspection. I saw beautiful china made from a white clay found in Florida only four months ago; also great blocks of salt as they were taken from the mine, that needed only to be crushed to fit them for immediate use.

"One of the things that has given a great uplift to the Cotton States has been the improvement of its railroads. A quarter of a century ago these were in a very depressed condition, crippled, bankrupt, and unremunerative, and about this time, H. B. Plant, of New York, interested Northern capitalists in them, bought, combined, reorganized, and improved them in every way, adding steamboat lines to the West Indies, and perfecting an express system unsurpassed in any part of the country, for the whole South. This so increased travel to the South, especially in the winter season, by health-seekers and pleasure-seekers, that better hotel accommodations were demanded. These were soon provided, at a large outlay, giving the South, especially Florida, the finest hotels in the world. St. Augustine, Palm Beach, and Tampa Bay, especially the latter, are unsurpassed for healthful, comfortable, and luxuriant appointments. Hence, Plant Day was one of the great days of the Exposition, when some two thousand of the more than twelve thousand employees of the Plant System came to do honor to the man who had done so much for the Southern section of our country. Receptions, addresses, silver cup, compass, and flowers, and a grand banquet in the evening at the Aragon Hotel, were cordially tendered to this benefactor of the Cotton States. Labor and capital clasped hands in the most friendly accord, and this problem of the age was here solved, where peace and good-will abounded among these men. We saw the man of war, the admiral of the fleet at Hampton Roads, pay his respects to this man of peace, whose guest we were, and whose power for good has been so widely felt in our land."—AN EAST ORANGE DOMINIE, *East Orange Gazette*, East Orange, New Jersey.

"EXPOSITION ECHOES.

"Mr. A. B. Wrenn, special agent of the Southern Pacific, who has been in Atlanta for the past few days, returned to the city yesterday, and gives a glowing account of the Exposition. He says that the number of people who visited the great show on President's Day was something over 78,000, and that on Atlanta Day the number will be considerably more.

"'One of the prettiest sights I saw while in Atlanta,' said Mr. Wrenn, 'was that of the thousands of the employees of the Plant System, when Plant Day was celebrated. Mr. H. B. Plant, president and owner of the Plant System of railroads, gave the thousands of his employees, who could possibly get off duty, a free trip to the Fair, and on Plant Day there were several thousands of them present. A grand reception was given, and section bosses, freight agents, clerks, and even negro laborers who worked on the sections, were given an opportunity of shaking hands with Mr. Plant, who is now an elderly gentleman. Mr. Plant made a speech and expressed his satisfaction at meeting so many of his men, and the affair passed off most pleasantly.'

"Mr. Wrenn says that the Exposition is well worth seeing."—*Daily Picayune,* New Orleans, Louisiana.

"THE ATLANTA EXPOSITION.

"BY THE REV. GEORGE H. SMYTH, D.D.

"Coming so soon after the great Exposition at Chicago,—the greatest the world has ever seen,—and considering the general depression of the country, and the short time taken for preparation, the Exposition of the Cotton States, at Atlanta, Georgia, is a marvel. The terraced ground, selected and laid out with such beautiful landscape effect, the architectural designs of the buildings, the artistic skill displayed in locating them, together with the drives, walks, ponds, fountains, lawns, and ornamentations of the whole Fair grounds, reflect great credit on the committee of distinguished gentlemen who had the matter in charge, and who spared neither pains nor expense to make the Exposition a great success. Atlanta alone contributed $1,000,000 to the enterprise.

"Plant Day was the great day of the Fair thus far. It was set apart by the Committee of Management in honor of Henry B. Plant, who has done so much for the progress, prosperity, and welfare of the Southern States. More than a quarter of a century has passed since he began his patriotic, not to say philanthropic, work of uplifting a prostrate section of our country. Up to this time the railroads of the Cotton States were poor, crippled, and some of them bankrupt. In 1879, Mr. Plant interested other capitalists in purchasing, reorganizing, and improving the railroads of the South. He organized and perfected an express system, steamboat system, railroad system—until now, the Plant System, as it is called, embraces nearly two thousand miles of railway lines and over twelve hundred miles of steamship lines. Of course, the facilities for comfortable travel to and through the South brought the health-seeker, the pleasure-seeker, investor, and permanent settler to the South; and this influx of population continues with increasing numbers each year. 'To-day, the South is universally acknowledged to be the most prosperous portion of the great Union, and that portion over which the Plant System ramifies itself is known as the garden-spot. Mr. H. B. Plant is the mainspring that moved the whole, and he is, in every sense, a public benefactor.' This is only the briefest intimation of the reasons for Plant Day at the Exposition.

"Sunday, October 27th, was Mr. Plant's seventy-sixth birthday. I had the pleasure of being one of a party of friends that filled his private car in going to the Exposition, and occupied one of the large and elegant rooms of his suite at the Aragon Hotel, Atlanta. On the morning of that day a few gentlemen—and they were gentlemen in every sense of the term—representing the more than twelve thousand employees of the Plant System, adroitly entertained their president in his own room, while the others took possession of his parlor. When everything was in readiness, Mr. Plant and his guests were invited into the parlor. He was most cordially greeted and congratulated on the seventy-sixth return of his birthday. Then written addresses, couched in choice language, were read from the three different departments—railroad, express, and steamboat—of the Plant System, followed by presentation of flowers, of a silver compass, suggesting the straight and upright course of his life, and a silver cup, large and massive,—a 'loving-cup,'—' filled, Mr. Plant, with the esteem, affection, and best wishes of your associates and employees, to whom you have been a benefactor and friend.' Mr. Plant's response was beautiful, tender, and touching, as kindly eyes looked through their tears at this grand old man whom they esteemed as a father.

"Next day, the reception given Mr. Plant in the Auditorium, by the employees of the Plant System, where addresses and resolutions of appreciation, esteem, and gratitude for what he had done for the South, were presented to him, was grand beyond description. In the evening of the same day a banquet was tendered him at the Aragon Hotel by the managers of the Exposition. Judges, lawyers, merchants, the mayor of Atlanta, and a large company of distinguished gentlemen sat down to a sumptuous repast. But it was 'the feast of reason and the flow of soul'—the eloquent and patriotic sentiments expressed in the after-dinner speeches that gave this choice chapter of Plant Day its chief significance and greatest charm. Never was Southern eloquence more eloquent or tongues more fluent in giving forth the overflow of heart. 'No North, no South, but one united, happy country —the land of the free and the home of the brave.'

"When, near the close, we were most unexpectedly called on for a speech, what could we say but express the pleasure experienced in all we had seen and enjoyed this whole day. We had witnessed the solution of the greatest problem of the age, a problem that many say will never be solved, that will yet bring on universal revolution. We had to-day seen labor and capital—employer and employed—clasp hands in mutual sympathy and most friendly accord. We had seen, everywhere we travelled in the South, the Plant System men vie with each other in doing honor to their chief. His presence was the signal for willing hands and happy faces in any service they could render him. Men felt better for his presence. The Czar of all the Russias might well envy this modest, quiet, Connecticut man, the connecting link between North and South, the harmonizer of differences, and the promoter of peace and good-will among men; and around whom cluster the respect and manly affection of 12,000 employees and many more thousands of invalids who find lost health travelling in the luxuriant cars and dwelling in the luxuriant hotels of the Plant System. Mr. Plant was first led to Florida in 1854 in search of health for his invalid wife, whose life he believes was prolonged many years by her residence in the soft, balmy air of this State. Travel then was so uncomfortable, and hotel accommodations so poor, that he began to think what could be done to improve both. Verily, 'There is a divinity that shapes our ends, rough hew them as we may,' and well is it when our own sufferings lead us to discover means of alleviating those of our fellow-men."—*The Christian Intelligencer*, New York.

CHAPTER XVII.

Some Changes that have Taken Place in the Configuration of the Globe—Islands Born and Buried—French Revolution—Napoleon's Influence on Europe—England's Long Wars—Barbarous Treatment of Prisoners—Slavery Abolished—English Profanity and Intemperance—Temperance Movements—Duelling—Penny Postage—Expansion of the Press—Canals, Erie and Suez—Railroads in England and the United States—First Steamer to Cross the Atlantic—First Steamship Line.

THE changes that have taken place on the globe itself, and in its inhabitants during the life of Mr. Plant, are varied, numerous, and wonderful.

The configuration of the earth has altered to a degree incredible to any but those observant of such changes. Winchell has tabulated some of these undulatory movements that have taken place along the Atlantic shore line of the American continent and elsewhere. "At St. Augustine, in Florida, the stumps of cedar trees stand beneath the hard beach shell-rock, immersed in water at the lowest tides. Some of the sounds upon the coast of North Carolina, which have been navigable within the memory of living sea-captains, are now impassable bars, or emerging sand-flats. Along the coast of New Jersey the sea has encroached, within sixty years, upon the sites of former habitations, and entire forests have been prostrated by the inundation. In the harbor of Nantucket the upright stumps of trees are found eight feet below the lowest tide, with their roots still buried in their native soil." Similar ruins of ancient submarine forests occur on Martha's Vineyard, and on the north side of Cape Cod, and again at Portland. In the region of the Saint Croix River, separating Maine from New Brunswick, the coast has been raised, carrying deposits of recent shells and sea-weeds, in one instance, to the height of twenty-eight feet above the present surface of the sea. The island of Grand Manan, off the mouth of the Saint Croix River, is slowly rotating on an axis, so that, while the south side is gradually dipping beneath the waves, the north is lifted into high bluffs. Near the River St. John is an area of twenty square miles containing marine shells and plants recently elevated from the sea. One hundred and fifty miles east of this place, the shore is experiencing a subsidence.

The north side of Nova Scotia is sinking, while the south is rising, insomuch that breakers now appear off the southern coast in places safely navigable in years gone by. The ancient city of Louisburg, on the island of Cape Breton, is another testimony to the uneasy condition of the land. This place was once the stronghold of France in America, and one of the finest harbors in the world. It was well fortified and had a population of twenty thousand souls within its walls.

It was destroyed during the French and Indian War, and the inhabitants dispersed, but Nature had herself ordained its abandonment. The rock on which the brave General Wolfe landed has nearly disappeared. The sea now flows within the walls of the city, and sites once inhabited have become the ocean's bed. In 1822, the entire coast of Chili was elevated to a height varying from two to seven feet, an area equal to that of New England and New York, having been lifted up bodily. In 1831, an island, since called Graham's Island, sprang from the bed of the Mediterranean between Sicily and the site of ancient Carthage. The island is now but a sunken reef. Another island, as recently as 1866, rose from the bottom of the Grecian Archipelago, before the very eyes of the American Consul, Mr. Chanfield, bearing upon its slimy back fragments of wrecks that had been sunken in the little harbor of Santorin.

"An island in the Missouri River, broken into fragments and washed away, was the unusual spectacle witnessed by the people of Atchison, Kansas. For years an island of 600 or 700 acres has been one of the attractions of Atchison. It was as fertile as a garden, and was known all over the West for the excellence of the celery, asparagus, sweet potatoes and melons it produced. It had the appearance of a veritable oasis in a desert, and its green shrubbery, generous shade trees, velvet lawns, and cool spring, were a perpetual joy. Upon this island a shooting club had a home, and the base-ball enthusiasts had their grounds, and grandstand. Altogether, it was a most pleasant resort. In a single night this island was dissolved into fragments.

"The big June rise in the Missouri River struck it, and to-day it is only a reminiscence. What was Kansas's loss, however, was Missouri's gain. With the obliteration of the island the current left the Missouri shore and struck hard against the Kansas bluffs. The result of this is that the Missouri banner has been planted a mile westward, and hundreds of acres of rich bottom land have been added to its domain, while Kansas mourns the loss of its green island and pleasant park."

The wonderful changes going on in the configuration of England are recorded in a well-known London paper (*Tit-Bits*) in the following words:

"Is England disappearing? Readers may pucker up their lips and ejaculate 'Absurd!' but facts, nevertheless, remain and show pretty clearly that England is positively disappearing, and may in years to come be marked on the map as a vanished isle.

"On the coast the sea is encroaching upon the land at an astonishing rate. Seaside towns and villages, holiday resorts, are gradually being eaten up and the inhabitants driven inland. In many parts the sea runs up on a beach which was once far inland. In other cases churches which were at one time far from the sea now stand at the edge of cliffs and have the sea lapping almost at their doors.

"The Goodwin sands, about five miles off the coast of Kent, were at one time a portion of the mainland itself and the property of Earl Goodwin. But the sea has swallowed them up.

"The coast of Norfolk is minus three villages which it once possessed — Shipden, Eccles, and Wimpwell—all of which have been taken into the arms of the encroaching ocean. The Cromer of to-day stands miles inland of the original Cromer.

"Auburn and Harlburn, two Yorkshire villages, once promised to develop into seaport towns of considerable importance; but, like the will of Canute, the will of the inhabitants of these villages was ignored by the rising sea, and Auburn and Harlburn now exist in mere names and sand-banks.

"Dunwich, on the coast of Suffolk, is gradually being swallowed up. Every now and then the inhabitants move a distance inland, rebuild their houses and shops and wait patiently and philosophically for the next "notice to quit" from the sea.

Many other seaside places have suffered or are suffering a similar fate.

"It may be argued, on the other hand, that some seaside towns are gradually becoming inland towns by the failure of the sea to 'come up to the mark,' and running out only to run in for a shorter distance. Winchelsea, Sandwich, Rye, and Southport are all suffering in this way. Winchelsea and Rye were originally two of our cinque ports, but the sea has left them standing high and dry. Sandwich was once a highly important seaport town. It now stands two or three miles inland.

"The sea is leaving Southport quite in the lurch— so much so indeed that the inhabitants have had to sink extensive lakes down on the beach to keep the sea from running off altogether and leaving merely an ordinary inland town.

"But the extension of our island in this way is very much less than the encroachment of the sea at other points, and while our land is certainly becoming more extensive in one direction, it is contracting, and with much greater rapidity, in some other. And the ultimate effect may be that our mountain peaks may form small islands, and eventually be pointed out by posterity as 'the position in which Great Britain is reputed to have stood.'"

The nineteenth has been the most remarkable century in the world's history. It was the most destructive and wasteful of life and property in the early part of its career, and in the latter half has been the most constructive and uplifting to the human race of any of the past centuries. The population of all Europe at the beginning of the century numbered one hundred and seventy millions, of whom four millions were engaged in the murderous work of war. The demoralization of society and the miseries inflicted on the people by these wars are beyond the power of pen to describe. France had an absolute monarchy. "The King held in his hands the unquestioned right to dispose, at his will, of the lives and property of the people. He was the sole legislator. His own pleasure was his only rule. He levied taxes, asking no consent of those who had to pay. He sent to prison men with no crime laid to their charge, and kept them there, without trial, till they died." Political corruption was rampant. For sixty years the court of Louis XV. had festered in the most filthy debauchery. Then followed the bloody Revolution, unparalleled in history. The guillotine, worn out with its butchery of more than a million lives stood idle, and peace—rather, the lull of an unfinished storm, for a time rested upon unhappy France. Then the tumultuous hurricane burst out anew in the wars of Napoleon, which terminated only at Waterloo in 1815.

"The influence which Napoleon exerted upon the

course of human affairs," says McKenzie, "is without a parallel in history. Never before had any man inflicted upon his fellows miseries so appalling; never before did one man's hand scatter seeds destined to produce a harvest of change so vast and so beneficient. It was he who roused Italy from her sleep of centuries and led her towards that free and united life which she at length enjoys. It was he, who by destroying the innumerable petty states of Germany, inspired the dream of unity which it has required more than half a century to fulfil." The progress made by these two countries during the century, in liberty, education, and all that conduces to the welfare of the individual and the strength of the nation, has been great beyond precedent.

England has perhaps outstripped all other nations in the advancement she has made during this period of the world's greatest progress. Her long and terrible wars with France and her allies had wasted her people and depleted her treasury. Taxes were enormous, food was high, wages low, and work scarce. The introduction of machinery in some departments reduced hand-labor a hundred-fold. The power loom threw thousands of people out of employment. England was badly governed. The laws were all made in the interests of the rich. Multitudes of the poor were famine stricken, one in eight being fed on charity, and many died of starvation.

Hunger maddens men, and hence crime abounded. Laws, numerous and terrible, were enacted for its prevention and punishment. Capital offences numbered two hundred and twenty-three. Some of the offences were ridiculous trifles. If a man appeared disguised in public, cut down young trees, shot rabbits, or stole property worth a dollar and a quarter, he was at once hanged. The treatment of prisoners was most barbarous. Young and old of both sexes were huddled together like cattle. Vermin, filth, and starvation were the common lot of all. John Howard and Elizabeth Fry inaugurated reforms in the interests of the prisoners that have since engaged the thought and effort of the best men and women of the nation.

War was carried on in the most cruel and brutal manner. Conscription and the press gang forced men from their families, and from peaceful occupation, and drove them to an unwilling military or naval, bloody field-servitude. Five hundred lashes was no uncommon punishment for some trifling offence. "The men who applied the torture were changed at short intervals, lest the punishment should be at all mitigated by their fatigue. The doctor stood by to say how much the victim could bear without dying. When that point was reached, he was taken down and carried to the hospital, to be brought back for the balance of his punishment when his wounds were healed. There is record of a soldier sentenced to one thousand lashes, seven hundred of which were actually inflicted. In the Crimean war two thousand six hundred British soldiers were killed, while eighteen thousand died in hospital of wounds and disease."

Scientific skill directed by generous-hearted Christian philanthropy has now mitigated these horrors, reducing them almost to a minimum. The same may be said of the brutality endured by women and little children working in mines from twelve to sixteen hours a day.

Slavery, which was almost universal at the beginning of the century, has been abolished. Forty millions in Russia, four millions in the United States, and many more millions in other lands have been made free.

Nor has this freedom been confined to the chattel slave. The courts of Europe were debauched beyond description. Even in England among the higher classes, "the supreme crowning evidence that an entertainment had been successful was not given till the guests dropped one by one from their chairs, to slumber peacefully on the floor till the servants removed them."

The temperance movement belongs to our present century, and while it has not yet accomplished all that could be desired, it has done much to lessen some of the grossest evils of society, and is full of promise for final triumph. The first temperance society was only eleven years old when the subject of this biography was born. It was organized in April, 1808, at Morean, Saratoga County, New York, with forty-three members. The American Temperance Society was formed at Boston, February, 1826, and, in 1829, the New York State Temperance Society, which in less than a year had one thousand local societies with a hundred thousand members. Soon the movement extended to the Old World, and a society was formed at New Ross, County Wexford, Ireland, and within a year sixty other societies were formed in different parts of the country. The Father Mathew crusade began in 1838, and it resulted in the enrollment of one million eight hundred thousand men and women in the temperance cause. The wave spread to Scotland, England, Wales, and the Continent. The Washington movement, started at Baltimore in 1840, doubtless advanced the cause of temperance in our country, half a million having signed the pledge. The great progress made in this direction is seen not so much in the number of temperance societies as in the fact that while there is difference of opinion as to the moderate use of wines and liquors, there is but one opinion among respectable people as to the immoderate use, and any one indulging in orgies such as those to which we have alluded would be excluded from all participation in decent society. No man of standing in good society glories in the shame of beastly intoxication; multitudes do not use liquor at all, and many others use it only as a medicine or aid to health.

The duel was made a legal way of settling disputes between gentlemen, and even, " Fox, Pitt, Castlereagh, Canning, O'Connell, and Wellington, had all attempted the slaughter of a foe."

Profanity was almost universal. " Erskine swore at the bar. Lord Thurlow swore on the bench. The King swore incessantly. Ladies swore orally and in their letters. The chaplain cursed the sailors, because it made them listen more attentively to his admonition." Obscene books were exposed for sale by the side of bibles and prayer-books.

Education was limited in its range and extent, and only the more wealthy could enjoy its benefits. In 1818, more than one half the children in England were without school advantages. In manufacturing districts, forty per cent. of the men and sixty-five per cent. of the women could not write their own names.

Penny postage, first proposed by Rowland Hill in 1837, adopted by Act of Parliament in 1839, and followed since then by every civilized country in the world, has proved to be a great adjunct in the education of the people.

The freedom and expansion of the press during this century have also been a great power for the enlightenment of mankind. True, it has not been an unmixed good, but let us hope the good has been, and will continue to be in the ascendant.

Canals, before the days of railroads and steamships, did much for the transportation of merchandise and intercommunication of the people. The Erie Canal, 363 miles in length, commenced in 1817, and finished in 1825, is said to have been one of the first impulses given to New York City in its ascendancy over every other city in the United States. On account of its great cost many of the people were opposed to it; "but in 1866, it was ascertained that besides enlarging many of the principal cities, and adding to the comfort and wealth of nearly all the people of the State, it had returned into the public treasury $23,500,000 above all its cost, including principle, interest, repairs, and superintendence."

In this same year, 1825, New York City was first lighted, partially only, with gas.

The Suez Canal, opened in 1870, was used by only 486 vessels, with a total net tonnage of 436,609, but its use was steadily increased, until in 1891, it rose to 8,698,777. When the canal was opened, it had cost $100,000,000, that is, $1,000,000 a mile, and since then $40,000,000 more have been expended in improvements. These are large amounts, but the canal pays annually from $4,000,000 to $5,000,000 over the interest of its bonded debt.

The introduction of railroads into England and the United States marks a great era in the progress of these two nations, not to say that of the whole world, though the event is of comparatively recent date, as the following account taken from a recent issue of the New York *Tribune* goes to show:

"The Chicago *Record* says that Edward Entwistle who has lived in Des Moines, Iowa, for forty years, ran the first passenger engine. He was born at Tilsey's Banks, Lancashire, England, in 1815, and was apprenticed to the Duke of Bridgewater, who had large machine shops at Manchester. The first railroad for general passenger and freight business was completed in 1831, between Manchester and Liverpool, a distance of thirty-one miles. The Rocket, the first locomotive or passenger engine, was built under the direction and according to the plans of George Stephenson, in the works where young Entwistle was serving as an apprentice. Stephenson engaged Entwistle as his assistant in the engine. The line being opened for general traffic, young Entwistle was put in charge of the Rocket, and for two years made two round trips every day between Liverpool and Manchester, one in the forenoon and the other in the afternoon. He came to this country in 1837."

When Mr. Plant was nine years old, there were only three miles of railroad in the United States. They were completed in 1827. Now there are 173,453 miles, and the speed of trains has been increased from ten miles an hour to more than seventy miles. The sleeping- and parlor-cars have made travel one of the great luxuries of this most luxuriant century. The first ocean steamer that crossed the Atlantic was the *Savannah*, which made the trip to Europe in the year 1819, the year Mr. Plant was born, and in 1838, the first regular line of Atlantic steamers was established.

CHAPTER XVIII.

Railroads Established—Engineering Progress—Steel, Iron Steamships—Horse Railroad—Kerosene Oil in Use 1830—Sewing Machines—Agricultural Implements 1831-51—Sanitary Progress—Philanthropic and Christian Progress—Higher Education—Medical Progress—Humane Care of the Insane—Sailors' and Seamen's Home—World's Fairs—Religious Reciprocity—Arbitration—Numerous Inventions and Discoveries—Concluding Remarks.

ENGINEERING skill has greatly improved, and by its daring achievements has added much to the progress of the world during the last forty years. This is seen in the construction of railroads of vast dimensions, four of which span our own continent, and stretch over vast prairies, deep chasms, and great rivers, penetrating through the Rocky Mountains, seemingly impassable as they rear their snow-capped peaks to the clouds. The Mont Cenis Tunnel connecting the railways of France and Italy, on the direct railway route from Paris to Turin, is a marvel of engineering skill. It is seven miles, four and three fourths furlongs in length. Fourteen years passed during its construction, and it cost about six millions and a half of dollars. It was begun in 1857 and completed in 1871. The Saint Gothard Tunnel which runs through a section of the Alps to Italy, six thousand feet below the top of these mountains, is another great achievement of engineering daring. The work consumed ten years' time, the labor of over three thousand men daily, and cost over eleven millions of dollars. The Sutro tunnel, in our own Rocky Mountains, was another grand feat of mechanical progress during the last half of the century.

In 1830, the first steel pen was made and the first iron steamship was built. One year before this, the first lucifer match was made; and nine years afterwards, envelopes were first used. In 1826, the first horse-railroad was built, and kerosene oil was first used for lighting purposes. In 1846, Howe's sewing-machine was given to the public, but it took eight years' hard work to convince the public that the new invention was of any great value. Many other sewing-machines have since come into use, but all are modifications of Howe's. They have revolutionized the whole "make up" of men's and women's wearing apparel, not to mention horse harness, upholstering, and all departments of life where fine stitching is called for. The delicate services of this wonderful machine have increased certain industries a thousand-fold, though at first, like all other improved methods of work, it was supposed to be the destroyer of these industries, and to bring untold miseries upon all who lived by the needle. The manufacture of these machines, sales, and repairs have employed tens of thousands of people, and added millions to the wealth of a nation; to say nothing of the comfort and betterment of the life of the people.

Agriculture has made great strides during the last half century by reason of the increasing use of scientific methods. Rotation of crops and artificial manures have preserved the land from exhaustion and maintained it at a high power of production. Machinery also has added largely to the facilities for its cultivation. Ploughing, sowing, reaping, threshing, and other machines have made it possible for the farmer of comparatively limited means to produce immense quantities of food for man and beast, so that starvation in almost any part of the globe can be averted by the over-production in other parts. In 1855, at a great trial of threshing-, reaping-, and mowing-machines in France, the American machines gained a complete victory. In 1862, the United States Government established the Agricultural Department at Washington. Agricultural societies and colleges, in many of the States, have greatly advanced this most important department of the nation's strength. It is as true now as when the wise Solomon spoke it, "The profit of the earth is for all: the king himself is served by the field." A better knowledge of agricultural chemistry has contributed much to the more profitable uses of the soil. The sanitary conditions of living have greatly improved, especially among the poor, during the last half-century. Underground sewerage in cities, drainage of swampy grounds, removal of the cesspool which often poisoned the well which supplied the family for cooking and drinking, and the introduction of pure water in abundance, cleaner streets, and better homes for the working-classes, have lessened the death rate about one half. From McKenzie we learn that "In 1842, the average length of life among the gentry and professional men of London, was forty-four years: in the laboring-class it was twenty-two years. Filth and bad ventilation cost England more lives annually than she had lost by death in battle or by wounds during the bloodiest year of her history. The annual waste of adult life from causes which ought to be removed was estimated at from thirty to forty thousand." Food is abundant and of great variety in our favored land, and the canning industry supplies the luscious fruits of summer at low prices throughout the entire year.

One noteworthy feature of the progress of the last fifty years is that it touches all classes; the workingman especially shares largely its advantages. The general and rapid diffusion of knowledge, by means of the greatly improved press, is one of the marvels of this most wonderful age. The "Hoe" octuple press can print 96,000 copies of a newspaper

per hour, or 1600 every minute; the paper travels through the press at the rate of 32½ miles an hour; is printed, pasted, cut, folded, counted, and delivered in bundles of twenty-five, automatically. Three of these presses would be able to print 748,000 eight-page sheets, equal to forty-two tons per hour of printed matter.

Mr. Plant might stand on the roof of his office at Twenty-third Street in New York City, and say, "How changed is this city since I first saw it when a boy." It had no horse-cars, no trolley-cars, no cable-cars, no elevated roads, no large hotels, no buildings of more than three stories in height, few stores more than twenty-five feet wide. It had no telegraph, telephone, phonograph, or electric lights, —only oil lamps,—no asphalt pavements. No steam-cars, no photograph galleries, no sewing-machines or type-writers, or bicycles, or horseless carriages, or public baths. No time-lock safes, stem-winding watches. No submarine cables, or Bessemer steel, or great suspension bridges. In 1820, the population of New York City was only 123,706; now it is over a million and a half. In the same time he has seen the population of the country grow from 9,628,131, (of whom 1,528,064 were slaves) to upwards of 70,000,000, and he has seen the inauguration of nineteen of the twenty-five Presidents of the United States. The territory of the United States has nearly doubled during his lifetime, and its accumulated wealth can hardly be measured during the same period. The development of our coal mines, iron mines, gold and silver mines, oil wells, natural gas stored up in the bowels of the earth— these, too, have made giant strides. The great railroad industries of the country, furnishing work for hundreds of thousands; the increase and enlargement of our manufactories, the great cities that have been built, some of them burned and rebuilt, as was the case with Boston, Portland, and Chicago; all these have added to the enormous wealth of the nation. In 1831, a dozen families around Fort Dearborn formed the nucleus of the present city of Chicago. Minneapolis this summer removed its first house, built in 1849, to a more convenient place, to be kept as an heirloom of that city of phenomenal growth. With the increase of wealth, large fortunes have been accumulated and have enabled their earners and owners to build the large railroads which have done so much for the development and progress of the country; to lay ocean cables, and work large mines, providing work and wages for millions of men.

The humane and philanthropic progress of this period is seen in the reforms instituted in prisons. Up to the present century punishment for crime seems to have been the leading idea of prison management. Instruction in the common-school elementary branches of education was introduced with encouraging results. Then libraries were established, and moral and religious instruction tended greatly to the reformation of the criminal. Wholesome rules and regulations were adopted. Various kinds of work, adapted to the prisoners' intelligence and strength, were given. Rewards were apportioned for good behavior, which shortened the period of confinement. Better classification was made of the inmates, and generally just and kind treatment was instituted. All this had an uplifting influence on the crushed and degraded men, and turned many from being the enemies of society to be its friends, and to appreciate the efforts made for their recovery from lives of vice. Reformatories for youthful offenders caused their separation from old and hardened criminals, and caused many of them to become useful members of society. The first of these was "The House of Refuge" on Randal's Island, in New York City.

The "Society for the Prevention of Cruelty to Animals," established by Henry Bergh in New York, proved to be the seed from which germinated hundreds of other similar societies throughout our country. Later, the "Society for the Prevention of Cruelty to Children" has saved many an unprotected child from inhuman treatment, often received from its own parents. It is by far the best age of the world for children. Many millions of dollars are invested in the manufacture of toys and in preparation of books, papers, and magazines especially devoted to the interests of children. Life-saving stations along the coast of dangerous seas have rescued thousands of lives from a watery grave, and saved many millions worth of property. Travel by sea and land has become one of the greatest luxuries and means of education in this most enlightened century. The circumnavigation of the globe is no longer the daring feat of the skilled mariner. The human race is coming closer together, and is massing into cities. Clubs are being formed for the discussion of literary, scientific, æsthetic, historic, political, dramatic, musical, and social topics, and admit to their membership young and old of both sexes.

It is also an age of conventions,—scientific, political, and religious. Christianity is exerting a mighty influence in various forms. Throughout the world this is shown by the multitudes it has lifted out of barbarism in India, China, Japan, Australia, Africa, and made them law-abiding, peace-loving, and self-governing Christian peoples. Cannibalism and human sacrifice have now disappeared from the earth, with many other practices too horrible to name. For the care of the poor and unfortunate, New York City alone spends annually more than $6,000,000. It has homes for the aged, for orphans and for half-orphaned children, also for crippled, and the deformed. Poor women about to become mothers may go to a suitable institute where medical attendance and trained nursing are furnished free, or they may have both free in their own homes. The advance in the higher education, as well as great improvement in our common-school system, is a marked feature of our times. Most of our colleges have greatly raised the course of study, and several have become fully equipped universities, while other new universities have been added to the number; one in Chicago, two in Washington City, one in California, and one in Baltimore. Probably the most marked feature in the education of our time is the throwing open the doors of so many colleges and universities to women. These have flocked thither to take equal stand with the men, who have had a monopoly of these privileges since colleges and universities were founded: and they have entered the learned professions of medicine, law, and divinity, professions once thought to be forever barred against their sex. Co-education, the higher education of women, and their aspiration to lead a professional life, fifty years ago would have been considered the dream of fanatics only. Some even now doubt the wisdom of the movement, but, good or bad, it is here to stay, and will advance with ever increasing velocity.

There are homes for incurables where their hopeless condition receives such treatment as not unfrequently returns them to their homes restored to a measure of health. The blind, deaf, and dumb are kindly cared for, educated, and made useful members of society. That class once considered hopeless, women fallen from virtue, are sought out, cared for, and restored frequently to society, and often become rescuers of their own sex from like degredation. Discharged criminals are looked after and provided with temporary homes, and work is sought out for them. The children of the street are taken up, taught, and placed in homes in the West, away from the city temptations that were destroying them. For young men, and now for young women, coming from the country to our large cities, the Christian Associations find safe lodgings, work, schools, and churches, and throw around them every safeguard. The reading-room, gymnasium, lecture course, evening classes, and devotional meetings are all intellectual and moral forces in character building, and in preparation for the great work of life.

The higher education of medical science has made rapid progress during the last century, and especially during the last half of it. Health boards have done much in the way of sanitation to prevent disease and protect communities against epidemics and virulent plagues that have scourged the world for centuries. The use of anæsthetics has saved an incalculable amount of agony, and has greatly aided physicians in improved methods of surgery. Operations are now performed, with almost universal success, which would not have been thought of fifty years ago. Improved medical apparatus and instruments for examining the body have proved of great value in the treatment of bronchial and internal affections. The Roentgen Ray, which can bring to light the whole inside of a man, is the latest and greatest discovery of the period under consideration. The discovery of disease-producing germs or microbes is worthy of mention in this connection. Pasteur's cure for hydrophobia has lessened the dread of one of the most terrible maladies that has afflicted the human family.

It might be supposed that humane treatment of those most unfortunate beings who have been deprived of their reason would be found even in the least civilized period of the world's history, but alas! the opposite has been true. Until within a comparatively recent date it was customary to confine these poor creatures in jail, along with the vilest criminals, a custom still prevailing in some places. "In 1826, a young clergyman, rendered insane by overwork, was found in the Bridewell Prison of New York, herded with ruffians and murderers. At that time there was in the prisons of

Massachusetts thirty lunatics. One had been in his cell nine years, had a wreath of rags around his body, and another around his neck. This was all his clothing. He had no bed, chair, or bench; a heap of filthy straw like the nest of a swine was in the corner. He had built a bird's-nest of mud in the iron grate of his den." Many were chained, kept in cages, "whipped, scourged, ironed, shut in close cells, and left for years in filth, naked, hungry, exposed to bitter cold, frozen," had lost toes or feet, and suffered torture until death ended their misery. All this is happily changed, and medical skill and intelligent, humane care, have taken its place, with some exceptions perhaps. Sailors were once the legitimate prey of the worst class of men and women the world ever produced, when they landed in large cities, often after most tempestuous voyages, and dangers most terrible to contemplate. In so-called sailor's boarding houses they were drugged, robbed, stripped naked, and thrown out on the street at midnight to groan and suffer and die.

Seamen's Friends Societies and Sailors' Homes, with hospitals, libraries, Christian ministry of godly men, and kindly care for the sick, disabled, or aged sailor until he enters the haven of eternal rest, is now in all Christian countries the provision made for this brave man to whom the world owes so much. Similar provision is made for the old or disabled soldier who has fought his country's battles. The "Soldier's Home" is one of the institutions for which America has reason to be proud.

The World's Fairs, first organized by Prince Albert in London in the year 1851 and continued in different countries until the present time, the last and greatest of them all held at Chicago in the United States in 1893, have done much to stimulate progress in every department of life, and to strengthen the spirit of friendly reciprocity that should bind the human family closer together in mutual helpfulness and good-will. The international congress of all religions held at the Chicago Fair, the first and only congress of the kind ever held, was in the line of the Fatherhood of God and the Brotherhood of Man.

The bitterness of the sectarian spirit among all Christian denominations is happily passing away, and a desire for closer relations, even for a union of all peoples of the Christian faiths, is fast taking its place. The Roman Catholic Church through its head, Leo XIII., and the Episcopal Church through its Bishops have both expressed their desire for the union of all Christian peoples. Arbitration for the settlement of disputes between labor and capital, and even between nations, is advancing towards a blessed consummation, and the day cannot be far distant when peace and good-will among men shall become universal, and Jesus of Nazareth shall reign, Prince of Peace and King of Nations through the whole world. Who knows but that the six hundred and one thousand miles of telegraph in the United States and the one hundred and sixty thousand miles of submarine telegraph in the world, shall soon flash the news round the globe, "The Lord is come."

The following item taken by permission of Charles Scribner's Sons from *The Last Quarter of the Century*, by Andrews, is significant in this connection:

"During the great Electrical Exposition in New York City, May, 1896, a message was transmitted round the world and back in fifty-five minutes. It was dictated by Hon. Chauncey Depew, and read— 'God creates, Nature treasures, Science utilizes electrical power for the grandeur of nations and the peace of the world.' Starting at eight thirty-five these words sped over the land lines to San Francisco, thence back to Canso, Nova Scotia, where they plunged under the sea to London. A click of the key four minutes later announced the completion of this part of the journey.

"Cannon were fired in honor of the achievement, while the throng on the floor of the Exhibition Building cheered.

"Meantime, the general manager of the Western Union Company had despatched the same message over his lines to Los Angeles, Galveston, City of Mexico, Valparaiso, Buenos Ayres, Pernambuco, across the Atlantic to Lisbon, and back to New York by way of London, a journey of ten thousand miles, in eleven and one half minutes.

"At nine twenty-five, just fifty minutes from the start, the receiving instrument clicked and Mr. Edison, for the nonce again a simple telegraph operator as of yore, copied from it the Depew message.

"It had travelled from London to Lisbon, thence to Suez, Aden, Bombay, Madras, Singapore, Hong Kong, Shanghai, Nagasaki, and Tokio, returning by the same route to New York, having traversed a distance of 27,500 miles."

We have thus tabulated, in the briefest manner, a few of the advances made in various departments of life during the period covered by this biography: and we have done so because Mr. Plant loves to recount the progress of the human family. He has kept in touch with it all, enjoyed it all, and has himself contributed no small share to its furtherance. It enhances one's estimate of the marvellous progress of the age in which we are living when we think how much has been accomplished in the comparatively brief period of one life. It gives ground for believing, too, that the next decade will surpass any that has preceded it, and that the twentieth century will outstrip the nineteenth as far as the nineteenth has outstripped any of its predecessors. It inspires the wish, also, that the subject of this biography may live to enjoy much of the world's era of peace and progress in science, art, industry, philanthropy, and Christian alleviation and uplifting power. May this very imperfect history of a very instructive life prove helpful to those taking their place in the onward march of the race towards its great and final destiny.

The wish expressed above for the continued health and life of the subject of this biography was written one year ago, and what follows affords strong hope of its realization.

The winter after the Atlanta Exposition found Mr. Plant with signs of failing health, somewhat alleviated by his sojourn in the South; but on his arrival in New York in the spring of 1896, he was taken violently ill and was constantly under the doctor's care for four or five months. The next winter he passed in the South, resulting in marked evidences of improved health. The next spring, however, another malady developed, greatly impairing health and threatening life for several weeks. Early in the spring he had so far recovered that he went by rail to San Francisco, in his own private car, thence by ocean to Japan and China, and, returning to Japan, spent a large part of the summer there, from whence he sailed for San Francisco and returned to New York early in November, nearly all evidences of past diseases having disappeared, and he has passed his seventy-eight birthday in apparently good health.

It is needless to say that honors, courtesies, and kindnesses were liberally tendered him throughout his whole trip in the East, which he enjoyed to the full.

The following incident is one among many that occurred to Mr. Plant during his very interesting tour in the land of the Rising Sun, and shows how promptly he improved every opportunity that came in his way, not only for learning all about the customs, manners, and ways of the Japanese, but of recalling old acquaintances, and renewing old friendships of his early boyhood in his native State, and town of Branford. On his return voyage via the Hawaiian Islands, the steamer stopped for a few hours at Honolulu. Mr. Plant at once set out to find a Branford lady who had long been a resident in these islands. Soon his search was rewarded by finding Mrs. Mary Parker, widow of a missionary of that name, and now in the ninety-fourth year of her age. Mr. Plant was present at the marriage of this good lady in Branford, Connecticut, when only a boy of seven, and doubtless some of the happy boyhood emotions of that occasion came back to him when he clasped the hand of this aged woman so far away from their native Branford.

HENRY B. PLANT IN WAR AND IN PEACE.

Few men are more blessed with a peaceful disposition and an inborn dislike of the antagonisms that arise so frequently between men and nations than is the subject of this sketch. Nor has it fallen to the lot of many to take such an important part in the two greatest wars of our country. In the former chapters of this biography we have spoken of the valuable services rendered to both sides of the contestants in our Civil War by the Plant System, then only in its embryo state of development. At the banquet given to Mr. Plant at the Atlanta Exposition we heard, from some of the representative men of the South, patriotic speeches full of native eloquence, that thrilled us in every fibre of our being. "Mr. Plant," said one of the distinguished speakers, "you have done more to bring the North and South together than any other man living." Mr. Plant has been privileged to have a large part in the present conflict that has completely cemented the whole nation as never before. This is by no means the smallest benefit that has come to our country out of this great conflict, for it is as true now as when it was uttered by one of the greatest American statesmen, "United we stand, divided we fall." The following description of the facilities afforded for shipment at Port Tampa is from the pen of one who is well acquainted with every foot of land and water about which he writes.

"The war with Spain directed attention more to Port Tampa than any one place in the United States. This was for the reason that the largest military expedition that ever left the shores of the United States was loaded and sailed from the docks there. The work was done in a very short time, considering the lack of experience of the government officials in charge.

"So much has been said and written about the loading of General Shafter's expedition, with its fleet of thirty-six steamships, that the public will appreciate some detailed information about the immense facilities which are found ready for use at Port Tampa. This was through the foresight and business sagacity of the head of the Plant System, for he built largely for the great business that must pass through that port at no distant day.

"The railroad yards of over thirty-six miles of track, at Port Tampa, Port Tampa City, and Tampa, belong to the Plant System, and have a capacity of over two thousand cars, leaving working room for all the business that this number of cars would bring to the place. The tracks are perfectly arranged, and experienced railroad men say that no railroad yard in the South will compare with this for conveniences in handling a big business. The business is in the hands of railroad men of experience, and no delays were traceable to them. Between Tampa and Port Tampa is a stretch of nine miles. To illustrate the perfect system employed in handling the business, it is only necessary to say that from six o'clock in the morning until 11:40 at night, twenty-six passenger trains passed over this nine miles every day. Besides this, the freight trains numbered more than this, comprising the various sections of regular trains and the large number of troop and supply-trains for the movement. There was no delay and not an accident.

"Of the facilities at the docks, as much can be said. It is the only port in the country where vessels drawing twenty-four feet of water can come alongside and load in such numbers. There is room for twenty-four vessels of that draught, three hundred and twenty feet long, to lie end for end, and receive cargoes at the same time. These steamers are all loaded from the railroad tracks, just twenty feet removed from the edge of the pier, and nothing stands in the way of the quick work. Vessels of less length make it possible to increase the number, and at one time there were thirteen vessels loading end to end at one side of the pier. According to this calculation, thirty-two vessels could be accommodated. At these docks are to be found berths for phosphate vessels where their cargoes are loaded from electric elevators, which are the latest improved. Just across the slip is the government coal dock, and here are electric elevators for handling this business. A large amount of coal is now stored in these docks for the government.

"It was not necessary to provide any of these facilities for the especial purpose of handling the government war business. They were all there and in use before the war, and the government used them in sending off this fleet of thirty-six vessels, under convoy of a large number of war vessels. It was one of the most imposing sights of the age to see this great fleet steaming down the bay; flags flying and bands playing, and sixteen thousand American soldiers cheering as they felt the vessels move over the waters of Tampa Bay, all bound for a victorious campaign against the enemy.

"The Plant System has done well its part in the great modern war, and is equally well prepared to do its part in carrying on the great commerce between the United States, Cuba, the West India Islands, and all of the South American countries."

The *Marine Journal* of New York of July 9, 1898, has the following editorial:

"PORT TAMPA—Phœnix-like Rose and Met the Occasion—Over Thirty Troop Ships Loaded and Departed from its Piers—The Largest War Fleet ever Sent from One Port at One Time in the Nation's History—The Port's Immense Facilities.

"It would take the entire reading space of the *Marine Journal* to describe the great amount of work done at Port Tampa, Fla., in getting Gen. Shafter's army afloat, and the exhaustive facilities that were found by the government to exist there available for this purpose; in fact, only those who have visited the West coast of Florida within ten years past have any idea of the extensive improvements that have been made at Port Tampa by the Plant System with a view to bringing the commerce of the United States within close communication with the Island of Cuba, Jamaica, and other nearby Gulf ports. Millions of dollars have been expended by Henry B. Plant and associates under the supervision of the best known experts in railroad and harbor improvements that could be obtained for this object, and the work was near completion when war was declared with Spain, and the Island of Cuba became the base of hostilities.

"Fortunately the government was well informed as to the superior facilities already in operation at Port Tampa, and the Quartermaster's Department of the Army was not slow in recommending this place for the mobilization of troops and their preparation and embarkation to Cuba therefrom. The vexatious delays caused by inexperience in handling such a large body of men and munitions of war, reports of spook Spanish fleets, etc., are more or less familiar to our readers, as well as the detail of the fitting out and embarking of over 12,000 troops and their supplies which were loaded on board over thirty transports at Port Tampa in a very short space of time. The wharf facilities at some times accommodated as many as thirteen of these troop ships strung along end on.

"Let the *Marine Journal* readers imagine for a moment that the Florida terminus of the Plant System of railroads at Port Tampa extends out into the harbor nearly a mile on two solidly built piers of sheet piling, earth, and rocks between which is a canal or basin with twenty-five feet depth of water its entire length, where a fleet of ships can lie and load or unload from or into cars night and day. The south pier is seventy feet wide, and has three tracks laid upon it, twenty feet of this width is set apart for working cargo from car to ship, and vice versa, also a promenade its entire length, midway of which is the famous "Inn," built out over the water, where passengers in transit to Cuba and Key West, as well as tourists, can enjoy a cool, delightful rest after a trip by sea or land. One can hardly imagine the amount of transportation facilities afforded at this immense terminus, with its mile in length railroad-yard, and Port Tampa is but twenty-four hours sail from Havana by steamers of fair average speed. The *Olivette*, of the Plant Line, has frequently made the trip in nineteen and a half hours.

"There is twenty feet of water on the shoalest part of the bar at the entrance of the (thirty feet) harbor of Port Tampa, and a very small expense in dredging, which is now being arranged for, will enable vessels to enter drawing twenty-five feet. Outside of the harbor, in Tampa Bay, is a roadstead where the entire naval and transport fleet of the United States could ride safely at anchor in the fiercest hurricane, thereby adding another valuable argument for Port Tampa as a naval as well as an army base.

"It is a well-known fact to mariners who are familiar with West Indian and Gulf navigation, that after July 15th, it is necessary to keep an eye to windward for hurricanes up to the middle of September; then more or less heavy weather occurs until the middle of March. And here comes in another great advantage in favor of Port Tampa as against all other ports in the United States as regards safety from the elements. With the present able weather bureau, and its complete arrangements for signaling the conditions of the weather from all important points, there is not the slightest danger of encountering a hurricane between Port Tampa and Cuba. The weather reports available make it not only easy to avoid them through reliable information of their coming, but enables the mariner to prepare for them in the harbor of Port Tampa or Key West if there is n't time to reach Cuba. If the government is wise it will ship no more troops to Cuba or Porto Rico this season from north or south of Hatteras, as there is no need of subjecting them to the risk of hurricanes. Our soldier boys should have as short and comfortable a sea voyage as possible, and that is only obtainable in first-class shape from Port Tampa, following down the west coast of Florida, always under the lee of the land in case of an eastern gale or hurricane."

The caution contained in the above against storms, and the desire for a safe and comfortable passage for our soldier boys, will find a tender response in many hearts for him who facilitated the embarkation of the brave men going from their native land to fight a foreign foe.

TESTIMONIAL ACCOMPANYING A SILVER SERVICE PRESENTED BY THE OFFICERS AND EMPLOYEES OF THE SOUTHERN EXPRESS COMPANY TO MR. AND MRS. H. B. PLANT ON THE CELEBRATION OF THEIR TWENTY-FIFTH WEDDING ANNIVERSARY.

"NEW YORK, July 2d, 1898.

"TO MR. AND MRS. H. B. PLANT.

"*The following officers and employees of the Southern Express Company ask that you accept this*

'SERVICE' *as an evidence of the affectionate regard in which they hold their honored President and his Wife.*

"*It has appeared to them that upon a day commemorative of the ceremony which twenty-five years ago united in affection your lives, they should give some enduring expression of the esteem in which they hold you both.*

"*They gratefully recognize the wise direction, the patient forbearance and the friendly counsel of their President, which has done so much to guide and aid them in their respective spheres of duty, and they are equally sensible of the fact that under advancing years, and multiplicity of duties, only the ceaseless care and affectionate heed of a devoted Wife has made this possible.*

"*They beg that you accept the testimonial in the spirit which has prompted it, and with the assurance that to your 'wedded love' is indissolubly linked their respect, admiration and affection.*

"H. Dempsey, J. Cronin, N. S. Woodward, W. J. Crosswell, C. A. Pardue, Mark J. O'Brien, W. A. Dewees, W. W. Allen, F. G. du Bignon, W. A. Blankenship, A. M. Richardson, H. E. Williamson, L. H. Black, J. L. S. Albright, L. Spaulding, A. Montgomery, J. B. Hockaday, G. C. Crom, F. de C. Sullivan, W. Buckner, W. E. McGill, G. A. Wilkinson, S. C. Hargis, G. W. Bacot, G. Sadler, C. C.

Wolfe, P. B. Wilkes, W. J. Brown, F. R. Osborne, O. M. Sadler, C. T. Campbell, V. Spalding, H. C. Fisher, M. F. Plant, F. J. Virgin, C. Pink, C. L. Loop, W. C. Agee, F. Q. Brown, J. C. Stuart, L. Minor, R. B. Smith, W. B. Menzies, John Lovette, E. J. Loughman, J. T. James, W. H. Hendee, S. R. Golibart, E. M. Williams, J. C. Barry, W. R. Twyman, E. C. Spence, L. Kuder, C. R. Smith, J. B. Gartrell, M. Culliny, A. Welsh, G. W. Agee, C. L. Myers, W. K. Haile, W. A. Mehegan, R. G. Erwin, C. H. Albright, W. M. Shoemaker, H. C. Mendenhall, G. H. Tilley, A. McD. Mullings, J. W. Gaines, T. W. Leary, C. G. McCormick, W. W. Hulbert, K. C. Barrett, M. F. Loughman, E. F. Cary, J. J. Crosswell, E. J. Michelin, T. T. Weltch, Thomas Grier, R. A. Buckner, H. M. Smith, M. J. O'Brien, W. S. McFarland, E. G. Williams."

MR. AND MRS. PLANT'S ACKNOWLEDGMENT OF TESTIMONIAL AND SERVICE.

"NEW YORK, July 2nd, 1898.

"ESTEEMED FRIENDS AND ASSOCIATES:

"*Twenty-five years ago, this second day of July, was a very happy one for us, and, to-day, on our Silver Anniversary, we are most pleasantly reminded of the occasion by the unexpected receipt of a handsome token indicative of the affection in which we are held by those who, during the last quarter of a century, have surrounded us as friends as well as business associates.*

"*The sentiments embodied in the testimonial accompanying the very beautiful 'Service' are highly appreciated and accepted by us as an evidence of the sincere feelings prompting your thoughtful recollection of this memorable mile-stone in our lives.*

"*In returning our deep gratitude for your remembrance and kind expressions, we indulge the hope that we will have many years together to enjoy the gift which your generosity has provided, and that while life lasts we may have the friendship of those whose acts in the past and present have brought them so near to us.*

"*Very sincerely,*
"HENRY B. PLANT,
"MARGARET J. PLANT."

PLANT GENEALOGY

PREPARED BY

G. S. DICKERMAN

THE PLANTS IN GENERAL

THERE are many families of the Plant name. This will be seen on looking into city directories and running the eye over lists there given. Accounts show that these families have come from several progenitors who arrived in this country at different times.

Attention is paid here more particularly to the descendants of John Plant, of Branford, Connecticut. But it may be of interest to glance at certain other families.

The Plants of St. Louis, Missouri, have occupied an honorable place in the history of that city during the last fifty years. One of their number * tells of having traced their ancestry back some three hundred years to the County Palatine, of Chester, in England, where, about 1600, were two brothers, Samuel Plant and John Plant. From the latter of these they are descended in the following line: John,[1] Thomas,[2] George,[3] Samuel,[4] who married Ann Haigh and lived in Macclesfield,

* Mr. Alfred Plant, of Webster Grove, Missouri, in a letter of December 11, 1897.

England, Samuel,[1] who came to Boston, Massachusetts, between 1790 and 1800, and married there Mary D. Poignaud, a Boston lady of Huguenot ancestry.

This Samuel[1] Plant was sent out by his uncle, Mr. Haigh, a manufacturer of woollen cloths at Leeds, to sell his goods, which he did, with his headquarters at Boston, though he travelled extensively, going once as far as Charleston, South Carolina. Some years later he brought over from England plans for cotton machinery and built, in 1808–9, the first cotton factory in Worcester County, Massachusetts, at Clinton.

He was the father of six sons and six daughters. The sons were George P.,[2] Frederick William,[2] Samuel,[2] Alfred,[2] William M.,[2] and Henry,[2] who all removed to St. Louis, and have been identified with the enterprise and development of that city since 1840. Of these sons Mr. Alfred[2] Plant is the only survivor.

Another family has a representative * in Chicago, who writes that his branch came from Ireland to Massachusetts early in this century. His father's name was Thomas Plant and he had an uncle Robert, who also settled in Massachusetts.

Again the name appears in the annals of Newbury, New Hampshire, where the Rev. Matthias Plant was rector of Queen Anne's Chapel from April, 1722, till his death on December 23, 1751, a period of twenty-nine years.† Previous to his time the church had been weak, but under his ministry its position became secure. St. Paul's Church was built in another part of the town from Queen Anne's, and he officiated there also. His wife was the youngest daughter of Samuel Bartlett, of Newbury. No further knowledge of this family has been obtained.

The name occurs twice in lists of persons embarking from

---

* Mr. George D. Plant, Principal of the Seward School in Chicago.
† *New Eng. Hist. and Gen. Reg.*, April 1886.

England in early times to settle in the colonies.* In one list William Plant is reported to have died on a plantation in Virginia in 1624. In another Matthew Plant, who was then twenty-three years old, was enrolled to sail on the *Assurance* from Gravesend for Virginia, July 24, 1635. Under the term "Virginia," in those times, were included the New England colonies as well as those in the South, so that it is quite supposable that Matthew Plant may have settled in New England.

THE PLANT FAMILY

OF BRANFORD, CONNECTICUT.

John¹ Plant, the progenitor of this family, was a soldier in the Narragansett war. The Connecticut General Assembly, in October, 1696, bestowed on the "English Volunteers" in this struggle a tract of territory six miles square, to be divided among them, which was located in New London County, and has since borne the name of Voluntown. In the list of those receiving these grants John¹ Plant was numbered 59 in the drawing of "Cedar Swamp Lots." †

The Narragansett war ended in 1676. Soon after this the name of John¹ Plant appears on the records of the town of Branford, January 21, 1677, when a lot of two acres was granted to him on condition that he should build upon it within three years. It seems unlikely that he was at Branford much before this date, for the reason that his name is not in the lists of residents enrolled in January, 1676. Nor do we find any others of the Plant name previous to this date. Subsequently his name occurs a number of times in connection with grants of land.‡

* *Lists of Emigrants*, by J. C. Hotten.
† *Soldiers in King Philip's War*, by George M. Bodge, page 442.
‡ His name appears, November 6, 1677, as a witness on the record of a

He died about 1691, as evidenced by the inventory of his estate taken June 4, 1691. The valuation of his property was £130 8s. 9d.

The indications concerning his family are not altogether clear.* He had a son John,² concerning whom accounts are somewhat full. There was a Martha Plant enrolled among the members of the church in 1704. She may have been his daughter. There was also an Elizabeth Plant,† who may have been another daughter.

payment. On February 20, 1683, he was given six acres on Mulliner's Hill, below the road, on condition of his improving it within two years. On February 4, 1688, he was given six acres more "on the way hill," that is, half way to the iron works at the outlet of the lake. He was sworn in as a freeman at Branford, April 8, 1690. His lot was laid out below the path, bounded on the west corner by a great white-oak-tree, on the north corner by a small walnut-, on the east by a black-oak-, and by a walnut-tree at the south.

The original home of the Plants seems to have been near George Plant's present residence. The old Plant house was once used as a hotel and again as a store. A tornado once tore down a fine orchard behind the house, and overthrew a cider mill near it. John ² Plant, Jr., sold the part of Mulliner's Hill, which had formerly belonged to Thomas Goodsell, to Deacon John Rose, July 13, 1713, and bought of John Goodsell, in 1727, three acres at Mulliner's Neck.

* Orcutt's *History of Stratford* says that John Plant's wife was Betty Roundkettle, and that he was probably of the Saltonstall company, but the authority is not stated.

† Elizabeth Plant married, July 23, 1712, John Coach, also of Branford, who died about 1728, as evidenced by the Probate Records. She was appointed administrator, June 14, 1728. The inventory exhibited June 26th following gives the valuation of his property at £118 14s. 4d. The children are named, Sarah, about twelve years of age, James, ten, Elizabeth, eight, Mary, five, John, three.

Sarah Coach married, September 20, 1738, Eleazer Stent.

Elizabeth Coach married, March 9, 1736, Jacob Carter.

Plant Genealogy

CHILDREN AND GRANDCHILDREN OF JOHN[2] AND HANNAH (WHEDON) PLANT.

JOHN PLANT, JR.
baptized March 3, 1678
died February 10, 1752
married
HANNAH WHEDON
died Nov. 5, 1754, aged 69

- HANNAH PLANT
  born July 16, 1708
  married
  ABRAHAM WHEDON
  - Reuben Whedon
  - William Whedon
  - Noah Whedon
  - Hannah Whedon
  - Martha Whedon
  - Submit Whedon
  - Sarah Whedon
  - Deborah Whedon

- JOHN PLANT
  born September 19, 1711

- JONATHAN PLANT
  born July 29, 1714

- JAMES PLANT
  born November 4, 1716
  died February 7, 1795
  married September 22, 1740
  BATHSHEBA PAGE
  - Solomon Plant
  - James Plant
  - Samuel Plant
  - Stephen Plant
  - Lois Plant
  - Ebenezer Plant
  - Sarah Plant
  - Moses Plant

- ELIZABETH PLANT
  born August 1, 1720
  married September 21, 1748
  JOSIAH PARRISH
  - Josiah Parrish
  - Elizabeth Parrish
  - Sibil Parrish
  - Hannah Parrish
  - Mary Parrish
  - John Parrish

- TIMOTHY PLANT
  born April 6, 1724
  married February 12, 1745
  LUCY PARRISH
  - Lucy Plant
  - Hannah Plant
  - Timothy Plant
  - Joel Plant
  - Ithiel Plant

- ABRAHAM PLANT
  baptized September 23, 1727
  married (1)
  HANNAH HOADLEY
  married (2)
  TAMAR FRISBIE
  - Eli Plant
  - Electa Plant
  - Lydia Plant
  - Abraham Plant
  - Anne Plant
  - Hannah Plant
  - Elizabeth Plant
  - Rebecca Plant
  - Jason Plant

- BENJAMIN PLANT
  born 1732
  died August 11, 1808
  married (1)
  LORANA BECKWITH
  married (2)
  ABIGAIL PALMER
  married (3)
  LOIS FRISBIE
  - Hannah Plant
  - John Plant
  - Benjamim Plant
  - Anderson Plant
  - Lorana Plant
  - Peggy Plant
  - Samuel Plant
  - Elias Plant

JOHN² PLANT, JR.—HANNAH WHEDON.

John² Plant, Jr., son of John¹ Plant, was baptized at Branford, March 3, 1678; died February 10, 1752, aged seventy-four; married Hannah Whedon, a daughter of Thomas and Hannah (Barnes) Whedon, who was born in 1686; died November 5, 1754, aged sixty-nine.*

Their children were born in Branford, and were as follows:

*Thomas Whedon, the grandfather of Hannah Whedon, came to New Haven with John Meigs, who, in 1648, bought the lot on the corner of Chapel and Church Streets, where the Cutler building now stands. Before leaving England Thomas Whedon had been bound to Meigs as an apprentice to learn his art of tanner. He took the oath of fidelity in 1657; married, May 24, 1651, Ann Harvey, at New Haven; moved to Branford, and his name appears on the lists of proprietors, January 17, 1676, as having five children, and an estate valued at £96; he died in 1691, leaving a wife and five children. Their son, Thomas Whedon, Jr., was born May 31, 1663, at New Haven, and died in 1692; his wife, Hannah Barnes, was the eldest daughter of John and Mercy (Betts) Barnes, and was born December 23, 1670.

John² Plant became a member of the church at Branford, September 2, 1716, and Hannah Plant, September 21, 1729. His will is in the Probate Records at Guilford, Connecticut, dated February 29, 1752, proved July 7, 1752. It names his wife, Hannah Plant, who was appointed administratrix, daughters Hannah Whedon and Elizabeth Plant, and sons John, Jonathan, James, Timothy, and Abraham. The inventory of the estate places the valuation at £1007 6s. 1¼d. whereof £891 8s. 11¼d. was real estate, of which one hundred acres of land was in Litchfield. In the distribution, which was made December 19, 1752, Elizabeth is called the wife of Josiah Parrish.

The will of Hannah Plant is also to be seen at Guilford, dated November 31, 1752, proved December 18, 1753, presented by John Plant, executor. It names sons John, Jonathan, James, Timothy, Abraham, and Benjamin, and daughters Hannah Whedon and Elizabeth Parrish. The distribution occurred February 18, 1754, when Hannah was called the wife of Abraham Whedon, and Elizabeth the wife of Josiah Parrish.

Benjamin's name occurs in his mother's will, but is omitted in his father's.

Plant Genealogy

I. Hannah³ Plant, born July 16, 1708; baptized August 7, 1715; married Abraham Whedon, who died about 1762.*

II. John³ Plant, born September 19, 1711; baptized August 7, 1715; died about 1788.†

III. Jonathan³ Plant, born July 29, 1714; baptized August 7, 1715; living in Branford May 29, 1753, as shown by the "ear mark" for his cattle entered on the records, May 29, 1753; died before October 7, 1772. ‡

IV. James³ Plant, born November 4, 1716; baptized November 18, 1716; died February 7, 1795; married, September 22, 1740, Bathsheba Page, daughter of Samuel and Mindwell Page, of Branford; born January 25, 1715–16; died, at Stratford, January 5, 1803. *Account continued on page 315.*

---

* His will, dated December 22, 1761, proved September 7, 1762, names wife Hannah Whedon, sons Reuben, William, and Noah, daughters Hannah, Martha, Submit, Sarah, and "youngest daughter Deborah, that still lives with me." William and Noah were minors, and chose their mother guardian.

Reuben Whedon's will, signed March 20, 1806, proved September 23, 1806, names wife Rachel, son Abraham, of Bolton, grandson Daniel, son of Abraham. The court appoints Captain William Whedon one of two commissioners to divide the estate.

William Whedon's will, dated February 6, 1821, names daughter Polly Page, son Captain Ozias Whedon, grandsons William N., Charles R., and Amaziah H., also five grandchildren, John, Catharine, Andrew, Noah, and George, children of son Edward Whedon.

Guardian's records of Amos Seward, January 20, 1822, and June 14, 1824, name Charles R. Whedon, minor son of Captain Noah Whedon, of New Haven, and grandson of Captain William Whedon, with his brother William N. Whedon, and Lucretia, the widow of Captain Noah Whedon.

† His will, signed at Branford, March 4, 1755, proved March 25, 1788, names his brother Benjamin executor and sole legatee.

‡ The deed of Timothy³ Plant to his son Timothy⁴ (page 313) names "heirs of Samuel Baker, deceased, assignee of my late brother Jonathan Plant, deceased."

V. Elizabeth³ Plant, born August 1, 1720 ; baptized August, 1720 ; married, September 21, 1748, Josiah Parrish, son of John and Hannah Parrish, of Branford.*

    1. Josiah⁴ Parrish, born April 6, 1749 ; married, December 25, 1770, Thankful Plant, perhaps the widow of Samuel Plant.
    2. Elizabeth⁴ Parrish, born August 3, 1751.
    3. Sibil⁴ Parrish, born March 28, 1753.
    4. Hannah⁴ Parrish, born July 11, 1756.
    5. Mary⁴ Parrish, born June 7, 1759.
    6. John⁴ Parrish, born May 16, 1762.

VI. Timothy³ Plant, born April 6, 1724 ; baptized May 17, 1724 ; married, at Branford, Lucy Parrish. *Account continued on page 317.*

VII. Abraham³ Plant, baptized September 23, 1727 ; married (1), May (or March) 9, 1751, Hannah⁴ Hoadley, daughter of John² and Lydia (Rogers) Hoadley (John², William¹); born May 8, 1733 ; died April 4, 1755 ; married (2), January 12, 1763, Tamar Frisbie ; born about 1740 ; died 1793, aged 53. Children by second marriage, and born at Branford.

    1. Eli⁴ Plant, born August 4, 1763 ; married, July 8, 1787, Sarah Stent.
    2. Electa⁴ Plant, born September 27, 1765.
    3. Lydia⁴ Plant, born December 20, 1767 ; baptized, with the younger children, May 2, 1784.
    4. Abraham⁴ Plant, born August 3 or 4, 1770.
    5. Anne⁴ Plant, born August 3 or 4, 1770, twin with Abraham.
    6. Hannah⁴ Plant, born March 14, 1773.
    7. Elizabeth⁴ Plant, born October 12, 1775.
    8. Rebecca⁴ Plant, born March 7, 1777.
    9. Jason⁴ Plant, born August 11, 1782.

* The will of John Parrish, the father of Josiah and also of Lucy Parrish, the wife of Timothy³ Plant, dated April 5, 1748, proved April 14, 1748, names wife Hannah Parrish, son Josiah, two younger sons, Gideon and Joel, and three daughters, Hannah, Lucia, and Abigail. In the inventory his estate was valued at £471 10s. 8d.

VIII. Benjamin⁸ Plant, born about 1732; died August 11, 1808, aged 76; married (1), April 5, 1758, Lorana Beckwith, of Lyme; born about 1736; died March 16, 1789, aged 53; married (2), June 17, 1790, Abigail Palmer; married (3), December 6, 1797, Lois Frisbie. *Account continued on page 318.*

Authorities.—New Haven and Branford Town and Church Records; Probate Records at New Haven, Branford, and Guilford; Atwater's *History of New Haven Colony;* Orcutt's *History of Stratford.*

JAMES⁵ PLANT—BATHSHEBA PAGE.

James⁵ Plant, son of John⁴ and Hannah (Whedon) Plant (John¹); born November 4, 1716; baptized November 18, 1716, at Branford; died there February 7, 1795; married, September 22, 1740, Bathsheba Page, daughter of Samuel and Mindwell Page, of Branford; born January 25, 1715–16; died January 5, 1803, at Stratford, Connecticut. *See page 313.*

He had a farm near the head of Lake Saltonstall and raised a family, most of whom left Branford. He was drowned while crossing the lake on the ice, and his farm was sold by John and Samuel Plant to George Townsend, of East Haven. His widow seems to have passed the closing years of her life with their oldest son in the home he had made at Stratford.

I. Solomon⁶ Plant, born May 1, 1741; died May 20, 1822; married (1), November 16, 1769, Sarah Bennett, of Stratford, who died September 15, 1815; married (2), November 19, 1816, Mrs. Esther (Frost) Botsford. *Account continued on page 320.*

II. James⁶ Plant, born September 10, 1742; living at Southington, Connecticut, as late as June 15, 1813, when he deeded land to his son Ebenezer⁷; married, January 9, 1772, at New Haven, Lucy Judd, daughter of Joseph and

Ruth (Thompson) Judd, of that place. *Account continued on page 321.*

III. Samuel[4] Plant, baptized February 10, 1745; married, July 2, 1769, Thankful Towner, of Branford. He was lost at sea.

IV. Stephen[4] Plant, baptized March 8, 1747; died before February 3, 1808, when his estate was admitted to probate in Litchfield, Connecticut, and his widow was appointed administratrix. *Account continued on page 322.*

V. Lois[4] Plant, baptized April 2, 1749; died April 21, 1833, aged 84, at South Hill, Onondaga County, New York; married Obed Fellows, of Canaan, Connecticut. Their son, Ephraim[5] Fellows, was the father of Lucy[6] Fellows, who became the wife of William Agur[6] Plant. *See page 328.*

VI. Ebenezer[4] Plant, born October 26, 1751; baptized December 15, 1751; died April or May, 1796; married, August 17, 1774, Esther[6] Bassett, daughter of Lieutenant John[5] and Naomi (Wooster) Bassett (Samuel,[4] Robert,[3] Robert,[2] John[1]), residence, Derby, Connecticut.*

Captain Samuel[5] Plant, his son, died at Norfolk, Virginia, in 1815. His wife was Dorothy[6] Gorham, daughter of Isaac[7] and Sarah (Atwater) Gorham (John,[6] Isaac,[5] Jabez,[4] John,[3] Ralph,[2] James[1]), born February 22, 1775; died August 4, 1832, aged 57. Their daughter, Sarah Atwater[6] Plant (born December 4, 1800, died June 16, 1880), married Nathaniel Jocelyn, of New Haven (born January 31, 1796, died January 18, 1881).

* On December 25, 1780, he was appointed by the town of Derby to collect the assessments to raise recruits for the Continental army.

His will, dated April 1, 1796, proved July 3, 1796, names widow Esther Plant, two sons, Samuel and David, daughters Lucy, Polly, and Sally. The estate was appraised at £313 4s. 11d. and includes seventy acres of land with a house and barn, in the parish of Great Hills.

Plant Genealogy

VII. Sarah⁴ Plant, born May 6, 1754; baptized June 9, 1754.

VIII. Moses⁴ Plant, born March 17, 1760; supposed to have settled at Niagara, New York, and died there. He was in the Revolutionary War, Sixth regiment, Connecticut line, Captain James Prentice, of New Haven; enlisted, April 20, 1777, for eight months; discharged, January 1, 1778; also enlisted, February 21, 1778, in the regiment of Artificers, from Branford, for three years.

Authorities.—New Haven, Branford, Guilford, Litchfield, and Southington Town and Probate Records; Branford Church Records; Orcutt's *History of Stratford;* Orcutt's *History of Derby; The Tuttle Family;* gravestones in Grove Street Cemetery at New Haven; private records of Hon. Livingston W. Cleaveland, of New Haven, a grandson of Mr. and Mrs. Nathaniel Jocelyn.

TIMOTHY³ PLANT—LUCY PARRISH.

Timothy³ Plant, son of John² and Hannah (Whedon) Plant (John¹), born April 6, 1724, at Branford; baptized May 17, 1724; married Lucy Parrish, daughter of John and Hannah Parrish of that place. *See page 314.*

I. Lucy⁴ Plant, born May 27, 1745; died February 26, 1825, aged 80, at Saybrook, now Westbrook, Connecticut; married, December 24, 1764, Daniel Dee, son of William Dee, of Saybrook; born about 1739; died August 23, 1823, aged 84. Their gravestone is in the old cemetery at Westbrook.

II. Hannah⁴ Plant, born March 15, 1747; married, at Saybrook, Jared Baldwin, son of Jerjah Baldwin, of Milford, where they afterward lived and are mentioned in the records, November 30, 1819, as occupying their house with their daughter, Hannah Bassett. *See The Baldwin Genealogy.*

III. Timothy⁴ Plant, born July 4, 1750; married, 1770, Mary

Ann Colberth, who died about 1788, residence, Litchfield, Connecticut. *Account continued on page 323.*

IV. Joel⁴ Plant, born March 25, 1753. He is supposed to have died young.

V. Ithiel⁴ Plant, born in 1755; married, November 20, 1783, at Saybrook, Connecticut, Hannah Denison, daughter of George and Jemima (Post) Denison of that place; born October 25, 1758.*

Authorities.—Town and Probate Records at Deep River; gravestone at Westbrook; *Early Connecticut Marriages*, by F. W. Bailey; *The Baldwin Genealogy*; *Record of Connecticut Men in the War of the Revolution;* United States Pension Records as given by Commissioner Evans.

BENJAMIN³ PLANT—LORANA BECKWITH.

Benjamin³ Plant, son of John² and Hannah (Whedon) Plant (John¹), born, about 1732, at Branford; died August 11, 1808, aged 76; married (1), April 5, 1758 (by Rev. Philemon

---

* Ethan Plant, of Saybrook, is recorded as in the Revolutionary army, from May 8, 1775, to December 18, of the same year.

Ethel Plant is also enrolled as enlisting at New London, May 24, 1778, in the Third troop of light dragoons, and is described as "a cooper, stature, 5 feet 8½ inches, complexion light, eyes light, hair dark."

On June 5, 1813, Ethel Plant made application for a pension, being at that time 63 years of age, and a resident of Delhi, New York. The pension was allowed for six years' actual service in the Connecticut troops in the Revolutionary War.

The town clerk of Delhi writes, January 26, 1898, that no traces of such a person are now to be found there.

His marriage was by the name of Ethiel Plant. The various spellings were no doubt due to the unusualness of the name.

The home of this family seems to have passed from Branford to Saybrook soon after the marriage of the elder daughter, devolving on her the care of her younger sister and brothers. In a similar way, after the marriage of Hannah Plant to Mr. Baldwin, her home in Milford may have become a place of frequent resort for her brothers. This would account in a measure for the marriage of Timothy to a person who seems to have been of a Milford family, probably that of Humphrey and Margaret Colebreath.

Robbins), Lorana Beckwith, of Lyme, Connecticut; born about 1736; died March 16, 1789, aged 53; married (2), June 17, 1790, Abigail Palmer; married (3), December 6, 1797, Lois Frisbie. He lived in Branford and his children were born there. *See page 315.*

I. Hannah[4] Plant, born January 26, 1759; baptized April 25, 1759; married, June 30, 1779, John Russell.

II. John[4] Plant, born December 1, 1761; baptized January 17, 1762; removed to Seneca Lake, New York; was twice married but left no children.

III. Benjamin[4] Plant, born October 1, 1763; died 1812; married, 1787, Lucinda Potter, daughter of Captain Stephen and Sarah (Lindley) Potter; born April 4, 1767, at Branford; died June 26, 1848. They removed to Utica, New York, about 1795.

    1. Sally[5] Plant, born 1790; died 1808.
    2. Stephen[5] Plant, died 1793.
    3. Benjamin[5] Plant, born April 28, 1794; died August 7, 1876; married, April 7, 1823, Sarah Mason, daughter of Arnold and Mercy Mason, 1798–1879.
    4. James[5] Plant, born June 16, 1798; died January 5, 1860; married, November 27, 1833, Hannah A. Mason, daughter of Arnold and Mercy Mason; born 1812.
    5. John[5] Plant, born June 16, 1789; died young.
    6. Mary Eliza[5] Plant, born June 9, 1800; died March 1, 1886; married, September 9, 1820, Roswell Keeler, son of Timothy and Luranay (DeForest) Keeler; 1791–1864.
    7. Frederick[5] Plant, born April 27, 1810; died January 31, 1884.

IV. Anderson[4] Plant, born November 18, 1765; baptized November 24, 1765; was drowned in the Susquehanna River at the age of about 25.*

* Anderson Plant, of Branford, bought three acres of land in Southington, October 3, 1787, and sold the same to Thomas Stow of Middletown, April 7, 1788. Witnessed by John Plant.—*Southington Land Records*, Vol. ii., pp. 302–321.

V. Lorana⁴ Plant, baptized August 30, 1767; married Henry Garret and went to Trenton Falls, New York. Their son Orrin Garret was a printer, and one of the early missionaries to the Sandwich Islands.

VI. Peggy⁴ Plant, born May 26, 1769; baptized June 4, 1769; married, March 23, 1793, Jonathan Frisbie.

VII. Samuel⁴ Plant, born April 1, 1772; baptized April 12, 1772; died July 29, 1862, aged 90; married, February 11, 1795, Sarah Frisbie; born May 15, 1774; died August 25, 1841, aged 67. *Account continued on page 324.*

VIII. Elias⁴ Plant, baptized August 7, 1774; married (1), March 31, 1799, Ruhama Hall, daughter of Elias and Ruhama Hall, and widow of Thomas Trowbridge; born January 16, 1776; married (2), November 10, 1843, Lydia Linsley. *Account continued on page 325.*

Authorities.—Town, Church, and Probate Records at Branford and Guilford; *History and Genealogy of the Potter Family*, Part V., p. 6.

SOLOMON⁴ PLANT—SARAH BENNETT.

Solomon⁴ Plant, son of James³ and Bathsheba (Page) Plant (John,² John¹), born, May 1, 1741, at Branford; died, May 20, 1822, at Stratford; married (1), November 16, 1769, Sarah Bennett, of Stratford, who died September 15, 1815; married (2), November 19, 1816, Mrs. Esther (Frost) Botsford.* *See page 315.*

I. Hannah⁵ Plant, born October 25, 1770; married, October 7, 1787, Asa Benjamin; born December 2, 1763.

II. Sarah⁵ Plant, born January 5, 1775; died August 14,

* He was a soldier in the French and Indian War, enlisted at the age of 19, April 10, 1760, under Captain Jonathan Baker, in Suffolk County, "from Brandford, New England, wheelwright." He served in Captain David Mulford's company. On returning from the war he settled in Stratford, where his children were born.

1857 ; married, September 10, 1797, Daniel Judson ; born November 24, 1763 ; died October 4, 1847.
III. Cata⁴ Plant, born December 30, 1777 ; died January 16, 1778.
IV. David⁴ Plant, born March 29, 1783 ; died October 18, 1851 ; married, December 5, 1810, Catharine⁴ Tomlinson ; born October 9, 1787 ; died June 2, 1835. *Account continued on page 327.*

Authorities.—Rolls of Soldiers in the State of New York ; Orcutt's *History of Stratford.*

JAMES⁴ PLANT—LUCY JUDD.

James⁴ Plant, son of James³ and Bathsheba (Page) Plant (John,² John¹), born September 10, 1742, at Branford ; died May 16, 1814 ; married, January 9, 1772, at New Haven, Lucy Judd, daughter of Joseph and Ruth (Thompson) Judd ; born 1742 ; died August 17, 1822. *See page 315.*

I. Lucy⁴ Plant, born May 14, 1773 ; died May, 1863.
II. Joseph⁴ Plant, born March 26, 1775 ; died March 30, 1803.
III. Rebekah⁴ Plant, born February 6, 1778 ; died September, 1862.
IV. James⁴ Plant, born February 16, 1781 ; died March 23, 1806 ; residence, Harwinton. Litchfield records say that he left a wife, Nancy, and an infant daughter, Laura.
V. Sally⁴ Plant, born April 14, 1784 ; died May 23, 1874 ; married, February 5, 1803, Zephi Brockett, son of Amos and Lucy (Dutton) Brockett. *See " The Tuttle Family," page 547.*
VI. Ebenezer⁴ Plant, born January 10, 1787 ; died April 30, 1821, at Southington, married, August 29, 1809, Lydia Neale, daughter of Jeremiah and Anna (Fuller) Neale, of that place ; born January 29, 1788 ; died February 22, 1857. *Account continued on page 329.*

VII. Vesta[5] Plant, born March 23, 1791; died January 30, 1815.

Authorities.—Town and Probate Records at Branford, Guilford, New Haven, and Southington; gravetones in Quinnipiack Cemetery at Plantsville; Letter of Mr. F. H.[7] Plant.

STEPHEN[4] PLANT—REBECCA ——.

Stephen[4] Plant, son of James[3] and Bathsheba (Page) Plant (John,[2] John[1]), baptized March 8, 1747, at Branford; died before February 3, 1808, when his estate was admitted to Probate in Litchfield, Connecticut, and his widow, Rebecca Plant, was appointed administratrix.* *See page 316.*

I. Naomi[5] Plant, born September 2, 1776.
II. Jerusha[5] Plant, born May 17, 1778.
III. Orpah[5] Plant, born July 24, 1780.
IV. Stephen[5] Plant, born June 25, 1782.
V. Ruel[5] Plant, born March 21, 1785; married (1), September 18, 1807, Phebe Spinyer; married (2), October 30, 1842, Hutsah Williams. Children by the first marriage, and born in Litchfield.

    1. Isaac[6] Plant, born August 13, 1808.
    2. Maryan[6] Plant, born February 7, 1811.
    3. Hariot[6] Plant, born March 10, 1814.
    4. Stephen[6] Plant, born January 31, 1817.
    5. Jane[6] Plant, born February 4, 1819.
    6. David[6] Plant, born January 30, 1821.
    7. Phebe[6] Plant, born September 1, 1823.
    8. Charlotte[6] Plant, born July 1, 1826.
    9. Abigail[6] Plant, born October, 21, 1828.

* On May 5, 1770, he, with John Smith, also of Branford, bought of Joseph Pickett forty acres of land in Litchfield, for which they paid £45. Soon after this he removed to Litchfield, and on July 13 following the land was divided, and he took the north half. Here he seems to have lived and reared his family.

VI. Rebecca⁵ Plant, born May 21, 1787.
VII. Ammi⁵ Plant, born November 5, 1789; married, December 7, 1820, Mary Barney, of Litchfield, the service being by Rev. Isaac Jones, of St. Michael's Church.
VIII. Isaac⁵ Plant, born March 31, 1793.

TIMOTHY⁴ PLANT—MARY ANN COLBERTH.

Timothy⁴ Plant, son of Timothy³ and Lucy (Parrish) Plant (John,² John¹), born July 4, 1750, at Branford; died about 1777; married, 1770, Mary Ann Colberth.* *See page 317.*

I. Margaret⁵ Plant, born December 11, 1771; married a Gleason.
II. Timothy⁵ Plant, born January 3, 1773; died April 7, 1836, aged 63; married, January 3, 1795, Chloe Dickerman, of New Haven. *Account continued on page 330.*

* He removed to Litchfield, Connecticut, about 1772, the occasion for which was as follows: On June 26, 1734, his grandfather, John² Plant, bought of Josiah Rogers, of Branford, a tract of one hundred acres of land in Litchfield on the west side of the Waterbury River. This land remained undivided at the settlement of John² Plant's estate, and passed in this manner to his six sons. Of these, Timothy³ Plant sold his share of one sixth to his son Timothy,⁴ October 7, 1772, for £17. A little later, January 13, 1773, Timothy⁴ Plant, Jr., bought also the share of his uncle James, which had been previously sold to David Wooster. Then, May 23, 1774, he bought of Asa and Harris Hopkins two thirds of another tract of one hundred acres. He afterward sold both of these tracts at a considerable advance on their cost. But having made his home in Litchfield, the family remained there.

In the Revolutionary War he entered the army, March 2, 1777, in the Fifth regiment, Connecticut line, Captain J. A. Wright's company, and was reported missing at Germantown, October 4, 1777. Tradition says that he was drafted, and that in the battle he was taken prisoner and confined in "the old sugar house" at New York, or in "the prison ship," and died there, no word having ever come from him to his family. The births of his children are registered in Litchfield, except of the youngest, who must have been born after he went to the war.

III. Lucy Parrish⁵ Plant, born November 6, 1774; married a Dickinson and went to the West.
IV. Joel⁵ Plant, born August 22 (or 24), 1776; died 1853, at Meridian, New York. *Account continued on page 332.*
V. Avis⁵ Plant, born 1777; unmarried; resided in Richmond, Virginia, for some years and died there.

Authorities.—Town and Probate Records at Litchfield; *Connecticut Soldiers in the War of the Revolution;* Family Records and Traditions.

SAMUEL⁴ PLANT—SARAH FRISBIE.

Samuel⁴ Plant, son of Benjamin and Lorana (Beckwith) Plant, born April 1, 1772; baptized April 12, 1772, at Branford; died July 29, 1862, aged 90; married, February 11, 1795, Sarah⁵ Frisbie, daughter of Joseph⁵ and Sarah (Rogers) Frisbie (Joseph,⁴ Joseph,³ John,² Edward¹); born May 15, 1774; died August 25, 1841, aged 67. They lived at Branford. He served as a coastguard in the War of 1812. *See page 320.*

I. Anderson⁵ Plant, born January 2, 1796; died October 29, 1826, aged 30; married, December 23, 1818, Betsey Bradley, of Branford. *Account continued on page 335.*
II. Polly⁵ Plant, born October 16, 1798; died April 20, 1800.
III. Sally⁵ Plant, born September 17, 1801; married Judah Frisbie, a merchant in New Haven.
IV. John⁵ Plant, born May 19, 1806; died May 22, 1881; married Angelina Beach, daughter of Asher S. and Statira (Baldwin) Beach; born October 9, 1807; died January 13, 1883. He was a deacon of the church.

1. Mary E.⁶ Plant, born October 13, 1826; died September 19, 1879; married, November 9, 1852, William Norton.
2. Anderson W.⁶ Plant, born March 21, 1829; died June 22, 1847.
3. Sarah J.⁶ Plant, born July 24, 1831; died May 30, 1846.

4. George W.⁶ Plant, born March 12, 1833; married, October 6, 1857, Eliza E. Lane, of New Haven; born November 16, 1832; she died March 17, 1895.
5. John B.⁶ Plant, born May 5, 1836; died December 28, 1836.
6. Angelina B.⁶ Plant, born December 24, 1838; died July 20, 1841.
7. Angelina B.⁶ Plant, married, October 5, 1858, Henry T. Swift.
8. Emily S.⁶ Plant, born August 9, 1842; died June 11, 1856.
9. Elizabeth R.⁶ Plant, baptized August 9, 1846; married, July 12, 1871, Edward A. Anketelle.
10. John A.⁶ Plant, born April 7, 1848; died September 16, 1852.

V. Mary R.⁵ Plant, born October 9, 1808; died October 1, 1825, aged 17.

VI. Samuel Orin⁵ Plant, born June 24, 1815; married, February 26, 1839, Mary Ann Blackstone, daughter of Captain James Blackstone.

1. Ellen Blackstone⁶ Plant.
2. Sarah Frisbie⁶ Plant, married Hon. Lynde Harrison, residence, New Haven.

Authorities.—Town and Church Records at Branford; gravestones at Branford; Family Records; *Baldwin Genealogy;* Rokeby's *History of New Haven County.*

ELIAS⁴ PLANT—RUHAMAH HALL.

Elias⁴ Plant, son of Benjamin³ and Lorana (Beckwith) Plant (John,² John¹), baptized August 7, 1774, at Branford; married (1), March 31, 1799, Ruhamah Hall, daughter of Elias and Ruhamah Hall,* and widow of Thomas Trowbridge; born January 16, 1776; married (2), November 10, 1843, Lydia

* Elias⁵ Hall was the eldest child of John⁴ and Abigail (Russell) Hall; (John,³ John,² John¹). Ruhamah was the only child of his second wife, who died at her daughter's birth. He served in the French and Indian War in Colonel Whiting's regiment, under Lord Amherst, and was on duty at Ticonderoga and Crown Point until 1759. He settled in Cheshire, Connecticut; removed in 1784 to Pittsford, Vermont, and died October 30, 1821, at the house of his son Elias, at Williston, Vermont.

Linsley. The children were by the first marriage. *See page 320.*

I. William[5] Plant, born January 4, 1800; baptized with the four younger children, September 30, 1810, at Branford; married Polly Beach, daughter of Asher S. and Statira (Baldwin) Beach. Children born at Branford.

> 1. Anna Louisa[6] Plant, born February 14, 1832.
> 2. Alonzo Austin[6] Plant, born October 27, 1834; married, July 2, 1857, Elizabeth Mary Hough, of New Haven.
> 3. Edwin Ezra[6] Plant, born February 6, 1837.
> 4. Margaret[6] Plant.
> 5. Lucerne[6] Plant.
> 6. William[6] Plant.
> 7. Albert E.[6] Plant married Bessie Upson, of East Haven, and had two children, Albert C. Plant and Mabel M. Plant.

II. Mary[5] Plant, born September 3, 1801.

III. Thomas[5] Plant, born April 14, 1804; died about 1873; married Sarah Chidsey. His will, dated April 4, 1867, proved June 26, 1873, appoints his brother James executor, and bequeaths all his estate to his sister, Jane Maria[5] Plant; residence, Guilford.

IV. Edward[5] Plant, born September 8, 1806; married, September 13, 1831, Harriette Jennette[7] Street, daughter of Elnathan[6] and Clarissa (Morris) Street (Nicholas,[5] Elnathan,[4] Samuel,[3] Samuel,[2] Nicholas[1]); born July 8, 1807; died June 14, 1866.

> 1. De Forest Edward[6] Plant, born June 27, 1832; died March 7, 1875; married, June 16, 1857, (by Rev. H. W. Beecher at Plymouth Church in Brooklyn), Harriet Ely, daughter of C. H. Ely, of Hanover, New Jersey.
> 2. Harriet Evelina[6] Plant, born January 18, 1834; died January 13, 1837.
> 3. Marian Albertina[6] Plant, born April 1, 1839; died November, 1863; married James La Hon.
> 4. Ella Alexina[6] Plant, born July 29, 1849; died 1864.

V. Jane⁵ Plant, born March 1, 1808.
VI. James⁵ Plant, baptized April 28, 1811.
VII. Harriet⁵ Plant, baptized May 23, 1813 ; married, February 28, 1839, James Morris.
VIII. Julianna⁵ Plant, baptized July 22, 1815 ; married, August 6, 1839, James T. Leete.
IX. Elias⁵ Plant, baptized June 27, 1817 ; married, December 31, 1848, Delia E. Beach. He died, and she married, November 24, 1874, Henry Doolittle.

1. Jane Frances⁶ Plant, baptized September 3, 1851.

X. Jane Maria⁵ Plant, baptized July 4, 1819.

Authorities.—Town and Probate Records ; *The Trowbridge Family ; Hall Family Record ; The Street Genealogy.*

DAVID⁵ PLANT—CATHARINE TOMLINSON.

David⁵ Plant, son of Solomon⁴ and Sarah (Bennett) Plant (James,³ John,² John¹), born March 29, 1783, at Stratford ; died October 18, 1851 ; married, December 5, 1810, Catharine⁵ Tomlinson, daughter of Dr. William Agur⁵ and Phebe (Lewis) Tomlinson (Agur,⁴ Zechariah,³ Agur,² Henry¹) ; born October 9, 1787 ; died June 2, 1835.* *See page 321.*

* "He prepared himself for college at the Cheshire Academy, and was graduated at Yale College in 1804, after which he studied law at the Litchfield Law School. He was a classmate and friend of John C. Calhoun, who was not only with him in college but also studied law at Litchfield. In 1819 and 1820 Mr. Plant was Speaker of the Connecticut House of Representatives, and in 1821 was elected to the Senate, after which he was twice re-elected. He was Lieutenant-Governor from 1823 to 1827, and from 1827 to 1829 was a member of the United States Congress. In politics he was a staunch Whig. Calhoun when Secretary of State offered him, for friendship's sake, any position within his gift, but he declined to hold office under the dominant party. He was one of the most influential men of his day in political circles of the State of Connecticut."

I. William Agur[6] Plant, born November 21, 1811, at Stratford; died January 29, 1898, aged 86, at Syracuse, New York; married (1), April 29, 1832, Lucy Fellows, daughter of Ephraim Fellows, and granddaughter of Obed and Lois (Plant) Fellows; she died in 1883, after a married life of over fifty-one years, and he married (2), September 5, 1886, Abbie Healey.*

II. Catharine Tomlinson[6] Plant, married John W. Sterling, son of David and Deborah (Strong) Sterling, residence, Stratford, Connecticut.

III. Sarah Elizabeth[6] Plant, married Lauren Beach, residence, Marcellus, New York.

---

* For several years of his early life he was in mercantile business in New York City. At the age of twenty he removed to Marcellus, New York, and engaged in farming until 1872, when he made his home in Syracuse, where he became a prominent member of the Brown Memorial M. E. Church.

" He was a man of strong character, honorable and upright, with clear intellect and much originality, fond of books, and well informed on the events transpiring in his country and throughout the world."

There were six children by his first marriage, two of whom were Charles H.[7] Plant and Mrs. W. R. Knowles, who died before him. The four others are Dr. William T.[7] Plant, Alfred D.[7] Plant, and Miss Ailda[7] Plant, of Syracuse, and Mrs. I. W. Davey, of Marcellus.

William Tomlinson[7] Plant, the eldest of these, was graduated from the University of Michigan in 1860, and began practice as a physician in Ithaca, New York. Early in the war he entered the United States Navy as surgeon, and continued till October, 1865, when he resigned, and in 1866 began the practice of medicine in Syracuse. This he followed till about 1894, when paralysis compelled him to retire from active life. He has filled many positions of honor and responsibility; has been on the medical staff of a large hospital, doing duty there four months in the year; was one of the founders of the Medical College of Syracuse, in which he held the chair of Jurisprudence and Pediatrics, and has contributed much to medical journals, having been the editor of one such periodical.

He has one son, John W.[8] Plant, who is in the graduating class of Syracuse Medical College for 1898.

IV. Henry⁵ Plant, married Eudocia ———. He was prominent as a business man in Minneapolis, Minnesota.

V. John David⁵ Plant, died February 29, 1860, at St. Anthony, Minnesota, where he was in business.

Authorities.—Orcutt's *History of Stratford;* *The Syracuse Press ;* Letter of Mrs. W. T. Plant, of Syracuse.

EBENEZER⁵ PLANT—LYDIA NEALE.

Ebenezer⁵ Plant, son of James⁴ and Lucy (Judd) Plant (James,³ John,² John¹), born January 10, 1787 ; died April 30, 1821, at Southington ; married, August 29, 1809, Lydia Neale, daughter of Jeremiah and Anna (Fuller) Neale, of that place ; born January 29, 1788 ; died February 22, 1857. *See page 321.*

I. Harriett⁶ Plant, born May 29, 1810 ; died September 30, 1816.

II. Laura Ann⁶ Plant, born April 20, 1812 ; died January 4, 1871 ; married, June 28, 1831, Alfred A. Hotchkiss.
  1. Edwin P.⁷ Hotchkiss, a manufacturer at Plantsville.

III. Amzi Perrin⁶ Plant, born July 2, 1816 ; died July 24, 1874 ; married (1), A. E. Shipman, who died April 3, 1849 ; married (2), March, 1850, Cornelia Dakin.
  1. Adelia⁷ Plant, born June 22, 1843 ; died July 1, 1846.
  2. Emily C.⁷ Plant, born May 4, 1853 ; died April 18, 1867.
  3. William Perrin⁷ Plant, born February 8, 1857.

IV. Ebenezer Howard⁶ Plant, born February 25, 1821 ; died January 12, 1891 ; married, September 28, 1843, Hannah K. Ives, daughter of Samuel and Abigail (Moss) Ives ; born January 6, 1823 ; died August 17, 1873.
  1. Frederick Howard⁷ Plant, born November 15, 1859.

Messrs. Amzi Perrin⁶ Plant and Ebenezer Howard⁶ Plant engaged in manufactures in the southern part of Southington, which developed into large industries, giving employment to many people. The village growing up about these establishments received their name, and is known as Plantsville.

Authorities.—Southington Town and Probate Records; gravestones in Southington; Trumbull's *History of Hartford County.*

TIMOTHY⁵ PLANT—CHLOE DICKERMAN.

Timothy⁵ Plant, son of Timothy⁴ and Mary Ann (Colberth) Plant (Timothy,³ John,² John¹), born January 3, 1773, at Litchfield, Connecticut; died April 7, 1836, aged 63, at New Haven; married, January 3, 1795, Chloe⁵ Dickerman, of New Haven, daughter of Stephen⁴ and Eunice (Tuttle) Dickerman (Isaac,³ Abraham,² Thomas¹); born July 7, 1773; died May 17, 1850; residence, Litchfield and New Haven. *See page 323.*

I. Mary Ann⁶ Plant, born February 17, 1796; died 1852; married, May 19, 1816, Samuel Westcott, of Providence, Rhode Island, died January 28, 1824.

    1. Susan⁷ Westcott.
    2. Mary Ann⁷ Westcott.
    3. Henry P.⁷ Westcott.
    4. George⁷ Westcott.

II. Benjamin Dickerman⁶ Plant, born February 8, 1798; married, November 6, 1828, Maria Kaigler, of South Carolina; born December 27, 1805. He was a bookseller in Columbia, South Carolina.

    1. Caroline Elizabeth⁷ Plant, married Samuel Rumph; residence, Marshallville, Georgia.
    2. George Benjamin⁷ Plant, married Lætitia McGehee; residence, Marshallville.
    3. Emily Maria⁷ Plant, married William I. Greene; residence, Fort Valley, Georgia.

III. Susan⁶ Plant, born September 19, 1800; died August 30, 1801.

IV. Susan⁶ Plant, born October 21, 1802; died January 20, 1831; married, November 6, 1828, Timothy McCarthy.
V. Caroline⁶ Plant, born January 27, 1806; died July 14, 1879; married, February 21, 1830, Fordyce Wrigley, son of Edward Wrigley, of England; born January 25, 1803; died October 1, 1846; residence, Macon, Georgia.

> 1. Benjamin Henry⁷ Wrigley, married, January 12, 1864, Lucy Knott.
> 2. Julia⁷ Wrigley, married, May 10, 1866, D. H. Peden; residence, Griffin, Georgia.
> 3. Lucia⁷ Wrigley, married, October 31, 1888, A. W. Blake.
> 4. William⁷ Wrigley, married (1), November, 1866, Annie Mellard; married (2), Ida McPherson.

VI. Timothy Henry⁶ Plant, born February 1, 1808; died January 4, 1871; married, August 28, 1834, Sarah Maria Peck, of Kensington, Connecticut, born September 14, 1814. He and his brother, Increase Cook⁶ Plant, were together at Columbia in the store of their older brother, and from there went to Augusta, Georgia, and established a book business under the firm name of "T. H. & I. C. Plant."

> 1. Augusta M.⁷ Plant, residence, Macon, Georgia.

VII. Ebenezer⁶ Plant, born April 28, 1810; died November 26, 1876; married Adeline Gibbs Nye, of New Bedford, Massachusetts.

> 1. Ida⁷ Plant.
> 2. Lucy⁷ Plant.
> 3. Annie⁷ Plant.

VIII. A child born April 8, 1812, died young.
IX. Increase Cook⁶ Plant, born February 27, 1814; died November 16, 1892; married (1), July 24, 1838, Charlotte

Walker; married (2), October 2, 1843, Elizabeth Mary Hazlehurst. *Account continued on page 335.*

X. A daughter, twin of Increase Cook⁶ Plant, died young.

Authorities.—Families of Dickerman Ancestry; Private family records.

JOEL⁵ PLANT—MARY JORDAN.

Joel⁵ Plant, born August 24, 1776, in Connecticut; died in 1853, at Meridian, New York; married, November 27, 1800, at Litchfield, Connecticut, Mary Jordan, of Woodstock; born December 4, 1776; died in 1846, at Peru, New York.* *See page 324.*

I. John⁶ Plant, born June 26, 1801; married twice; a physician at Hyde Park, Pennsylvania.

* A tradition represents him to have been the son of Joel⁴ Plant, the brother of Timothy,⁴ but no records confirm this view, while a number of points in his story seem to identify him with Joel,⁵ the son of Timothy,⁴ born at Litchfield, according to one entry there, August 22, 1776, and according to another, August 24, 1776. The following account is from his son, Mr. Lauren Plant, of Cicero, New York, December 25, 1897.

"Timothy, the son of John Plant, married Lucy Parrish, settled in New Haven, and was in the bookbinding business. Among their children were two sons, Timothy, born July 4, 1750, who subsequently settled in Litchfield; and Joel, born March 25, 1753, who was a soldier in the Revolutionary War, and died, or was killed, on Long Island in 1779, leaving a wife and two children in New Haven. A daughter, Margaret, afterward married Benoni Gleson and went to Vermont. Joel was born August 24, 1776; his mother died when he was twelve years old, and at the age of fourteen he was bound out to work in the bookbindery that his grandfather had established long before. Not liking the business, he ran away, at the age of seventeen, and went west to the banks of the Susquehanna River, where he remained two seasons, returning to his Uncle Tim's in Litchfield and attending school in the winter, where he made the acquaintance of Mary Jordan, whom he married. They lived two or three years in Worthington, Massachusetts, then moved to Benson, Rutland County, Vermont, and, in 1837, to Onondaga County, New York."

Plant Genealogy

II. Lorenzo⁶ Plant, born April 17, 1803 ; died July 2, 1836, at Orwell, Vermont ; married (1), October 7, 1829, Louisa Hall, who died May 9, 1830, aged 21 ; married (2), October 11, 1831, Harriet M. Cook ; born December 29, 1812 ; died March 11, 1888, at Georgia, Vermont. (She married (2), February 13, 1844, Noah R. Parker.)

    1. Azro Melvin⁷ Plant, born May 25, 1835; married, November 29, 1864, Annie Fairchild, of Milton, Vermont, born March 27, 1846. He was Assistant Surgeon, 14th Regiment, Vermont Volunteers in the war, and served in hospitals at Washington, after which he was a druggist at St. Albans, Vermont. Residence, in 1898, Milton.

III. Alanson⁶ Plant, born March 28, 1805 ; died in 1844 ; married Betsey Hiscock, of Onondaga Hill, New York ; residence, Kenyonville, New York.

IV. Althea Mariah⁶ Plant, born May 7, 1807 ; died June 27, 1862 ; married William M. Taylor (died December, 1850), who had previously married her sister Mary, who died ; residence, Dudley, Massachusetts.

    1. Mary P.⁷ Taylor, born August 11, 1839 ; died July 2, 1843.
    2. William A.⁷ Taylor, born about 1841 ; died July 20, 1864.
    3. Martha O.⁷ Taylor, born January 15, 1843; died August 2, 1848.
    4. Mary A.⁷ Taylor, born November 2, 1844 ; married, October 19, 1871, ——Prentice, Norwich, Connecticut.
    5. Helen⁷ Taylor, born July 27, 1846 ; married Henry Holt ; residence, Hartford, Connecticut.
    6. Hyram⁷ Taylor, born July 27, 1846 ; died July 22, 1863.
    7. Annie Maria⁷ Taylor, born November 2, 1847 ; died July 19, 1849.
    8. Lorenzo P.⁷ Taylor, born December, 1850 ; died March 30, 1851.

V. Almira⁶ Plant, born April 30, 1809 ; died December, 1891 ; married A. G. Wheeler.

VI. Mary⁶ Plant, born March 8, 1811 ; died 1837, at New Boston, Connecticut ; married William M. Taylor.

VII. Lucy⁶ Plant, born June 26, 1813; died 1843, at Peru, New York.

VIII. A. Joel⁶ Plant, born May 15, 1815; died 1872, in Cortland County, New York; married, 1845, Margaret Phillips, of Locke, New York.

    1. Adin⁷ Plant, residence, Binghamton, New York.
    2. Leona⁷ Plant, residence, Binghamton, New York.

IX. Lauren P.⁶ Plant, born March 7, 1817, in Rutland County, Vermont; died at Cicero, New York, January 29, 1898; married, February 25, 1836, Mrs. Sarah R. Smiley, of that place, who died there December 5, 1877. He was a Republican in politics and held the offices, at different times, of Town Clerk, Constable, and Deputy Sheriff.

    1. Byron⁷ Plant, born April 29, 1839; married, September 25, 1861, Minerva Saunders.
    2. Mary Elizabeth⁷ Plant, born January 18, 1842, at Sullivan, New York; died February 25, 1891; married, April 11, 1867, Job Fuller, of Syracuse.
    3. Almira⁷ Plant, born September 2, 1844, at Cicero; married, October 6, 1886, John S. Botsford, of Clay, New York.

X. Arunah H.⁶ Plant, born October 25, 1819; died September 5, 1873; married, April 19, 1848, at Maumee, Ohio, Mrs. Amelia Lane. In 1866 he wrote to his niece in Vermont, "I have not accumulated much of this world's goods, but have a pleasant home and am contented."

    1. Mary Sedate⁷ Plant, born December 31, 1848; married, January, 1885, J. M. McCann, of Toledo, Ohio.
    2. Helen M.⁷ Plant, born September 12, 1850; married, September 1, 1880, Elijah Lee Jaquis.

Authorities.—Letters from members of the family.

ANDERSON⁵ PLANT—BETSEY BRADLEY.

Anderson⁵ Plant, son of Samuel⁴ and Sarah (Frisbie) Plant (Benjamin,³ John,² John¹), born January 2, 1796, at Branford; died there October 29, 1826*; married, December 23, 1818, Betsey⁵ Bradley, daughter of Levi⁵ and Lydia (Beach) Bradley (Timothy,⁴ Daniel,³ Isaac,² Francis¹), born August 28, 1799; died January 20, 1886, at New Haven. She married (2), Philemon Hoadley, born March 31, 1797, at Southampton, Massachusetts; died January 28, 1862, at New Haven. *See page 324.*

I. Henry Bradley⁶ Plant, born October 27, 1819; married (1), September 25, 1843, Ellen E. Blackstone, who died February 28, 1861; married (2), July 2, 1873, Margaret Josephine Loughman, only daughter of Martin Loughman of New York City. *Account continued on page 336.*
II. Eliza Ann⁶ Plant, baptized September 26, 1824, died young.

Authorities.—Branford and Guilford Town and Probate Records; *The Hoadley Family.*

INCREASE COOK⁵ PLANT—MARY E. HAZLEHURST.

Increase Cook⁵ Plant, son of Timothy⁴ and Chloe (Dickerman) Plant (Timothy,⁴ Timothy,³ John,² John¹), born February 27, 1814, at New Haven; died July 23, 1883, at Macon, Georgia; married (1), July 24, 1838, Charlotte Walker, of Leamingston, Vermont, who died March 12, 1839; married (2), October 2, 1843, Elizabeth Mary⁵ Hazlehurst, daughter of Robert⁴ and Elizabeth Pettingale (Wilson) Hazlehurst

---

* Anderson Plant's estate was in probate, June 13, 1827. Mr. Samuel Plant was chosen and appointed guardian of Henry Bradley Plant, who with his mother, Mrs. Betsey Plant, were the only heirs.

(Robert,[1] Isaac,[2] Robert[3]), born April 20, 1819, at Brunswick, Georgia; died July 23, 1883, at Macon.

Beginning business in a bookstore with his brother at Augusta, Georgia, he soon entered upon a banking business, which he followed at Columbus and Brunswick, and finally at Macon, where his name is held in honor not only as a banker but as an influential, public-spirited citizen. *See page 331.*

I. Mary Hazlehurst[7] Plant, married, October 6, 1875, Marshall de Graffenried; residence, Atlanta, Georgia.

II. Robert Hazlehurst[7] Plant, born December 21, 1847; married, July 25, 1871, Margaret Redding Ross, daughter of John Bennett and Martha (Redding) Ross, of Macon. He succeeded his father in the banking business, and has engaged in other enterprises, insurance and manufacturing, which are highly prosperous.

III. George Henry[7] Plant, married Minnie Leila Wood; residence, Macon, where he is engaged in banking in the firm with his brother.

IV. Elizabeth Wilson[7] Plant, married Alonzo D. Schofield; residence, Macon.

HENRY BRADLEY[6] PLANT— { ELLEN E. BLACKSTONE. / MARGARET J. LOUGHMAN.

Henry Bradley[6] Plant, son of Anderson[5] and Betsey (Bradley) Plant (Samuel,[4] Benjamin,[3] John,[2] John[1]), born October 27, 1819, at Branford; married (1), September 25, 1843, Ellen E.[7] Blackstone, daughter of Captain James[6] and Sarah (Beach) Blackstone (Timothy,[5] John,[4] John,[3] John,[2] Rev. W. T.[1]); born February 21, 1821; died February 28, 1861; married (2), July 2, 1873, Margaret Josephine Loughman, only daughter of Martin Loughman, of New York City. *See page 335.*

I. A boy; ——, born ——, died June 17, 1846, aged 17 mo., 4 days.

II. Morton F.⁷ Plant, born August 18, 1852; married Nellie⁷ Capron, daughter of Col. F. B.⁶ Capron, of Baltimore, Md. They have a son, Henry Bradley⁸ Plant, Jr., born May 18, 1895.

Banfield¹ Capron, born in Chester, England, in 1640. In 1654 he came to America, to Barrington, Mass.; married a lady named Callender, of Rehoboth, Mass. They had twelve children, six sons and six daughters. He died August 20, 1752; gravestone in Attleboro.

Jonathan² Capron, farmer, sixth son, of Attleboro, Mass., born March 11, 1705; married Rebecca Morse, who died August 29, 1772. (See gravestone, Attleboro.) They had eight children.

Elisha³ Capron, third son, married Abigail Makepeace, of Norton, Mass., and resided at Attleboro, Mass.; had nine children.

Seth⁴ Capron, first son, born September 23, 1762; married Eunice Mann, of Attleboro, Mass., daughter of Jesse Brown, of Cumberland, R. I. They had six children. Fought in the Revolutionary War; died at Walden, Orange County, N. Y., September 4, 1835.

Newton Mann⁵ Capron, first son, born August 24, 1791, at Cumberland, R. I.; married Maria Brown, May 29, 1815; had two children.

Francis Brown⁶ Capron, first son, born May 17, 1816; married Olivia Royston at Baltimore, Md., and had three children.

Nellie⁷ Capron, first daughter; married Morton Freeman⁷ Plant, June 23, 1887.

INDEX.

Adams Express Company, organized March, 1853, and April, 1854; list of shareholders, 52: in 1861 this company sold and transferred its entire interests in the South to H. B. Plant, 54

Atlanta Exposition of 1895, object of, 157; Mr. Plant's interest in, and exhibit at, said Exposition, 157, 158; "Plant Day" at the Exposition; Mr. Plant's seventy-eighth birthday; importance of "Plant Day," 159; Plant System described, 160; opening up of Florida by this System, 161; purchase of railroads; extending the System; Plant Investment Company, 161, 162; purchase of railroads and establishment of steamboat lines, 161-163; steamship line to Canada, 164; Exposition described by the press; various newspaper accounts, 221-263; Atlanta Exposition's recognition of Mr. Plant's services to the Exposition, 253; he is appreciated, feasted, and honored, 254; Florida's truest friend, 254

Blackstone family: William Blaxton only one in State of Massachusetts; lived in wilderness among wild beasts and savage men; Boston Common; Blackstone's beautiful character, 23: Captain Blackstone was father of Mr. Plant's first wife; his son Timothy's gift of a library (memorial to his father); his education and successful career, 26, 27: history of Blackstone family in Massachusetts, Rhode Island, and Branford, Connecticut, 29, 30; five generations lived and died on the old family farm in Branford; James a strong character in politics and patriotic service; Timothy, his son, donor of library, 31-33: Ellen Elizabeth, second daughter of James Blackstone, married Henry B. Plant; Sir William Blackstone, author of *Law Commentaries*, was fifth cousin of James Blackstone, 34

Board of Trade, Savannah, resolutions, 221; Mr. Wiley's address, 222; Mr. Plant's acknowledgment, 226

Branford, Connecticut, purchased from Indians in 1638; first settled, 1644, by people from New Haven, 15: first church; danger from Indians; records of; colony from, 16: John Plum first town clerk; resembles Harlem, N.Y., in customs, 2: second church built, its architecture, seating, etc., 17; its pulpit; foot stoves, 18: Rev. Timothy Gillett, its pastor, taught an academy also; strained relations with his congregation, 19: he and wife buried at Branford, 20; this

Index

Branford, Connecticut—*Continued* town rendered patriotic service in Revolution, 20, 21; once shipbuilding flourished; seaport town; seat of colonial governor, 22

Bullock, Ex-Governor: description of H. B. Plant, 99-101

Canals: Erie; Suez, 276

Changes that have taken place in the configuration of the globe during Mr. Plant's lifetime, 264-269

Cotton States, development due largely to H. B. Plant, 165, 248-251

Cuba: scenery; architecture, Moorish, Saxon, and Doric; Morro Castle; Santa Catalina warehouses; mail service by the Plant line of steamers, 114-116

Duelling once legalized, 275

Engineering skill, great achievements of, 279

England's bad laws; favored the rich; severe in punishing crime; cruel treatment of prisoners, 271, 272; war barbarities, inhuman treatment of soldiers, 272, 273; educational progress, 275

Frisbee family, sketch of; Edward Ebenezer; Elisha; Professor Levi; James; Richard; John; Joseph; President Edward S., of Wells College; O. L. Frisbee, 4-7

Nineteenth century: demonstration at its beginning, 269, 270; political and social condition of France, 270; Napoleon's bad and good influence on Europe, 271

Penny postage originated, 275

Plant, A. P., his industry, religion, and success in life, 1-2

Plant, David, 2; education and career, 3

Plant, Henry Bradley: birth and parentage, 1; descended from J. Frisbee, a major in Washington's army, 4; right to join the "Sons of the American Revolution," 13; the Plants settled in Branford over two hundred years ago; their descendants still own the lands of the first settlers; Anderson Plant, father of Henry B., 35: died when Henry was six years old, 36; death of father's sister, and also Henry's sister; Henry's first recollections of his mother, 36: enduring and tender impressions of an hour; poem, 37; poet's mother, 38; the boy Henry's first day at school, 38; his courage fails him, 39; diffident all his life, 39; his mother's second marriage, 40; moved from Branford to Martinsburg; lived part of the time there with mother and stepfather, and part with grandmother Plant at Branford, 40: here he was thrown from a plow horse and badly injured, 40, 41; testimony of A. P. B., "one of the noblest and best of men," 41; parents moved to New Haven, 41; declined grandmother's offer of a course in Yale College, 41; studies under Rev. Gillett and John E. Lovell, 42; his first attempts at business did not succeed, 42; in 1837 began as captain's boy on New York and New Haven line of steamers, 42; manly boy, 42, 43; first experiences in express business, 43; it was hard at first, but improved after a time, 44; his development of Southern Express, 44; enlargement of responsibility by addition of railroads, steamship lines, and hotels, 45; Captain Stone's fondness for young Plant, 45; marries Miss Blackstone in 1842; first child died, aged eighteen months; second son, Morton Freeman,

Index

Plant, Henry Bradley—*Continued*
now associated with his father, 45; removes from New Haven to New York; is employed by Beecher Express Co., 46: next by Adams Express Co., 46; his mother banked his savings, 46; bought some New Haven bank stock, which he still owns, 46; buys a pew in a new church, 46; stepfather died at New Haven in 1862 or 1863; failure of his wife's health takes him to Florida in 1853; the journey took eight days by three different steamers, 47: Mrs. Plant's improved health and return to New York, 47; landing at Jacksonville, and romantic experiences while in Florida, 48; lost their way in the woods five miles from boarding-house; sail in a "dug-out," 48: drive in a buggy; Indian girl, 49: boarding at the Judson Hotel, New York; Captain Stone leaves his son in Mr. Plant's care; Plant returns South on account of wife's failing health; appointed superintendent of Harnden's Express, at Savannah, 51: appointed superintendent of Adams Express Company, 1854, 52; large development of the company under his superintendence; difficulty of the work, 53: extent of business of the Southern and Texas Express Companies, of which Mr. Plant is president, 54; formed, and became president of, Southern Express Co. in 1861, 55; death of wife at Augusta, Ga., February 28, 1861; remains afterward removed to Branford, Conn., 55; buys a slave, who proves a good nurse to Mr. Plant, 58; impaired health, and change of climate ordered by doctor; pass from President Davis to pass through Confederate lines at any point, 59: goes to Bermuda, Halifax, and Montreal; son Morton brought to him; visits his mother at New Haven, Conn.; in fall sails for Liverpool; a stranger in a strange land, 59: goes to Paris; courtesy of French officials in passport; visits Rome, Naples, Leghorn, Barcelona, Milan, and Venice, 60: travelled in Switzerland, 60, 61; returned by way of Canada, and was in New York when President Lincoln was assassinated, 61; his second marriage and trip to Europe in 1873, accompanied by his wife, mother, and son, 61; his third visit to Europe, 1889; represented the United States as juror in Class Six, at the Paris Exposition, 61: medals for Plant System, diploma to Mr. Plant, and many courtesies extended, 61; his busy life in Augusta; difficulties of express work caused by the war; bravely met and adjusted, 62: hotel life in Augusta; letter of a friend, 63: his health fails, 64; rewards a kindness done to his wife and child thirty-six years ago, 65; his second wife Miss Loughman; her ancestors; her interest and impress on some achievements of the System, 67: Mr. Plant's intuitive knowledge and keen insight illustrated, 68, 69; after-dinner speeches, Tampa Board of Trade banquet, 70–72; Florida Mr. Plant's hobby; banquet given him at Ocala, in 1896, at Ocala Hotel, 87, 88: his reply to many addresses of welcome on the subject, "The Plant System," 88–94; reception, excursion, and banquet given Mr. Plant and friends by the mayor and leading citizens of Leesburg, 95; reception next day at Eustis, 95; his words of cheer to the people who had suffered great loss from the freeze of the previous winter de-

Plant, Henry Bradley—*Continued*
stroying their orange groves, 96; their grateful appreciation of his visit, 96; honesty, importance of; testimonies to this quality of his character, 97, 98; his power and influence over employees and associates, 99; Ex-Gov. Bullock's description of Mr. Plant's ability, fidelity, and gentlemanly character, 99, 100; industry and power of endurance, 102-104; character and manner of answering his large mail, 102-104; missionary letter from Japan, 103; his private car; comfort, elegance of, 103; old darkie "shining up 100," 104; keen intuition, and great power of self-control, 105; calm, quiet spirit, kindly nature, and efficient performance of all he does, 105; testimony of an employee, of respect and appreciation of Mr. Plant's character and work for the South, 105, 106; his calm and kindly spirit saved him the consuming force of friction which grinds some men, 106; not a pessimist or recluse; loves music and social life, 107; medical benefactor, 107, 108; much pain saved by medical progress, 108; Mr. Plant's share in alleviating suffering, 109; testimony of physicians to healthfulness of Florida for invalids, 110; Mr. Plant facilitates travel, and provides hotels healthful and luxurious, 111-113; furnishes comfortable transit from Florida to Cuba and Jamaica; press notices of Mr. Plant and his philanthropic work for the South in railroads, steamship lines, hotels, etc., 121, 122; promoted orange-growing by the facilities afforded for getting the fruit soon and safe to market, 123; railroads induced many people to settle in the South, 124; various railroads bought, built, and combined in the Plant System, 126; steamer *Mascotte*, elegant and comfortable, 127; railroad topics; notes, characteristics, and success of his life, 128; largely a pioneer in his work of opening up the South, 131; the Plant Investment Company's president, 132; his palatial residence in New York City, 132; never speculates in Wall Street, 133; analysis of his disposition, temper, spirit, and pleasant manner, 133, 134; *Home Journal;* Ocala *Evening Star;* similar descriptions, 134-140; his close and constant contact with the Plant System, 141; notes of his voyage from New York to Key West, 142-146; also from Port Tampa to Jamaica; attentions of distinguished people, 146; Lady Blake's garden party at King's House on February 1st, 146, 147; entertainment and enjoyment at Jamaica, 147-149; his economical management of the Plant System, 150; riding in a baggage-car saw expressman handle carelessly a box marked "glass," etc.; gentle rebuke; saved the man from discharge by superior officer, 152, 153; generous treatment of an honored employee, 153; horrors of strikes contrasted with "Plant Day" at Atlanta Exposition in 1896, 153; spent over forty years of his life in developing the South, 166; eulogies on his character and work, 166-168; "Loving Cup" and other presentations, 169-178; Mr. Plant's response, 178-181; programme of "Plant Day" at Atlanta Exposition, 204, 205; ringing of the "Liberty Bell," 206; services at the Auditorium; enthusiastic reception, 207; music and speeches, 208-210; Mayor King and others, 210-212; Mr. Plant's response, 212-217; resolutions, complimen-

Index

Plant, Henry Bradley—*Continued*
tary, 217–220; Judge Falligant's speech, 220–221
Profanity and drunkenness lessened, 275

Railroads: waste of railroad strikes, 150; losses to employers and employed, 150, 151; damage to commerce, demoralization of labor, inconvenience and losses to the public, 151; no strikes on Plant System, 151; due to President Plant, 152; strikes contrasted with "Plant Day" at Atlanta Exposition, 153; "Plant Day" as described by employees of the System, 154; introduction to this description, 154–156; railroads, introduction of in England, and United States, 277; Edward Entwistle ran the first train in England, came to this country, 277; railroad mileage in the United States increased from three miles to 173, 453 in Mr. Plant's lifetime, 278; first steamship that crossed the Atlantic; first regular line established, 278

Southern Express Company formed, 1861, 54, 55; its relations to and services for the Southern Confederacy; given the custody of all government funds, it collected tariffs, and had soldiers detailed for its service, 56; President Davis' proclamation for all noncitizens of Confederacy to leave its bounds; permission given Mr. Plant to remain and conduct express business, 57; generous service of the company to soldiers in the war, 65–66; presentation of silver service by the company to its president, 66; Southern development due largely to H. B. Plant, 165; history of the company, 233–236; the company's building and exhibit on the fair grounds, 236; reception in this building to Mr. Plant and friends, 237, 238; thanks tendered the press, 239; telegrams and congratulations, 239–241; honors to Mr. Plant, 243; list of employees present, 245; sketch of Mr. Plant published in Atlanta *Chronicle*, 247–248; slavery abolished, 273

Tampa, progress of, 70–72; speech of Mr. Plant, 73, 74; growth of Tampa, Mr. Plant's share in its growth, 74, 75; cigar-making industry, 76; phosphate mines, 76; the town as Mr. Plant found it in 1885, 77; description of the great hotel, 78; grounds, 80; description of Tampa, streets, buildings, water supply, brick-making, 81; population, character of; Spaniards, Cubans, colored, Americans, 81–82; Ybor City, its tobacco factories, 82–83; rapid increase of population and wealth, 83; colored people thrifty and well-to-do, 84; own their homes, have schools, churches, and are respected by their white neighbors, 85; Port Tampa, its inn, or hotel, open all the year, 85; good fishing, bass, tarpon or silver king, 85; Tampa's boards of trade, health, and education, 86; Tampa Bay Hotel, —described by W. C. Prime, 183–186; also by Henry G. Parker, 187–192

Tampa Bay, De Soto's dream, Aladdin's Lamp, 192–195; description of the Palace Hotel, architecture, furniture, 196–203

Tampa's historical interest: De Soto landed here on May 25, 1539, discovers the Mississippi River afterwards, 191; Navarez obtains grant of land from Charles V. of Spain, 191

Temperance societies formed, 273–275

Tunnels, 279, 280

Varied progress: steel pens, steamships, iron, lucifer matches, kerosene oil used, machine sewing, agriculture, 280; Mr. Plant on roof of office in New York noting progress, 283; sanitary progress, life lengthened by it, 282; territorial extension of our country, increase of wealth, rapid growth of cities, 283-284; philanthropic and Christian progress; higher education, better care of the insane, aged, orphans, sailors, neglected children, seamen, and others by societies, 285, 286; conventions for mutual counsel in reform and charitable work, clubs multiplied, social, scientific, 286, 287; female education, co-education, 287; homes for all classes of dependent human beings, 288; progress of medical science, lessening disease and suffering, 288-290

World's Fairs, International, 291; arbitration; better Christian spirit, among all who bear the name, 291: Electrial Exposition, 292; message round the world in 55 minutes, 292, 293

www.ingramcontent.com/pod-product-compliance
Lightning Source LLC
Chambersburg PA
CBHW020229240426
43672CB00006B/465